Preparing Teachers and Developing School Leaders for the 21st Century

LESSONS FROM AROUND THE WORLD

OECD

This work is published on the responsibility of the Secretary-General of the OECD. The opinions expressed and arguments employed herein do not necessarily reflect the official views of the Organisation or of the governments of its member countries.

This document and any map included herein are without prejudice to the status of or sovereignty over any territory, to the delimitation of international frontiers and boundaries and to the name of any territory, city or area.

Please cite this publication as:
Schleicher, A. (ed.) (2012), *Preparing Teachers and Developing School Leaders for the 21st Century: Lessons from around the World*, OECD Publishing.
http://dx.doi.org/10.1787/9789264174559-en

ISBN 978-92-64-17421-4 (print)
ISBN 978-92-64-17455-9 (PDF)

The statistical data for Israel are supplied by and under the responsibility of the relevant Israeli authorities. The use of such data by the OECD is without prejudice to the status of the Golan Heights, East Jerusalem and Israeli settlements in the West Bank under the terms of international law.

Photo credits:
Getty Images © Dave & Les Jacobs
Getty Images © Fuse

Foreword

Nations around the world are undertaking wide-ranging reforms to better prepare children for the higher educational demands of life and work in the 21st century.

What are the skills that young people demand in this rapidly changing world and what competencies do teachers need to effectively teach those skills? What can teacher preparation and continuing professional development do to prepare graduates to teach well in a 21st-century classroom? What are the different roles and responsibilities of 21st-century school leaders and how do countries succeed in developing these leaders?

To answer these questions we need to rethink many aspects of our education systems: the quality of recruiting systems; the type of education recruits obtain before they start working; how they are monitored and what education and support they get; how their compensation is structured; how to improve performance of struggling teachers and enhance development among the best ones.

To help governments effectively address these and other key issues, placing teachers and school leaders at the center of improvement efforts, the U.S. Department of Education, the OECD and Education International brought together education ministers, union leaders and other teacher leaders together in the second International Summit on the Teaching Profession in March 2012. This publication summarizes the evidence that underpinned the Summit, bringing together data analysis and experience for better education policies for better lives.

Angel Gurría
OECD Secretary-General

Acknowledgements

The volume was edited by Andreas Schleicher, in consultation with the Summit co-sponsors – the U.S. Department of Education, Education International, the National Education Association, the American Federation of Teachers, the Council of Chief State School Officers, the Asia Society, the New York Public Television station WNET and the National Board for Professional Teaching Standards. The volume is mainly based on data and comparative analysis from the OECD. Chapter 1 was drafted by Beatriz Pont in collaboration with Pauline Musset, Andreas Schleicher, Diana Toledo Figueroa and Juliana Zapata. Chapter 2 was drafted by David Istance and Stephan Vincent-Lancrin in collaboration with Dirk Van Damme, Andreas Schleicher and Kristen Weatherby. Chapter 3 was drafted by Andreas Schleicher in collaboration with Dirk van Damme and Pauline Musset. Marilyn Achiron provided editorial input while Elizabeth Del Bourgo, Rebecca Tessier and Elisabeth Villoutreix co-ordinated its production.

Table of Contents

8

Introduction

Many countries have seen rapidly rising numbers of people with higher qualifications. But in a fast-changing world, producing more of the same education will not suffice to address the challenges of the future. Perhaps the most challenging dilemma for teachers today is that routine cognitive skills, the skills that are easiest to teach and easiest to test, are also the skills that are easiest to digitize, automate and outsource. A generation ago, teachers could expect that what they taught would last for a lifetime of their students. Today, where individuals can access content on Google, where routine cognitive skills are being digitized or outsourced, and where jobs are changing rapidly, education systems need to place much greater emphasis on enabling individuals to become lifelong learners, to manage complex ways of thinking and complex ways of working that computers cannot take over easily. Students need to be capable not only of constantly adapting but also of constantly learning and growing, of positioning themselves and repositioning themselves in a fast changing world.

These changes have profound implications for teachers, teaching and learning as well as for the leadership of schools and education systems. In the past, the policy focus was on the provision of education, today it is on outcomes, shifting from looking upwards in the bureaucracy towards looking outwards to the next teacher, the next school. The past was about delivered wisdom, the challenge now is to foster user-generated wisdom among teachers in the frontline. In the past, teachers were often left alone in classrooms with significant prescription on what to teach. The most advanced education systems now set ambitious goals for students and are clear about what students should be able to do, and then prepare their teachers and provide them with the tools to establish what content and instruction they need to provide to their individual students. In the past, different students were taught in similar ways, today teachers are expected to embrace diversity with differentiated pedagogical practices. The goal of the past was standardization and conformity, today it is about being ingenious, about personalizing educational experiences; the past was curriculum-centered, the present is learner centered. Teachers are being asked to personalize learning experiences to ensure that every student has a chance to succeed and to deal with increasing cultural diversity in their classrooms and differences in learning styles, taking learning to the learner in ways that allow individuals to learn in the ways that are most conducive to their progress.

The kind of teaching needed today requires teachers to be high-level knowledge workers who constantly advance their own professional knowledge as well as that of their profession. But people who see themselves as knowledge workers are not attracted by schools organized like an assembly line, with teachers working as interchangeable widgets in a bureaucratic command-and-control environment. To attract and develop knowledge workers, education systems need to transform the leadership and work organization of their schools to an environment in which professional norms of management complement bureaucratic and administrative forms of control, with the status, pay, professional autonomy, and the high quality education that go with professional work, and with effective systems of teacher evaluation, with differentiated career paths and career diversity for teachers.

Results from the OECD's Programme for International Student Assessment (PISA) have shown that the degree to which education systems succeed in equipping students with important foundation skills varies significantly (for data see the Annex). Since the quality of teaching is at the heart of student learning outcomes, it is an appealing idea to bring together education leaders from high performing and rapidly improving education systems to explore to what extent educational success and some of the policies related to success transcend the specific characteristics of cultures and countries. To this end, in March 2012 the second *International Summit on the Teaching Profession* was held in New York, hosted by the U.S. Department of Education, the OECD and Education International.

The Summit brought together education ministers, union leaders and other teacher leaders from high-performing and rapidly improving education systems, as measured by PISA, to review how to best improve the quality of teaching,

teachers and school leaders. This publication underpinned the Summit with available research about what can make educational reforms effective, and highlights examples of reforms that have produced specific results, show promise or illustrate imaginative ways of implementing change. The Summit was organized around three interconnected themes:

Developing Effective School Leaders. As more countries require better achievement from their schools and grant greater autonomy to schools in designing curricula and managing resources, the role of the school leader has grown far beyond that of administrator. Developing school leaders requires clearly defining their responsibilities, providing access to appropriate professional development throughout their careers, and acknowledging their pivotal role in improving school and student performance. What are the different roles and responsibilities of 21st-century school leaders and how have countries succeeded in developing effective school leaders at scale? Chapter one summarizes findings from OECD's comparative policy reviews on these questions.

Preparing Teachers to Deliver 21st-Century Skills. Many nations around the world have undertaken wide-ranging reforms of curriculum, instruction, and assessments with the intention of better preparing all children for the higher educational demands of life and work in the 21st century. What are the skills that young people need to be successful in this rapidly changing world and what competencies do teachers need, in turn, to effectively teach those skills? This leads to the question what teacher preparation programs are needed to prepare graduates who are ready to teach well in a 21st-century classroom. While comparative evidence on this is still scarce, Chapter two highlights a range of promising policies and practices.

Matching Teacher Demand and Supply. Many education systems face a daunting challenge in recruiting high-quality graduates as teachers, particularly in shortage areas, and retaining them once they are hired. How have countries succeeded in matching their supply of high-quality teachers to their needs? How have they prepared teachers for priority subjects or locations? The issue of teacher demand and supply is both complex and multi-dimensional, as it reflects several interrelated challenges: how to expand the pool of qualified teachers, how to address shortages in specific subjects, how to recruit teachers to the places where they are most needed, how distribute teachers in equitable and efficient ways, and how to retain qualified teachers over time. Chapter three summarizes available data and examines policy response at two levels: The first concerns the nature of the teaching profession itself and teachers' work environment. Such policies seek to improve the profession's general status and competitive position in the job market and are the focus of this paper. The second involves more targeted responses and incentives for particular types of teacher shortage, which recognizes that that there is not a single labor market for teachers, but a set of them, distinguished by school type and characteristics, such as subject specialization.

Chapter 1

DEVELOPING EFFECTIVE SCHOOL LEADERS

As more countries grant greater autonomy to schools in designing curricula and managing resources to raise achievement, the role of the school leader has grown far beyond that of administrator. Developing school leaders requires clearly defining their responsibilities, providing access to appropriate professional development throughout their careers, and acknowledging their pivotal role in improving school and student performance. What are the different roles and responsibilities of 21st-century school leaders and how have countries succeeded in developing effective school leaders at scale? This chapter summarizes OECD research on these questions.

A CHANGING PROFILE OF SCHOOL LEADERSHIP

PISA shows that a substantial proportion of students in OECD countries now attend schools that have high degrees of autonomy in different areas of decision making. PISA also finds that high-performing and equitable school systems tend to grant greater autonomy to schools in formulating and using curricula and assessments.[1] In some countries, the development and adaptation of educational content has been the main expression of school autonomy (Figure 1.1a). Others have focused on strengthening the management and administration of individual schools through market-oriented governance instruments or collaboration among schools and other stakeholders in local communities even while, in some cases, moving towards centralized governance of curricula and standards (Figure 1.1b). But effective school autonomy depends on effective leaders, including system leaders, principals, teacher leaders, senior teachers and head teachers, as well as strong support systems. That, in turn, requires effectively distributed leadership, new types of training and development for school leaders, and appropriate support and incentives. As a result, it is crucial for the quality of the education provided that school leaders are well-equipped to meet these demands and that leading a school is regarded as a valued profession. In some countries, focusing on the development of effective school leaders has become a key part of education reform (see Box 1.1).

Box 1.1 Ontario – Improving education through more effective school leaders

With the election of a new government in 2004, the provincial government of Ontario designed and implemented an education-improvement strategy (Energizing Ontario Education) that focused on three main goals: raising the level of student achievement, defined as 75% of students achieving the provincial standard in Grade 6 and achieving an 85% graduation rate; narrowing the gaps in student achievement; and increasing public confidence in publicly funded education.

To meet its goals, Ontario developed a coherent leadership strategy, adequate contextual support frameworks and concerted actions to include key actors, such as school boards, teachers' unions, academics and practitioners, in the reform process. Within the strategy, a specific leadership framework defines five domains for effective leaders: setting direction; building relationships and developing people; developing the organization; leading the instructional program; and being accountable.

The leadership strategy focuses on attracting good candidates, preparing them for their tasks, and supporting them as they work to improve the quality of instruction. School boards overtly plan for leadership succession. The process of attracting and preparing the right people begins before there is a vacancy to be filled. Potential candidates for school leader need to have an undergraduate degree; five years of teaching experience; certification by school level; two specialist or additional honor specialist qualifications (areas of teaching expertise) or a master's degree; and completion of a Principal's Qualification Program (PQP), offered by Ontario universities, teachers' federations and principals' associations, which consists of a 125-hour program with a practicum.

Mentoring is available during the first two years of practice for principals, vice-principals, supervisory officers and directors. Principals and vice-principals are required to maintain an annual growth plan, and their performance is appraised every five years, based on student achievement and well-being.

Source: OECD (2010b).

School leaders can define the school's educational goals, ensure that instructional practice is directed towards achieving these goals, observe and evaluate teachers, suggest modifications to improve teaching practices, shape their professional development, help solve problems that may arise within the classroom or among teachers and liaise with the community and parents. They are also in a position to provide incentives and motivate teachers to improve the quality of instruction.[2] PISA asked school leaders to report on their level of involvement in several issues, including making sure that teachers' work and development reflects the educational goals of the school, monitoring student performance and classroom activities, and working with teachers to resolve problems (Figure 1.2).

Figure 1.1a

How much autonomy individual schools have over curricula and assessments

Percentage of students in schools whose principals reported that only "principals and/or teachers", only "regional and/or national education authority" or both "principals and/or teachers" and "regional and/or national education authority" have a considerable responsibility for the following tasks:

- A Establishing student assessment policies
- B Choosing which textbooks are used
- C Determining course content
- D Deciding which courses are offered

- 1 Only "principals and/or teachers"
- 2 Both "principals and/or teachers" and "regional and/or national education authority"
- 3 Only "regional and/or national education authority"

Range between top and bottom quarter

◆ Average index

	A			B			C			D			Index of school responsibility for curriculum and assessment	Variability in the index (Standard Deviation)
	1	2	3	1	2	3	1	2	3	1	2	3		
Australia	65	33	2	92	8	0	46	40	14	75	24	1		0.9
Austria	57	27	15	94	5	1	37	40	23	32	40	29		0.8
Belgium	78	19	4	94	4	1	32	42	26	40	46	13		0.8
Canada	28	62	10	40	49	11	12	51	38	44	54	3		0.6
Chile	72	21	6	73	20	7	43	22	35	64	20	16		1.0
Czech Republic	95	5	0	89	11	1	83	16	1	88	11	1		0.8
Denmark	61	28	11	100	0	0	56	32	12	47	39	14		0.9
Estonia	63	33	3	66	32	2	66	30	4	79	20	2		0.9
Finland	50	43	7	98	2	0	32	52	16	55	39	6		0.8
France	w	w	w	w	w	w	w	w	w	w	w	w		w
Germany	71	21	9	84	13	3	21	47	32	80	18	2		0.7
Greece	20	12	68	7	8	85	1	3	96	6	5	88		0.3
Hungary	94	6	0	98	2	0	49	36	15	43	28	29		0.9
Iceland	92	8	1	93	4	3	61	26	13	48	42	10		0.9
Ireland	87	13	0	97	3	0	29	37	34	78	21	1		0.7
Israel	80	20	0	53	43	4	52	44	5	44	50	6		1.0
Italy	91	8	1	99	1	0	59	27	14	49	25	27		0.9
Japan	98	2	0	89	8	3	93	6	1	94	5	2		0.7
Korea	92	6	2	96	4	0	89	8	2	79	17	4		0.8
Luxembourg	9	33	58	13	80	7	9	72	20	18	61	21		0.6
Mexico	56	15	29	63	11	26	14	7	79	5	5	91		0.5
Netherlands	99	1	0	100	0	0	87	12	1	89	10	1		0.6
New Zealand	81	17	2	99	1	0	79	20	1	92	8	0		0.8
Norway	38	36	27	97	2	1	30	40	30	23	33	44		0.7
Poland	92	8	0	92	8	0	93	7	0	40	31	29		0.8
Portugal	35	37	28	98	2	0	5	3	92	10	5	86		0.4
Slovak Republic	76	21	3	56	39	5	48	47	5	52	48	1		1.0
Slovenia	46	48	5	72	27	1	34	59	6	28	52	20		0.8
Spain	44	34	23	95	5	0	32	31	37	30	31	39		0.8
Sweden	66	30	3	99	1	0	66	26	8	53	25	22		1.0
Switzerland	57	27	16	40	40	20	21	41	38	24	50	27		0.7
Turkey	42	29	30	14	18	68	9	15	76	14	21	65		0.4
United Kingdom	88	12	0	98	2	0	77	20	2	86	14	0		0.8
United States	46	40	13	62	28	10	36	46	18	58	37	4		0.9
OECD average	66	23	11	78	15	8	45	31	24	50	28	21		0.8
Albania	51	16	33	91	8	1	35	7	57	35	12	53		0.8
Argentina	74	20	6	81	16	3	28	43	29	8	30	61		0.6
Azerbaijan	54	8	38	50	6	43	27	9	64	37	5	58		0.8
Brazil	47	27	26	88	9	2	35	25	40	18	17	65		0.8
Bulgaria	25	37	38	88	12	1	10	26	65	10	15	75		0.4
Colombia	39	21	39	92	3	4	69	23	8	64	14	23		0.8
Croatia	26	36	38	63	34	3	11	50	39	2	25	72		0.4
Dubai (UAE)	77	10	13	55	17	27	62	13	26	59	16	25		1.1
Hong Kong-China	93	7	0	93	7	0	81	17	2	87	13	0		0.8
Indonesia	67	28	6	80	13	7	75	18	7	49	23	28		0.9
Jordan	27	4	70	4	1	95	7	1	93	7	1	92		0.5
Kazakhstan	31	22	47	16	14	70	11	18	71	40	22	37		0.5
Kyrgyzstan	65	8	26	68	8	23	59	10	31	44	7	49		1.0
Latvia	56	40	4	71	27	2	19	46	36	30	42	28		0.6
Liechtenstein	69	25	6	54	5	40	41	0	59	53	9	38		1.1
Lithuania	75	20	5	89	11	1	50	35	15	75	20	5		0.9
Macao-China	95	0	5	100	0	0	94	6	0	81	14	4		0.8
Montenegro	40	32	28	5	30	65	5	34	61	20	36	44		0.6
Panama	41	25	34	52	26	22	41	23	36	26	23	51		0.8
Peru	75	15	10	52	12	37	53	23	24	45	18	37		1.0
Qatar	45	18	37	37	16	47	31	9	60	35	17	48		0.9
Romania	42	36	22	86	13	1	46	33	20	31	41	29		0.7
Russian Federation	63	25	12	65	27	8	21	40	39	71	22	7		0.8
Serbia	49	44	7	19	59	23	2	41	57	0	12	87		0.2
Shanghai-China	86	9	5	49	17	34	45	22	33	52	28	20		1.0
Singapore	57	41	2	72	24	3	44	38	18	66	31	4		0.9
Chinese Taipei	74	17	8	92	8	0	81	16	3	68	25	7		0.9
Thailand	79	18	2	89	10	1	89	11	0	91	8	1		0.8
Trinidad and Tobago	50	45	5	29	62	10	21	40	39	34	51	15		0.7
Tunisia	11	11	78	0	1	99	3	14	83	4	9	87		0.1
Uruguay	23	30	47	31	36	33	3	26	71	21	19	59		0.4

-2.0 -1.5 -1.0 -0.5 0 0.5 1.0 1.5 2.0 2.5 Index points

Source: OECD, *PISA 2009 Database*, Table IV.3.6.

Figure 1.1b

How much autonomy individual schools have over resource allocation

Percentage of students in schools whose principals reported that only "principals and/or teachers", only "regional and/or national education authority" or both "principals and/or teachers" and "regional and/or national education authority" have a considerable responsibility for the following tasks:

- **A** Selecting teachers for hire
- **B** Dismissing teachers
- **C** Establishing teachers' starting salaries
- **D** Determining teachers' salaries increases
- **E** Formulating the school budget
- **F** Deciding on budget allocations within the school

- **1** Only "principals and/or teachers"
- **2** Both "principals and/or teachers" and "regional and/or national education authority"
- **3** Only "regional and/or national education authority"

Range between top and bottom quarter

◆ Average index

	A			B			C			D			E			F			Index of school responsibility for resource allocation	Variability in the index (Standard Deviation)
	1	2	3	1	2	3	1	2	3	1	2	3	1	2	3	1	2	3		
Australia	61	20	19	43	12	45	12	5	84	13	6	81	68	16	16	93	6	0		0.9
Austria	13	35	52	5	26	68	1	0	99	1	0	99	11	9	80	84	12	4		0.3
Belgium	75	13	12	63	21	17	0	1	99	0	1	99	56	18	26	63	19	17		0.3
Canada	54	39	7	17	35	48	3	5	92	4	6	91	25	30	45	76	19	5		0.5
Chile	69	8	23	59	3	38	37	1	62	37	1	62	55	9	36	71	9	20		1.2
Czech Republic	100	0	0	99	1	0	77	15	8	65	25	11	55	36	9	75	24	1		1.2
Denmark	97	2	0	69	15	16	20	10	70	16	14	70	80	13	8	98	2	0		0.9
Estonia	98	2	0	95	5	0	7	20	73	12	33	55	37	54	9	85	15	1		0.6
Finland	32	43	25	18	19	63	8	7	84	5	15	80	36	41	23	92	6	1		0.5
France	w	w	w	w	w	w	w	w	w	w	w	w	w	w	w	w	w	w		w
Germany	29	36	34	7	14	79	3	0	97	4	15	81	29	4	67	97	2	2		0.5
Greece	0	1	99	0	2	98	0	0	100	0	0	100	34	7	59	59	7	34		0.1
Hungary	99	1	0	97	2	1	49	7	44	56	7	37	73	15	12	92	5	2		1.2
Iceland	94	6	0	93	7	0	7	13	80	4	16	80	57	30	13	77	22	0		0.5
Ireland	61	25	14	36	14	50	0	2	98	1	0	99	60	13	27	89	5	6		0.2
Israel	67	30	3	49	38	13	9	4	87	13	6	80	15	26	59	66	24	11		0.8
Italy	9	10	82	9	6	84	3	0	97	3	0	96	7	7	86	69	11	21		0.5
Japan	25	2	73	22	1	77	13	0	87	16	3	80	28	4	69	89	3	8		1.0
Korea	32	6	62	23	4	74	8	0	92	6	0	94	29	12	58	86	6	8		0.7
Luxembourg	21	41	38	19	36	45	6	0	94	6	0	94	31	57	12	78	14	8		0.8
Mexico	34	5	61	22	4	73	8	0	92	6	0	94	46	6	48	71	7	22		0.8
Netherlands	100	0	0	99	1	0	72	8	20	55	12	33	99	1	0	100	0	0		1.0
New Zealand	100	0	0	89	7	4	9	3	88	15	21	64	95	4	1	99	1	0		0.7
Norway	72	21	6	44	22	34	8	4	88	6	13	81	55	28	17	88	12	1		0.6
Poland	87	12	1	90	10	0	9	20	71	4	20	77	7	42	51	26	43	31		0.4
Portugal	13	57	30	14	0	86	5	0	94	5	0	94	63	10	27	89	3	8		0.7
Slovak Republic	98	2	0	98	2	0	39	27	34	32	33	35	45	40	15	70	27	3		1.1
Slovenia	96	4	1	88	10	1	7	11	82	13	31	56	26	49	26	78	21	1		0.6
Spain	31	3	66	32	1	67	3	2	95	3	2	95	63	4	33	93	4	3		0.6
Sweden	96	4	0	63	17	20	57	16	27	69	22	9	64	20	16	93	5	2		1.1
Switzerland	82	15	3	60	26	15	8	8	84	8	13	79	35	30	35	83	13	4		0.7
Turkey	1	1	99	2	2	96	1	0	99	1	0	99	34	19	47	56	16	28		0.2
United Kingdom	90	9	0	70	22	8	52	23	25	67	17	15	57	29	14	95	5	1		1.1
United States	88	12	0	75	19	6	17	5	78	18	6	75	54	29	16	83	13	4		0.9
OECD average	61	14	25	51	13	37	17	7	77	17	10	73	46	22	32	81	12	8		0.7
Albania	8	14	78	7	14	79	3	0	97	3	1	96	33	12	55	61	8	31		0.5
Argentina	44	5	51	27	3	70	2	1	97	1	4	96	22	5	73	64	12	24		0.4
Azerbaijan	40	22	38	61	17	22	35	6	59	13	3	84	5	6	89	20	4	76		0.3
Brazil	17	7	76	14	8	78	8	1	91	7	1	92	14	5	80	21	6	73		0.8
Bulgaria	93	5	2	97	2	1	66	20	14	84	12	4	73	22	5	92	7	1		1.1
Colombia	21	5	75	21	1	78	14	0	86	13	1	86	58	5	36	87	5	8		1.0
Croatia	90	10	0	84	11	5	1	1	98	2	1	97	26	34	40	68	23	9		0.4
Dubai (UAE)	65	12	23	67	9	24	62	3	34	68	1	31	75	2	22	92	3	5		1.2
Hong Kong-China	83	15	2	79	17	4	18	24	58	15	12	74	84	15	2	91	9	0		0.9
Indonesia	29	12	59	26	11	63	20	9	70	23	11	66	83	11	5	78	14	8		1.0
Jordan	6	1	93	4	1	95	1	1	98	2	0	98	83	1	17	70	2	28		0.4
Kazakhstan	88	10	2	95	4	2	17	10	73	8	10	82	8	13	79	17	19	64		0.7
Kyrgyzstan	74	14	11	68	13	19	18	4	77	13	3	84	12	7	81	19	7	74		0.6
Latvia	94	4	2	96	4	0	10	15	75	18	25	57	62	25	12	81	16	3		0.7
Liechtenstein	41	0	59	37	0	63	0	6	94	39	17	45	37	0	63	100	0	0		1.0
Lithuania	96	4	0	99	1	0	11	7	81	6	8	86	25	27	48	42	29	28		0.5
Macao-China	92	4	4	91	5	4	91	4	5	90	4	5	95	5	0	84	16	0		1.0
Montenegro	89	11	0	82	18	0	0	5	95	10	11	78	12	21	68	65	22	13		0.3
Panama	22	3	76	20	8	72	14	5	81	14	8	79	70	15	15	43	10	47		0.9
Peru	38	15	47	30	9	61	22	2	76	22	2	77	60	9	31	79	6	15		1.3
Qatar	52	3	44	54	5	41	42	5	53	47	4	50	43	4	53	52	4	44		1.2
Romania	1	9	91	4	11	86	0	2	97	1	4	95	7	25	68	40	13	47		0.1
Russian Federation	95	4	1	95	5	0	35	15	50	29	20	51	8	30	63	46	28	27		0.7
Serbia	72	28	1	64	30	7	1	8	90	16	19	65	9	27	64	74	16	10		0.3
Shanghai-China	98	2	0	99	1	0	36	5	59	43	6	51	91	2	6	98	1	1		1.1
Singapore	14	38	48	14	24	62	4	3	93	7	17	75	49	22	29	91	8	1		0.6
Chinese Taipei	73	13	14	74	14	12	18	7	75	23	7	70	50	13	37	78	8	14		1.0
Thailand	30	20	50	59	12	28	29	14	56	72	24	5	70	20	10	90	7	2		1.1
Trinidad and Tobago	17	14	69	6	4	90	2	1	96	6	5	89	46	28	26	75	12	12		0.6
Tunisia	2	0	98	1	0	99	1	1	99	1	0	99	10	18	72	78	13	9		0.3
Uruguay	17	5	78	13	1	86	3	1	96	2	1	96	13	12	75	49	16	35		0.6

-2.0   -1.5   -1.0   -0.5   0   0.5   1.0   1.5   2.0   2.5 Index points

Source: OECD, *PISA 2009 Database*, Table IV.3.5.

Figure 1.2

School principals' views of their involvement in school matters

Index of school principal's leadership based on school principals' reports

- **A** I make sure that the professional development activities of teachers are in accordance with the teaching goals of the school.
- **B** I ensure that teachers work according to the school's educational goals.
- **C** I observe instruction in classrooms.
- **D** I use student performance results to develop the school's educational goals.
- **E** I give teachers suggestions as to how they can improve their teaching.
- **F** I monitor students' work.
- **G** When a teacher has problems in his/her classroom, I take the initiative to discuss matters.
- **H** I inform teachers about possibilities for updating their knowledge and skills.
- **I** I check to see whether classroom activities are in keeping with our educational goals.
- **J** I take exam results into account in decisions regarding curriculum development.
- **K** I ensure that there is clarity concerning the responsibility for co-ordinating the curriculum.
- **L** When a teacher brings up a classroom problem, we solve the problem together.
- **M** I pay attention to disruptive behavior in classrooms.
- **N** I take over lessons from teachers who are unexpectedly absent.

Percentage of students in schools whose principals reported that the following activities and behaviors occurred "quite often" or "very often" during the last school year

Range between top and bottom quarter
◆ Average index

	A	B	C	D	E	F	G	H	I	J	K	L	M	N	Variability in the index (Standard Deviation)
OECD															
Australia	98	99	64	93	76	58	89	95	81	81	97	93	94	32	1.0
Austria	89	92	41	60	67	86	84	79	67	22	75	92	87	53	0.8
Belgium	95	97	43	42	68	33	89	90	82	46	74	98	96	4	0.8
Canada	98	98	77	91	86	60	95	95	86	63	87	99	98	19	1.0
Chile	97	98	55	93	95	73	90	96	82	84	94	97	97	62	1.1
Czech Republic	95	98	57	81	79	93	86	98	83	59	93	96	75	23	0.8
Denmark	86	89	25	44	53	39	94	91	76	25	76	99	95	29	0.6
Estonia	92	94	59	84	58	75	72	93	57	62	87	83	79	24	0.9
Finland	64	75	9	46	40	61	77	95	59	13	77	98	94	39	0.7
France	w	w	w	w	w	w	w	w	w	w	w	w	w	w	w
Germany	82	94	40	57	53	82	80	85	57	33	73	95	84	42	0.7
Greece	40	78	12	61	53	46	97	96	67	34	69	98	96	63	1.0
Hungary	93	99	54	84	62	84	89	91	65	73	86	94	91	41	0.8
Iceland	88	89	39	78	77	69	87	96	54	58	87	100	75	26	0.7
Ireland	88	88	14	64	41	50	88	92	62	78	88	97	97	39	0.9
Israel	94	99	46	87	85	81	94	89	86	90	94	97	98	26	0.9
Italy	97	99	39	86	75	87	96	98	88	77	92	98	98	18	0.9
Japan	43	51	37	30	38	40	29	50	31	37	29	61	60	17	0.9
Korea	80	85	42	64	68	56	75	69	60	46	63	79	68	7	1.2
Luxembourg	87	98	32	65	52	64	96	67	74	32	47	98	98	23	1.0
Mexico	95	97	68	94	89	90	95	91	92	62	90	97	96	43	1.0
Netherlands	95	97	52	66	73	50	76	82	79	75	80	86	71	16	0.7
New Zealand	99	98	68	98	73	42	78	84	74	87	97	83	94	12	1.0
Norway	81	88	24	70	49	55	90	91	48	47	81	98	95	28	0.6
Poland	94	97	39	95	89	96	91	99	92	71	80	97	93	37	0.8
Portugal	93	97	9	94	65	49	91	89	48	82	97	99	97	7	0.7
Slovak Republic	97	99	86	87	86	90	86	98	91	76	96	91	91	15	0.7
Slovenia	99	100	77	78	85	90	90	95	85	65	93	98	94	23	0.8
Spain	86	97	28	85	55	45	86	86	66	71	92	99	99	63	0.9
Sweden	90	96	38	83	63	29	89	90	52	68	93	98	87	13	0.8
Switzerland	72	82	64	34	60	61	85	80	59	17	54	92	83	31	0.8
Turkey	85	95	70	93	85	90	75	90	87	78	93	97	99	36	0.9
United Kingdom	100	100	93	100	92	88	90	96	95	97	99	96	97	29	0.9
United States	98	98	95	96	94	72	95	97	94	88	90	97	96	16	1.1
OECD average	88	93	50	75	69	66	86	89	72	61	82	94	90	29	0.9
Partners															
Albania	97	100	98	99	94	94	90	88	93	87	93	96	96	47	0.8
Argentina	95	98	63	90	96	84	94	91	86	66	87	98	96	43	0.9
Azerbaijan	95	96	97	89	97	99	86	96	99	86	90	90	99	77	1.0
Brazil	99	99	60	94	94	91	97	97	91	94	94	99	99	44	1.1
Bulgaria	100	100	92	95	79	93	87	98	94	71	98	91	96	29	0.8
Colombia	98	99	45	85	92	88	90	96	82	87	92	96	96	31	1.2
Croatia	94	98	70	80	92	96	96	95	98	76	95	99	100	19	0.8
Dubai (UAE)	100	100	95	97	98	93	98	99	98	90	93	98	97	39	1.2
Hong Kong-China	99	99	99	97	100	93	96	98	95	92	97	96	96	45	0.9
Indonesia	94	99	88	91	99	77	89	96	96	95	96	81	93	47	1.0
Jordan	99	100	100	99	100	98	99	99	99	81	81	100	99	90	1.1
Kazakhstan	96	98	98	95	97	97	85	98	99	60	87	86	89	17	0.8
Kyrgyzstan	90	92	98	90	94	98	89	96	95	82	87	86	81	29	0.9
Latvia	96	97	80	97	83	86	85	94	85	75	83	76	85	30	0.8
Liechtenstein	53	21	3	15	14	46	82	16	10	0	13	96	58	44	0.7
Lithuania	97	98	47	92	75	60	74	89	55	65	89	95	83	7	0.8
Macao-China	100	100	88	74	82	86	93	76	86	52	88	90	90	45	0.9
Montenegro	95	100	88	97	97	100	92	100	99	84	100	100	96	23	0.7
Panama	91	95	86	88	95	84	90	92	95	85	88	97	94	43	1.1
Peru	94	98	86	88	93	80	80	94	92	84	91	91	95	45	1.1
Qatar	96	100	100	98	97	94	95	95	98	84	87	96	98	28	1.1
Romania	98	100	87	98	90	90	96	98	99	91	99	100	99	40	0.8
Russian Federation	99	99	92	89	87	95	80	99	97	55	97	96	86	31	0.9
Serbia	97	100	67	90	91	82	97	99	87	93	91	97	97	44	0.8
Shanghai-China	98	98	94	57	99	69	91	93	96	70	98	99	89	14	0.8
Singapore	100	100	80	99	94	66	93	93	93	98	98	97	96	8	0.9
Chinese Taipei	98	98	92	84	86	94	86	98	88	90	95	97	95	20	0.9
Thailand	94	99	88	95	97	94	94	96	98	97	97	97	97	45	0.9
Trinidad and Tobago	97	98	60	86	88	71	94	95	84	92	95	97	98	26	1.0
Tunisia	84	97	92	92	97	60	97	82	84	40	59	99	99	45	1.1
Uruguay	85	98	89	90	90	81	92	94	84	45	73	98	100	25	1.0

-3 -2 -1 0 1 2 3 4 Index points

Note: Higher values on the index indicate greater involvement of school principals in educational issues.
Source: OECD, *PISA 2009 Database*, Table IV.4.8.

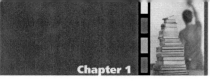 

Among OECD countries, 93% of students attend schools whose leaders reported that he or she ensures that teachers' work reflects the school's educational goals "quite often" or "very often"; over 86% of students attend schools whose leader "quite often" or "very often" takes the initiative to discuss a problem teachers may have in their classrooms; half of students attend schools whose leader "quite often" or "very often" observes classes; 61% of students attend schools whose leader "quite often" or "very often" considers exam results when making decisions regarding curriculum development; and over a quarter of OECD students attend schools whose leaders "quite often" or "very often" take over lessons from teachers who are unexpectedly absent. Variation in the role of school leaders within the school system is greatest in Chile, Korea and the United States; the role of school leaders is relatively more homogeneous across schools in Denmark and Norway.

Studies in some OECD countries have shown how school leaders are affected by the growing demands on their time. In England, 61% of head teachers described their work-life balance as poor or very poor.[3] Some have attributed this to long working hours or to deficiencies in working practices, such as school heads not knowing how to prioritize or delegate their work. In New Zealand, a study found that, eight years after major education reforms were introduced, school leaders' administrative work had increased substantially and they were working ten hours longer per week, on average, than before the reforms. This and other research finds that administrative demands are taking up 34% of school leaders' time, clearly competing with educational leadership as their top priority.[4]

SUPPORTING, EVALUATING AND DEVELOPING TEACHER QUALITY

The OECD's comparative review of school leadership[5] identifies a focus on supporting, evaluating and developing teacher quality as the core of effective leadership. This includes co-coordinating the curriculum and teaching program, monitoring and evaluating teaching practice, promoting teachers' professional development, and supporting collaborative work cultures. In Sweden, for example, school leaders often spend much of their time giving feedback to teachers about their work. They also tend to frequently challenge the assumptions of their staff. By asking questions such as "How do we know that?", "Could we test another way of doing it?" and "What do we know about how people in other schools do it?" they help to foster a learning atmosphere in the school.

The OECD's comparative review of school leadership finds that teacher monitoring and evaluation are increasingly important responsibilities of school leaders. In general, regular teacher evaluations involve the school leader and other senior school staff; but in countries such as France and Belgium, they also involve a panel with members from outside the school. While the nature and consequences of teacher evaluation vary widely across countries, there are now formal provisions for teacher evaluation in the majority of the countries studied. The form, rigor, content and consequences of evaluation vary greatly across countries – and sometimes within them. In most countries where teacher evaluation is carried out, it is conducted as a part of a larger quality review or school-improvement process. The purposes of evaluation are relatively evenly distributed among formative evaluation, performance appraisal, professional-development planning and support for promotion.

The criteria for evaluations differ, sometimes involving an assessment of teaching performance, in-service training and, in some cases, measures of student performance. Classroom observation, interviews and documentation prepared by teachers are the typical methods used in the evaluations. In the OECD leadership study, the weight given to the school leaders' observations or monitoring varies among participating countries from considerable (Slovenia) to slight (Chile, where the input counts for only 10% of the total). School leaders can rely almost exclusively on their observations (Slovenia) or on a wide range of other data, such as reviewing teaching plans, observing meetings, reviewing communications with parents, pupil performance data, peer review and teacher self-evaluations, among others (such data is used, for example, in Denmark, England, Korea, New Zealand and Scotland). The frequency of observations ranges from as often as three to six times per year in England to once every four years in Chile, with several countries settling on annual observations. Where teacher evaluation is conducted, it almost always entails some form of annual formal meeting between leader and teacher.

PISA shows that, on average across OECD countries, 61% of 15-year-olds are in schools where the practices of mathematics teachers were monitored over the preceding year through school leader or senior staff observations. Student achievement on PISA tended to be higher when teachers were held accountable through the involvement of school leaders and external inspectors in monitoring lessons.

The OECD's comparative review of school leadership also finds that school leadership plays a vital role in promoting professional learning and development for teachers. There have always been different types of professional-development activities, but the perception of their relative effectiveness has changed over the years.

School-based professional development activities involving the entire staff or significant groups of teachers are becoming more common, while teacher-initiated personal development is becoming less so, at least in terms of programs supported through public funds. Most countries now link professional development to the developmental priorities of the school and co-ordinate in-service training in the school accordingly. School leaders and, in some cases, local school authorities play an important role in planning professional-development activities. Some countries, including England, are also ensuring that teachers identify their own professional-development needs.

Last but not least, supporting collaborative work cultures is an increasingly important and recognized responsibility of school leaders. Some OECD countries, and in particular Denmark, Finland, Norway and Sweden, have more of a history of teamwork and co-operation among their teaching staff, especially in primary schools. Others, such as Ireland, are shifting to encourage such practice. When surveyed, school leaders in Finland spoke enthusiastically about the benefits of collaboration. Sharing resources and ideas helped them to face the many demands on their time and energy, and mutual support helped them to cope with difficulties. One of the heads "loves data", another "hates it" and leaned on her colleague for help with statistics. In exchange, she offered expertise in workforce development.

GOAL-SETTING, ASSESSMENT AND ACCOUNTABILITY

Aligning instruction with external standards, setting school goals for student performance, measuring progress against those goals and making adjustments in the school program to improve performance were identified as other important aspects of school leadership.

While most countries establish a core curriculum or curriculum framework at national or state level, it is usually up to school leaders to implement curricula and instruction effectively. PISA shows that, on average across OECD countries, more than half of 15-year-olds are in schools where school-level stakeholders have the responsibility to decide which courses are offered, and more than 40% of students are in schools that determine course content. School leaders generally have a degree of discretion in how they design curriculum content and sequencing, organize teaching and instructional resources, and monitor quality. As noted before, PISA data suggest that in countries where school leaders reported higher degrees of responsibility, performance tended to be better, even if that relationship can be affected by many other factors.

School leaders also played a key role in integrating external and internal accountability systems by supporting their teaching staff in aligning instruction with agreed learning goals and performance standards. For example, a group of schools reviewed in England used data as a vehicle to engage the leadership team and teachers in school improvement, and used student-outcome information to develop strategies for learning for individual students and classrooms. Information was reviewed every six weeks. Data was analyzed at the individual and classroom levels, providing an overview of where problems lay. Intervention teams then stepped in to look into potential underperformance and respond to challenges.

Most countries also have a long tradition of school inspections where leaders are held accountable for their use of public funding and for the structures and processes they establish. Most OECD countries report that they have or are developing some form of national goals, objectives, or standards of student performance. To assess these, accountability frameworks tend to rely on both school and student information.

To evaluate school performance, two-thirds of OECD countries have regulations that require lower secondary schools to be inspected regularly; a slightly smaller number of countries have regulatory requirements for schools to conduct periodic school self-evaluations. In around three-quarters of OECD countries, these school inspections and school self-evaluations also have a high level of influence on the evaluation of school administration and individual teachers. In more than half of all OECD countries, school inspections are also used to make decisions about whether or not to close schools.

In two-thirds of OECD countries, periodic standardized assessments of students in compulsory education are conducted to obtain information on student performance. In slightly fewer than half of all OECD countries, national examinations have a real impact on lower secondary school students, such as allowing them to proceed to a higher level of education. Only a few countries, including Belgium (Flemish Community), Chile and the Czech Republic reported that school inspections influenced decisions about providing financial rewards or sanctions.

STRATEGIC RESOURCE MANAGEMENT

The strategic use of resources and their alignment with pedagogical purposes can help to focus school activities on the objective of improving teaching and learning. However, where devolution has put greater discretion for maintenance, repair and substantial capital projects in the hands of school leaders, they are often asked to fulfill responsibilities that call for expertise many do not have. Even where such tasks are the responsibility of the governing board, they are often formally or informally delegated to the school leader.

PISA shows that, on average across OECD countries, 84% of 15-year-old students are enrolled in schools that have full autonomy in deciding how their budgets are spent, and 57% are in schools that are fully autonomous in formulating their budgets. However, PISA also shows that school leaders only have a modest role in setting teachers' salaries or awarding salary increases, which somewhat undercuts the notion that school leaders enjoy great discretion in budgetary matters. Across countries, fewer than 60% of students are enrolled in schools that have the authority to hire teachers, and half are in schools with the authority to dismiss teachers. Moreover, the lack of transparent and accepted procedures for dealing with ineffective teachers can mean that those teachers may remain in their posts, often without being offered any professional development assistance, with all the adverse consequences this has for student learning, the reputation of schools and the teaching profession.

School leaders who have the responsibility, whether formal or informal, for managing resources should be trained so that they can effectively align resources with pedagogical purposes. The OECD's comparative review of school leadership found that the capacity of school leaders to shift financial and human resources strategically is often limited by a lack of training in the field. School leaders often reported having to engage in operational delivery issues and put aside the strategic planning that is necessary to provide an overarching vision and allocate resources.

LEADERSHIP BEYOND SCHOOL WALLS

The OECD's comparative review of school leadership suggests that an important role for school leaders is that of collaborating with other schools or communities around them. Schools and their leaders strengthen collaboration, form networks, share resources, and/or work together. These engagements enlarge the scope of leadership beyond the school to the welfare of young people in the city, town or region. They can also nurture a culture where improving school leadership is accomplished across communities, to the benefit of all concerned. For example, in some Finnish municipalities, school leaders also work as school district leaders, with one-third of their time devoted to the district and two-thirds to their own schools. Management and supervision are shared, as are evaluation and development of education planning. The aim is to align schools and municipalities to think systemically in order to promote a common vision of schooling and a united school system.

At the same time, experience in these municipalities also shows that for school leaders to be able to take on this larger system-level role, leadership at the school level must be better distributed, so that deputy heads and leadership teams can assume some of the school leaders' tasks when he or she is taking on larger roles. Overall, the study suggests that leaders' collaboration with other schools and with the local community can help to improve problem-solving through intensified processes of interaction, communication and collective learning. It can also help to develop leadership capacity and address succession and stability issues by increasing the density of and opportunities for local leadership in the school and at the local level.

Figure 1.3

How selected countries have defined school leaders

Leadership Academy, Austria	Ontario School Leadership Framework	National Professional Qualification for Headteachers, England
• Strategic leadership • Instructional leadership • Human resource management • Organizational development • Change management • Aspects of lifelong learning • Administrative	• Setting direction • Building relationships and developing people • Developing the organization • Leading the instructional program • Securing accountability	• Shaping the future (strategically) • Leading learning and teaching • Developing self and others • Managing the school • Securing accountability • Strengthening community

Figure 1.3 shows how a few countries have defined the roles of school leaders and Box 1.2 describes one of them, Australia, in more detail.

**Box 1.2 Australia's approach to school leadership and
its National Professional Standard for Principals**

The Australian Institute for Teaching and School Leadership was created in 2010 to promote excellence in the teaching and school leadership profession. A public, independent institution supported by the Ministry of Education, its role is to develop and maintain national professional standards for teaching and school leadership, implement an agreed system of national accreditation of teachers based on those standards, and foster high-quality professional development for teachers and school leaders.

The National Professional Standard for Principals, introduced in July 2011, is based on three requirements for leadership: vision and values; knowledge and comprehension; and personal qualities and social and communication skills. These are made manifest in five areas of professional practice: leading teaching-learning processes; developing self and others; leading improvement, innovation and change; leading school management; and engaging and working with the community.

Excellence in school leadership

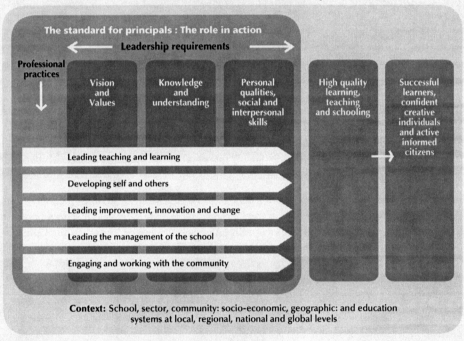

Source: Australian Institute for Teaching and School Leadership (2011).

DISTRIBUTING LEADERSHIP

As greater responsibility and accountability is demanded of school leaders, leadership needs to be distributed effectively within and across schools. School leaders need to develop a network and share their tasks with vice-principals or co-principals, deputy principals, assistant principals, vocational/technical department heads, workshop managers and/or co-coordinators and teachers with special duties. Leadership structures or more informal *ad hoc* groups based on expertise and current needs can be formed to encourage a distribution of power among these actors.

Hallinger and Heck have concluded that 'collaborative leadership, as opposed to leadership from the principal alone, may offer a path to school improvement.'[6] There is also emerging evidence of the impact of teacher leadership on teacher self-efficacy where teachers are encouraged within their schools and within education systems to show leadership in relation to such areas as pedagogy, the curriculum and its assessment, evaluation and student behavior.[7] There is also debate about the nature of standards which could be used to define collaborative leadership. One such example is the work of the Teacher Leadership Exploratory Consortium in the United States, involving higher education institutions and teacher unions, which has published a set of teacher leader model standards for use by the teaching profession itself. Last but not least, education unions are increasingly engaged in encouraging teachers to take the lead in their own learning.[8]

In Norway, some schools have a three-person school leader group: one responsible for pedagogy, one for personnel matters and one for finance. In Portugal, schools tend to be grouped together with a collective management structure such that school leaders are regarded as co-coordinators of their schools with teaching responsibility; they have little decision-making power. In the Netherlands, which has a decentralized education system, the role of school leaders varies among schools, which are free to distribute tasks and functions to several leaders. In Scotland, the devolved government introduced a distributed-leadership arrangement among school leaders, deputy-head teachers and teacher leaders under the new standards for school leaders, *A Teaching Profession for the 21st Century*.[9]

In a distributed-leadership arrangement, principals and other actors, with different responsibilities, can play a role in school development and improvement:

- *Principals, vice-, deputy and assistant school leaders* : In Korea, the role of vice-principal and the scope of his or her authority are flexible, depending on the school leader's leadership style. In secondary education in France, the school leader is supported by a leadership team that includes one or several deputy principals, an administrative manager and one or more educational counselors. In certain cases, such as in the Flemish Community of Belgium and Korea, the number of vice-principals might depend on the number of students, and they might be responsible for some specific area of administration, such as student discipline or curriculum co-ordination.

- *Teacher leaders* also assume a formal role and responsibilities for managing and leading in schools. In Australia, teacher leaders are responsible for teams, year levels, or curriculum areas. New Zealand designates senior practitioners for grade clusters, curriculum leaders and specialist classroom teachers. In Korea, chief teachers handle mid-level supervisory duties; while in Spain, teachers with a reduced workload assume the role of leadership assistants to free school leaders from some administrative tasks.

- *School boards*, which are generally composed of teachers, members of the community, parents and students, also play a role in distributing school leadership. In the Flemish Community of Belgium school boards have a high degree of responsibility over schools and school resources; while in Hungary, Korea, Portugal and Spain, they are largely advisory bodies. In the Netherlands and Scotland, the roles of the school boards are defined by the local community or by the schools.

DEVELOPING LEADERSHIP FOR TOMORROW'S EDUCATION SYSTEMS

How have countries succeeded in developing effective school leaders at scale? The OECD's study of innovative leadership development programs[10] found that the more effective ones:

- prepare and develop school leaders using innovative approaches that address the broader roles and responsibilities of leaders and the purposes of schooling, and that use core technologies to achieve intended outcomes;

- are designed to produce leaders who work to build student-centered schools with the capacity for high performance and continuous improvement towards that end; and

- take a system-wide perspective, so that the programs are aligned with the larger goals and processes of the system concerning school improvement, student performance, and enhanced efficiency and effectiveness.

Effective leadership-development programs often also include networking among participants, which can help to foster collaborative problem-solving and alleviate the sense of isolation that some school leaders feel. Based on studies of what works for teachers' professional development, coaching and mentoring could also have a place in these programs.[11] Through mentoring, newly appointed school leaders have access to the counsel and advice of those with years of experience in leading schools.

While many of the studies suggest that leadership-development programs influence student achievement only indirectly, they do show that school leaders who participate in such programs change practices within the school that ultimately lead to better teaching and learning outcomes. The Stanford Educational Leadership Institute,[12] for example, found that directors who participate in "exemplary programs" (see Box 1.3) are better prepared and are more consistent in their use of effective practices in school.

Box 1.3 Characteristics of leadership-development "exemplary programs"

All of the initial training programs categorized as "exemplary" by the Stanford Educational Leadership Institute share the following characteristics:

- a comprehensive and coherent curriculum aligned with state and professional standards, particularly the Interstate School Leaders Licensure Consortium standards, which emphasize instructional leadership;

- a philosophy and curriculum emphasizing instructional leadership and school improvement;

- active, student-centered instruction that integrates theory and practice and stimulates reflection. Instructional strategies include problem-based learning; action research; field-based projects; journal writing; and portfolios that feature substantial use of feedback and assessment by peers, faculty, and the candidates themselves;

- faculty who are knowledgeable in their subject areas, including both university professors and practitioners experienced in school administration;

- social and professional support in the form of a cohort structure and formalized mentoring and advising by expert principals;

- vigorous, targeted recruitment and selection to seek out expert teachers with leadership potential; and

- well-designed and supervised administrative internships that allow candidates to engage in leadership responsibilities for substantial periods of time under the tutelage of expert veterans.

Source: Darling-Hammond, et al. (2007).

Box 1.4 Cultivating school leadership in the United States

Founded in 2000 by a team of social entrepreneurs, New Leaders (formerly "New Leaders for New Schools") is a national non-profit organization that develops school leaders and designs leadership policies and practices for school systems across the United States. In its first decade, New Leaders trained almost 800 leaders in 12 urban areas through its Aspiring Principals Program, affecting a quarter of a million students in high-need schools across the country. New Leaders was the first principal-training program to track and measure its success based on the student-achievement results of its graduates. It is the only national principal-training program that prepares leaders for both district and charter schools.

The goal of New Leaders is to improve student achievement by recruiting, selecting, training and supporting outstanding school leaders while also working with partner school systems to create the conditions that will enable these leaders to succeed once on the job. To achieve this goal, New Leaders:

Attracts high-quality candidates. The Emerging Leaders Program provides free, high-quality professional development for successful teachers and assistant principals interested in improving their leadership skills and possibly becoming a principal. The idea is to create a pathway to school leadership for effective teachers and other top instructors who may not have considered the job.

...

Selects carefully. Both the Emerging Leaders Program and the Aspiring Principals Program have highly selective processes for admission. For both programs, New Leaders looks for candidates who believe in the potential of every child, and have strong instructional knowledge, a track record of improved learning outcomes, and adult leadership potential.

Trains for what matters most. After selecting the most promising candidates, the Aspiring Principals Program provides future leaders with coursework combined with a full-time residency year in a high-need school. Local staff create an individualized learning plan for each resident.

Fosters a supportive network. New Leaders partners with school systems that have similar priorities in order to build a network of leaders. Working with these systems, the organization designs and puts in place principal-performance standards and evaluations systems, and defines the roles and provides support and training for principal managers.

In 2011, New Leader schools were among the top 10 highest-gaining schools in eight U.S. cities.

Several school systems have adopted elements of the New Leaders' model in developing their own principal-training programs, and more plan to do so in the near future. In addition, New Leaders works to influence key decision makers and public education policies in order to improve school leadership and promote educational excellence at scale.

THE URBAN EXCELLENCE FRAMEWORK™ (UEF)

In 2007, New Leaders created the Urban Excellence Framework™ (UEF) to articulate what leaders in successful schools do to improve student achievement. The UEF now informs the organization's leadership training programs and recommendations to system partners. The UEF was developed based on more than 100 visits to and case studies of schools that achieved dramatic gains; an extensive review of the available research on the practices of effective schools and leadership; and the collective knowledge of the New Leaders staff and participants.

Source: New Leaders, website: *www.newleaders.org*.

There are many examples illustrating the efforts countries are investing in this (see Box 1.4 for one example from the United States). Leadership programs can have a substantial impact on how schools work and on the quality of the school. A longitudinal study of 35 schools in Sweden[13] shows that such training led to more collaborative work among teachers. In England, research on the impact of leadership-development programs shows that schools whose leader participated in the National College for School Leadership's development program improved more quickly than others. Assessment outcomes of 16-year-old students in schools that had engaged in the program improved by 8.1% between 2005 and 2009, compared with a 5.8% improvement in schools that had not engaged. Similarly, 43% of schools with a leader who had been certified with a National Professional Qualification for Headship showed an improvement in their overall performance rating between 2005 and 2008, compared with only 37% of non-NPQH-led schools. A study[14] with data from the United States found that better-trained school leaders recruit, select and retrain teachers with stronger academic backgrounds, especially in schools in low-income areas, which leads to better student outcomes.

Selecting suitable candidates

Many countries rely on self-selection to fill enrolments in training and development programs. While this approach rewards initiative, it can be inefficient. Self-selected candidates may or may not be the best qualified. In countries where additional training implies higher salaries, the incentive to attend such programs may be less the leadership role than the possibility of earning a raise in pay. Self-selection also does not address a school's or a jurisdiction's specific needs for succession planning. Other countries, such as Singapore, use a planning model, continuously assessing teachers for different leadership positions and providing them with the opportunity for training (see Box 1.5).

Box 1.5 Selecting and training school leaders in Singapore

To ensure that Singapore has the best school leaders, young teachers are continuously assessed for their leadership potential and are given the opportunity to develop their leadership capacity. Future school leaders are chosen from successful teachers already in the education system. Moreover, all education leadership positions are part of the teaching-career structure. Potential school leaders can serve on committees, be promoted to middle-level leadership positions (e.g. head of department), and be transferred to the ministry for a period.

Successful potential school leaders are selected to attend the Management and Leadership in Schools program at Singapore's National Institute for Education, based on interviews and leadership-situation exercises. Once accepted, aspiring school leaders can attend the four-month executive leadership training. Potential vice principals attend a six-month Leaders in Education program. Candidates in both programs are paid during their training. Only 35 people are selected for the executive leadership training each year.

More experienced school leaders mentor recently appointed leaders; and principals are periodically transferred among schools as part of Singapore's continuous improvement strategy. Experienced school leaders are offered the opportunity to become Cluster Superintendants, which is the first step toward a system-level leadership role.

Source: Mourshed M., C. Chijioke and M. Barber (2010); OECD (2011a).

To respond to shortages or a lack of qualified candidates, some institutions that provide development training screen potential candidates for leadership. Another approach to pre-screening and selecting candidates is to provide short "taster" courses for those who may be interested in leadership (see Box 1.6).

Box 1.6 Sampling school leadership in Denmark and the Netherlands

Denmark is introducing a "taster" course for aspiring school leaders. Danish teachers who may want to have a leadership position can begin to understand the different components of becoming a school leader through a "taster" course offered by local school districts or municipalities. Participants take part in one or more modules of a Leadership Diploma of Education. The course consists of theoretical assignments, case studies, personal reflections, discussions with a mentor about career opportunities, personal strengths and areas for development, and networking. Participants must also conduct a project in their own school. Those who want to continue can attend a two-year Diploma in Leadership course that includes seminars on economy, personal leadership, coaching, strategy implementation, change-management and problem-solving. The program is managed by School Leadership Development, but is organized by the Local Government Training and Development Denmark, which is the center for training and development for all of the country's municipalities and regions.

In **the Netherlands**, training institutes offer orientation courses to allow teachers interested in leadership functions to discover whether they have the required capabilities. For example, *Orientation towards Management* is a brief training program offered by the Association of School Leaders for the Sectoral Board for the Education Labour Market (a fund of employers and employee organizations in the education sector). School boards, upper-school managers and school leaders are asked to select candidates from their own schools. After participating in a two-day training course on various leadership topics, candidates draw up a personal development plan based on a competence analysis. *Orientation towards Management* then offers further training for candidates who are interested and suitable.

Source: Moos L. (2011).

The availability of training

Until recently, most education systems did not demand that school leaders have a specific leadership qualification (see Figure A.21 in the Annex). In some countries, while having a qualification is not mandatory, it may be actively encouraged. For example, in Finland, school leaders are encouraged to have a Certificate in Educational Administration or sufficient knowledge of education administration before applying for a leadership post. Until recently, the only formal requirement for school leaders in Australia was a four-year teaching qualification.[15] Since 2006, however, a national program for school leaders has been available. In Japan, current education reforms include the establishment of graduate schools with teacher-training programs that are also for school leaders. These programs equip leaders with pedagogical theory and practical skills to help them improve teaching in their schools. In England, new school leaders can obtain a National Qualification for Professional Headship awarded by the National College for School Leadership.

Despite the availability of training, school leaders across OECD countries have often reported that they felt they had not been adequately trained to assume their posts. Although most candidates for school-leadership positions have a teaching background, they are not necessarily competent in pedagogical innovation or in managing financial or human resources. Much of the gap between the skills candidates bring to the position of leader and the skills required of them once they're in the post can be filled once the role and responsibilities of school leader are clearly defined and specific training in those skills is made available to them.

Types of training

Experts in leadership and development argue that school leaders' "professional development activities should be ongoing, career-staged and seamless".[16]

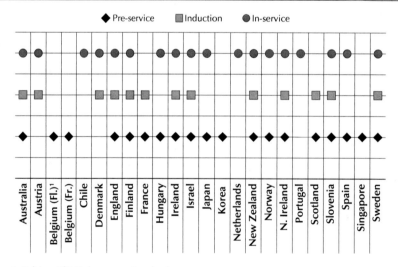

Figure 1.4

Leadership development in selected countries

1. Belgium (Fl.): Only community schools.
Source: Updated from Pont, Nusche and Moorman (2008a).

England, Ontario (Canada), Ireland, Northern Ireland, Scotland and Victoria (Australia) all have relatively comprehensive training that include pre-service qualification programs, induction programs to support the initial phase as leader, and in-service training programs for established school leaders. Victoria and Ontario have integrated these comprehensive training programs into their national strategies to improve schools. Most of these approaches were designed and are led by a leading institution, such as England's National College for School Leadership, the Regional Training Unit in Northern Ireland or the Department for Education in Victoria (Australia). In England, a leadership-development strategy establishes five stages of school leadership. Each has a range of related development opportunities based on preparatory, induction and further training for school leaders. In Northern Ireland, there is training for emergent and aspirant leaders as well as serving leaders and managers. The Scottish approach is described in Box 1.7.

Among the countries with comprehensive programs, program participants, schools, central or regional authorities provide the financial support for the programs. Participants and other agencies might share the cost of the program or subsidies might be granted, as in England. Incentives for participating in training should be offered.

Box 1.7 Leadership development in Scotland

Scotland has two national training programs for aspiring headteachers both of which are accredited against the Standard for Headship. The Standard for Headship defines the professional actions required of effective headteachers. These training programs will result in successful participants being awarded the Standard for Headship. These training programs are not mandatory. However, we expect local authorities, who appoint headteachers, to ensure that those teachers appointed to their first headteacher posts meet the Standard for Headship. This can be done through the formal national routes or by other local interview and assessment procedures. There is no national induction program for new school leaders. Each local authority will have their own arrangements which can include coaching and mentoring support. In 2003, it introduced a new framework for leadership development that includes learning opportunities for those involved in leadership teams as well as more senior staff. *Continuing Professional Development for Educational Leaders* is based on the notion of professional progression in education leadership through four broad areas:

- **Project Leadership,** for teachers who have, or may take on, responsibility for leading a small-scale project. This refers to teachers possibly quite early in their careers, who wish to develop their leadership skills, for instance in an area related to curriculum development or supporting pupils' learning, or through a small school-based research project.

- **Team leadership**, for teachers who, in addition to leading small-scale projects, have regular responsibility for leading either permanent teams of staff or task groups/working parties. This might be particularly relevant to aspiring and established principal teachers, whether their responsibilities are primarily in the areas of curriculum or of guidance.

- **School leadership**, for staff who lead projects and teams and who have, or are seeking, overall responsibility for an aspect of leadership across an establishment. This might include teachers or principal teachers who aspire to membership of a senior leadership team and established members of such teams. Some members of senior leadership teams will aspire to become school heads.

- **Strategic leadership**, for staff who, in addition to project, team and school-leadership responsibilities, have overall responsibility for leading an establishment or are leading strategic initiatives at the local or national level. This is particularly relevant to head teachers and to those working in the education service who have a strategic role in improving Scottish education.

Source: Scottish Executive Education Department (2007).

Training for school leaders is particularly important in countries where schools and school leaders have a high degree of autonomy. New Zealand, which has a highly decentralized school system, established four development initiatives for school leaders: an induction program for first-time school leaders; an electronic network for sitting school leaders (LeadSpace); development centers for school leaders (Principals' Development Planning Centre); and guidelines on professional development for school leaders.[17]

Initial training

Many countries offer pre-service leadership-preparation programs that often lead to a university degree or specialized qualification (see Box 1.8). The education ministries in France and Korea offer such programs to groups of pre-selected candidates who will become school leaders after the training. Other countries' programs are offered in partnership with universities, local municipalities or other providers. Spain recently made participation in such programs mandatory, but the country's regional governments are responsible for providing the training.

There is some debate about whether initial training should be mandatory. Those in favor argue that it can be seen as a way of professionalizing school leadership. It can also help to align programs with national goals and priorities. Those against say that mandatory training often does not encourage flexibility and innovation, that such development is more effective when initiated by the individual and not imposed by legislation, and that local and regional authorities, rather than national authorities, may be better placed to determine the training needs of school leaders.

Box 1.8 Leadership-preparation programs in Finland and Norway

Finland started a program in 2010 in 76 education networks to re-design the country's school leadership-development model. The main objective of the program is to give greater responsibility to schools to implement staff-development activities that meet the individual or organizational needs of the school and its personnel. It also empowers teachers to create and implement their own professional-development program. The program initially targeted school leaders, teaching staff over 55 years of age, and persons who had not participated in professional-development activities in recent years. The program encourages collaboration and the use of innovative learning methods and institutionalizes professional development within the school.

In 2009, **Norway**'s central authorities introduced a new two-year program to develop instructional leadership skills for school principals. The program covers student learning outcomes and environment; management and administration; collaboration and organization; guidance for teachers; development and change; and leadership identity. It was initially offered to new school principals with less than two years of experience, and will eventually be offered to more experienced school leaders as well.

Source: Hamalainen K., K. Hamalainen and J. Kangasniemi (2011); OECD (2011b).

Induction programs

Many countries provide leadership training for newly appointed school leaders, however most of these programs are optional. By targeting new school leaders, these programs can help to shape initial school-leadership practices and build networks through which the leaders can share their concerns. They should provide a combination of theoretical and practical knowledge and self-study, and should be designed to cohere with the broader development framework.

In the United States, more than half of the 50 states now require that new school leaders receive some form of induction support. In Australia and Hungary, induction programs are short courses organized by local authorities to introduce school leaders to their surroundings. In Denmark, the courses may run to about a month, but in other countries, they may run from one to three years.

Ireland launched an induction program for newly appointed school leaders in 2001. *Misneach* (Gaelic for "courage") focuses on managing self, leading learning, leading the organization and leading people. Only 18% of those who attended the program felt that they had been well-prepared to assume their role as school leader before they participated in the training.[18]

In-service training

In-service training can respond to specific needs. As such, it should be available periodically for school leaders and leadership teams to allow them to update their skills and/or share new practices. Australia, Austria, Chile, England, Finland, Ireland, New Zealand, Northern Ireland, Slovenia and Sweden provide systematic in-service training programs for school leaders. In Finland, the minimum annual requirement for development training is three days; in Hungary, it is 120 hours every seven years. In Scotland, to ensure that school leaders and teachers undertake in-service training, they must participate in an additional 35 hours of training per year, and teachers must maintain a record of their professional development activities. But in most places, there are no requirements.

In-service training covers a range of different aspects of school management and education leadership; it can also focus on new national requirements. For example, Austria's Leadership Academy was established to provide school leaders, who had just acquired greater autonomy, but had little experience operating outside a hierarchical, bureaucratic structure, with the capacity to act more independently, take more initiative, and help their schools navigate though government reforms. Inspectors, the staff of in-service training institutes, executives from the Ministry of Education and provincial education authorities were invited to participate.

Countries offer course-based training, group training, self-study and other arrangements. Professional networks can also be used to develop school leaders and leadership teams informally. In Australia, England, New Zealand and Northern Ireland, for example, virtual networks help school leaders to share best practices.

APPRAISAL OF SCHOOL LEADERS

Appraising the performance of school leaders can help to improve practice. Most OECD countries evaluate school leaders through systematic performance-appraisal processes. Denmark's performance-appraisal system for primary schools is under the discretion of the municipality; but for secondary schools, it is defined by a results-based contract. Rewards for good performance are determined by the municipality, and leaders in secondary schools can receive a monetary reward. In Ireland, appraisals are conducted by the Inspectorate, which bases them on predefined school objectives. If schools are underperforming, further evaluations are conducted. In Slovenia, the annual performance appraisal is conducted at the discretion of the school governing board, and achievement criteria are predetermined by the school program. Under-performance or under-achievement are reflected in the school leader's salary. Austria, the French Community of Belgium and Finland do not conduct systematic performance appraisals. In England, Northern Ireland and Scotland, performance data is used to track and monitor student progress and guide ongoing improvement, although Northern Ireland notes that internal-assessment data are not used enough to review students' progress over time or to modify classroom practice and improve the quality of students' work. In Scotland, the HM Inspectorate of Education works alongside Learning and Teaching Scotland, which develops guidelines for the national curriculum, to promote improvement in standards, quality and achievement for all students. It does so through annual inspections that evaluate the quality of pre-school, school and teacher education, community learning and development, and further education.[19]

For accountability systems to lead to improvements, they need to focus on information relevant to teaching and learning, motivate individuals and schools to use that information to improve practice, and build the knowledge necessary for interpreting and applying the information. That requires the participation of school leaders who are skilled in interpreting test results and in using data to plan and design appropriate strategies for improvement. It also demands that school leaders involve their staff in the use of accountability data in order to strengthen professional learning communities within schools and engage those who need to change their practice.

CONCLUSIONS

School leaders can make a difference in school and student performance if they are granted the autonomy to make important decisions. To do this effectively, they need to be able to adapt teaching programs to local needs, promote teamwork among teachers, and engage in teacher monitoring, evaluation and professional development. They need discretion in setting strategic direction and must be able to develop school plans and goals and monitor progress, using data to improve practice. They also need to be able to influence teacher recruitment to improve the match between candidates and their school's needs. Last but not least, leadership preparation and training are central and building networks of schools to stimulate and spread innovation and to develop diverse curricula, extended services and professional support can bring substantial benefits.

Notes

1. OECD (2010a).

2. Hallinger, P. and R. Heck (1998).

3. PricewaterhouseCoopers (2007).

4. Wylie, C. (2007).

5. Pont, B., D. Nusche and H. Moorman (2008a). Much of this chapter is based on this study which covered Australia, Austria, Belgium (Flanders and French Community), Chile, Denmark, Finland, France, Hungary, Ireland, Israel, Korea, The Netherlands, New Zealand, Norway, Portugal, Slovenia, Spain, Sweden and the United Kingdom (England, Northern Ireland and Scotland).

6. Hallinger, P. and R. Heck (2010).

7. Frost, D. (2011).

8. Bangs, J. and J. MacBeath (2012).

9. Ingvarson, L., et al. (2006).

10. Pont, B., D. Nusche and H. Moorman (2008b).

11. OECD (2009).

12. Darling-Hammond, L., et al. (2007).

13. Blossing, U. and M. Ekholm (2005).

14. Baker, B. and B. Cooper (2005).

15. Dinham, S., et al. (2011).

16. Davis S., et al. (2005).

17. New Zealand Ministry of Education (2002).

18. Morgan, M. and C. Sugrue (2005).

19. *http://www.hmie.gov.uk/NR/rdonlyres/0980BB93-8806-40D9-806C-AA35532BA931/0/PrinciplesofInspectionandReview2010FINAL.pdf*

References

Anderson, M., et al. (2006), *Standards for School Leadership: a Critical Review of Literature*, Teaching Australia.

Augustine, C., et al. (2009), *Improving School Leadership: The Promise of Cohesive Leadership Systems*, RAND Education, The RAND Corporation .

Australian Institute for Teaching and School Leadership (2011), "National Professional Standard for School Leadership", public statement endorsed by Ministers at the Ministerial Council for Education, Early Childhood Development and Youth Affairs (MCEECDYA) on 8 July 2011, transcript available at *http://www.aitsl.edu.au/verve/_resources/NationalProfessionalStandardForPrincipals_July25.pdf*

Baker, B. and B. Cooper (2005), "Do Principals With Stronger Academic Backgrounds Hire Better Teachers? Policy Implications for Improving High-Poverty Schools", *Educational Administration Quarterly*, August, Vol. 41, No. 3, pp. 449-479.

Bangs, J. and J. MacBeath (2012), "Collective Leadership: the role of teacher unions in encouraging teachers to take the lead in their own learning and in teacher policy", *Professional Development in Education,* Vol. 38, No. 2, April, pp. 331-343.

Barber, M. and M. Mourshed (2007), *How the World's Best-Performing School Systems Come Out on Top*, McKinsey, London.

Blossing, U. and M. Ekholm (2005), "School Reforms and Local Response in the Long Run: A Twenty-year Longitudinal Study of 35 Swedish 'Grund' Schools", paper presented at the Second OECD Conference on Evidence-Based Policy Research, Stockholm, 27-28 January.

Bush, T. and D. Glover (2004), "Leadership Development: Evidence and Beliefs", National College for School Leadership, Nottingham.

Bush, T. and D. Jackson (2002), "A Preparation for School Leadership: International Perspectives", *Educational Management Administration and Leadership*, Vol. 30.

Darling-Hammond, L., et al. (2007), *Preparing School Leaders for a Changing World: Lessons from Exemplary Leadership Development Programs,* Stanford University.

Davis, S., et al. (2005), *Review of Research, School Leadership Study: Developing Successful Principals,* Stanford Educational Leadership Institute, and the Wallace Foundation.

Day, C., et al. (2009), "The Impact of School Leadership on Pupil Outcomes", *Research Report DCSF-RR108,* University of Nottingham.

Dinham, S., et al. (2011), "Breakthroughs in school leadership development in Australia", in *School Leadership and Management*, Vol. 31, No. 2, pp. 139-154.

Frost, D. (2011), "Supporting Teacher Leadership in 15 Countries, International Teacher Leadership project Phase 1, Leadership for Learning", University of Cambridge Faculty of Education.

Fry, B, G. Bottoms, and K. O'Neill (2004), "The Principal Internship: How Can We Get it Right?", Southern Regional Education Board (SREB), Atlanta.

Gorham, M., M. Finn-Stevenson and B. Lapin (2008), "Enriching School Leadership Development through Coaching", *Research and Policy Brief,* The School of the 21st Century, Yale University.

Hallinger, P. and R. Heck (1998), "Exploring the Principal's Contribution to School Effectiveness: 1980-1995", School Effectiveness and School Improvement, Vol. 9, pp. 157-191.

Hallinger, P. and R. Heck (2010), "Collaborative Leadership and School Improvement: Understanding the impact on school capacity and student learning", *School Leadership and Management,* 30:2, pp. 95-110.

Hamalainen K., K. Hamalainen and J. Kangasniemi (2011), "2011 Annual Conference of the Association for Teacher Education in Europe", 24 - 28 August 2011: 12 December 2011, *www.ppf.lu.lv/pn/files/articles/ATEE%202011%20Hamalainen.doc,* "Osaava verme", 3 July 2011, *http://ktl.jyu.fi/ktl/verme/osaavaverme.*

Heck, R. and P. Hallinger (2009), "Assessing the Contribution of Distributed Leadership to School Improvement and Growth in Math Achievement", *American Educational Research Journal,* Vol. 46, No. 3 (September), pp. 659-689.

Hess, F. and A. Kelly (2007), "Learning to Lead: What gets taught in principal-preparation programs", *The Teachers College Record*, Columbia University.

Ingvarson, L., et al. (2006), "Standards for School Leadership: A Critical Review of the Literature", *Teaching Australia,* Australian Institute for Teaching and School Leadership Ltd., Canberra.

Karstanje, P. and **C. Webber** (2008), "Programs for school principal preparation in East Europe", *Journal of Educational Administration*, Vol. 46, No. 6.

Leithwood, K., et al. (2004), *How Leadership Influences Student Learning*, Minneapolis, Minnesota: Center for Applied Research and Educational Improvement, University of Minnesota.

Leithwood, K., et al. (2006), *Seven Strong Claims about Successful School Leadership*, National College of School Leadership, Nottingham.

Levine, A. (2005), *Educating School Leaders*, The Education Schools Project, *http://www.edschools.org/reports_leaders.htm.*

Matthews, P. (2009) *Twenty Outstanding Primary Schools: Excelling against the Odds,* Ofsted, United Kingdom.

Matthews, P. (2009) *Twelve Outstanding Secondary Schools: Excelling against the Odds,* Ofsted, United Kingdom.

Moos L. (2011), "Educating Danish school leaders to meet new expectations?", *School Leadership & Management,* Vol. 31, Issue 2.

Morgan, G. and **R. Hawkins** (2004), "Generational Change in the Principalship", Leadership Fellowship 2004, Frank Farrell Award, New South Wales Department of Education and Training.

Morgan, M. and **C. Sugrue** (2005), "Evaluation of the MISNEACH Program", Clare Education Centre, Ennis, Ireland.

Mourshed M., C. Chijioke and **M. Barber** (2010), *How the World's Most Improved School Systems Keep Getting Better,* McKinsey and Company.

Murphy, J. (1992), "The landscape of principal preparation: Reframing the education of schools administrators", Newbury Park.

New Zealand Ministry of Education (2002), "Principals' Development Package", unpublished paper.

OECD (2009), *Creating Effective Teaching and Learning Environments: First Results from TALIS,* OECD Publishing.

OECD (2010a), *PISA 2009 Results: What Makes a School Successful? Resources, Policies and Practices* (Volume IV), PISA, OECD Publishing.

OECD (2010b), *Improving Schools: Strategies for Action for Mexico,* OECD Publishing.

OECD (2011a), *Strong Performers and Successful Reformers in Education: Lessons from PISA for the United States,* OECD Publishing.

OECD (2011b), *Improving Lower Secondary Schools in Norway,* OECD Publishing.

Olson, L. (2007), "Getting Serious About Preparation" in *Leading for Learning,* Supplement to the 12 September 2007 issue of *Education Week.*

Paredes, R. and **V. Paredes** (2010), "Chile: Educational Performance and Management under a Rigid Employment Regime", *CEPAL Review,* No. 99.

Pont, B., D. Nusche and **H. Moorman** (2008a), *Improving School Leadership: Volume 1: Policies and Practices,* OECD Publishing.

Pont, B., D. Nusche and **H. Moorman** (2008b), *Improving School Leadership: Volume 2: Case Studies on System Leadership,* OECD Publishing.

PricewaterhouseCoopers (2007), "Independent Study into School Leadership: Main Report", Department for Education and Skills, London.

Reeves, P. and **J. Berry** (2008), "Preparing, Developing and Credentialing K-12 School Leaders: Continuous Learning for Professional Roles", National Council of the Professors of Educational Administration, Eastern Michigan University, Ypsilanti.

Robinson, V., C. Lloyd and **K. Rowe** (2008), "The Impact of Leadership on Student Outcomes: An Analysis of the Differential Effects of Leadership Types", Educational Administration Quarterly, December 2008, Vol. 44, No. 5 635-674.

Ross, J. and **P. Gray** (2006), "School Leadership and Student Achievement: The Mediating Effects of Teacher Beliefs", *Canadian Journal of Education,* Vol. 29.

Scottish Executive Education Department (2007), OECD Review of the Quality and Equity of Education Outcomes in Scotland: Diagnostic Report, available at *www.oecd.org/edu/reviews/nationalpolicies.*

Smith, B., R. Harchar and **K. Campbell** (2006), "Reality Check: Designing a New Leadership Program for the 21st Century", National Council of the Professors of Educational Administration, Eastern Michigan University, Ypsilanti.

Witziers, B., R. Bosker and **M. Kruger** (2003), "Educational Leadership and Student Achievement: the Elusive Search for an Associaton", *Educational Administration Quarterly,* Vol. 39.

Wylie, C. (2007), *School Governance in New Zealand: How Is It Working?,* New Zealand Council for Educational Research, Wellington.

Chapter 2

PREPARING TEACHERS
TO DELIVER 21ST-CENTURY SKILLS

Many nations around the world have undertaken wide-ranging reforms of curriculum, instruction, and assessments with the intention of better preparing all children for the higher educational demands of life and work in the 21st century. What are the skills that young people need to be successful in this rapidly changing world and what competencies do teachers need, in turn, to effectively teach those skills to their students? The question that arises from this is, of course, what teacher preparation programs are needed to prepare graduates who are ready to teach well in a 21st-century classroom. This question is, however, still difficult to answer with available comparative evidence.

CHANGES IN THE DEMAND FOR STUDENT SKILLS

The world is rapidly becoming a different place, and the challenges to individuals and societies imposed by globalization and modernization are widely acknowledged. Perhaps the most challenging dilemma for educators in the 21st century is that routine, rule-based, knowledge, which is easiest to teach and to test, is also easiest to digitize, automate and outsource. The issue of 21st-century skills[1] is by no means orthogonal to traditional school subjects but, in fact, equally relevant to the latter. Take *mathematics* as an example. Traditionally mathematics is often taught in an abstract mathematical world, using formalism first, removed from authentic contexts, and discouraging to the students that do not see its relevance – for example, students are taught the techniques of arithmetic, then given lots of arithmetic computations to complete; or they are shown how to solve particular types of equations, then given lots of similar equations to solve. In contrast, in the 21st century, students need to have an understanding of the fundamental concepts of mathematics, they need to be able to translate a new situation or problem they face into a form that exposes the relevance of mathematics, make the problem amenable to mathematical treatment, identify and use the relevant mathematical knowledge to solve the problem, and then evaluate the solution in the original problem context. Further, their creativity can be enhanced by devising novel solutions, and even new problems with non-standard solutions. *Literacy* provides another example. In the past, literacy was mainly about *learning to read*, a set of technical skills that individuals would acquire once for a lifetime in order to process an established body of coded knowledge. In the 21st century, literacy is about *reading for learning*, the capacity and motivation to identify, understand, interpret, create and communicate knowledge, using written materials associated with varying situations in continuously changing contexts. In the past, it was sufficient to direct students to an encyclopedia to find the answer to a question, and they could generally rely on what they found to be true. Today, literacy is about curiosity and self-direction, managing non-linear information structures, building one's own mental representation and synthesis of information as one finds one's own way through hypertext on the Internet, about dealing with ambiguity, developing healthy skepticism, an inquiring mindset, and interpreting and resolving conflicting pieces of information.

Similarly, the conventional approach of schools to problems was to break these down into manageable bits and pieces, and then teaching students the techniques to solve them. But today individuals create value by synthesizing the disparate bits. This is about openmindedness and making connections between ideas that previously seemed unrelated, which requires being familiar with and receptive to knowledge in different fields. The world is also no longer divided into specialists and generalists. What counts today are the versatilists who are able to apply depth of skill to a progressively widening scope of situations and experiences, gaining new competencies, building relationships, and assuming new roles. They are capable not only of constantly adapting but also of constantly learning and growing, of positioning themselves and repositioning themselves in a fast changing world.

Box 2.1 ATC21S – Assessment and Teaching of 21st-Century Skills

Starting from the premise that learning to collaborate with others and connecting through technology are essential skills in a knowledge-based economy, the Assessment and Teaching of 21st-Century Skills project brought together more than 250 researchers across 60 institutions worldwide who categorized 21st-century skills internationally into four broad categories:

Ways of thinking. Creativity, critical thinking, problem-solving, decision-making and learning

Ways of working. Communication and collaboration

Tools for working. Information and communications technology (ICT) and information literacy

Skills for living in the world. Citizenship, life and career, and personal and social responsibility

The project also outlines the nature of assessment systems that can support changes in practice, illustrates the use of technology to transform assessment systems and learning, and proposes a model for assessing 21st-century skills.

For further information, see *www.atc21s.org.*

...

Charles Fadel[2] identifies the following dimensions of a 21st-century education, and the related challenges for curricula:

Knowledge – relevance required: students' lack of motivation, and often disengagement, reflects the inability of education systems to connect the content to real-world relevance. The author suggests a need to rethink the significance and applicability of what is taught, and in concert to strike a better balance between the conceptual and the practical.

Skills – necessity for education outcomes: higher-order skills ("21st-Century Skills") such as the "4 C's" of Creativity, Critical thinking, Communication, Collaboration. The author notes that curricula are already overburdened with content, which makes it much harder for students to acquire (and teachers to teach) skills via deep dives into projects. He notes further that, while there is some consensus on what the skills are, and how teaching methods via projects can affect skills acquisition, there is little time available during the school year given the overwhelming nature of content curricula, and that there is little in terms of teacher expertise in combining knowledge and skills in a coherent ensemble, with guiding materials, and assessments.

Character (behaviors, attitudes, values) – to face an increasingly challenging world: as complexities ramp up, humankind is rediscovering the importance of teaching character traits such as performance-related traits (adaptability, persistence, resilience) and moral-related traits (integrity, justice, empathy, ethics). The author describes the challenges for public school systems as similar to those for skills, with the extra complexity of accepting that character development is also becoming an intrinsic part of the mission, as it is for private schools.

Meta-Layer (learning how to learn, interdisciplinarity, systems thinking, personalization, etc.) – often neglected, or merely mentioned and not acted upon deterministically, this "meta-layer" enveloping the other three dimensions is essential for establishing lifelong learning habits, activating transference, building expertise, fostering creativity via analogies, enhancing versatility, addressing individual students' needs, and so on.

Of all 21st-century skills, creativity and innovation deserve a special mention: At the country, organization, and personal levels, the two have become the recognized hope for solving employability, personal, and societal crises. Schools need to nurture creativity and innovation in their students, deliberately and systematically, and across all disciplines not only through the Arts.

Last but not least, in today's schools, students typically learn individually and at the end of the school year, schools certify their individual achievements. But the more interdependent the world becomes, the more important the capacity of individuals to collaborate and orchestrate becomes. In the flat world, everything that is proprietary knowledge today will be a commodity available to everyone else tomorrow. There is a shift from a world of stocks – with knowledge that is stacked up somewhere depreciating rapidly in value – to a world in which the enriching power of communication and collaborative flows is increasing.

While there have been numerous efforts to systematize 21st-century skills (see Box 2.1 for an example) most of the resulting frameworks share the above features.

A DEMANDING AGENDA FOR TEACHERS

Changes in the demand for skills have profound implications for the competencies which teachers themselves need to acquire to effectively teach 21st-century skills to their students. A generation ago, when teachers could reasonably expect that what they taught would last for a lifetime, teaching a fixed syllabus of content was at the center of education in most countries. Today, where individuals can access content on search engines, where routine rule based knowledge is being digitized or outsourced, and where jobs are changing rapidly, teachers need to enable people to become lifelong learners, to manage non-rule-based complex ways of thinking and complex ways of working that computers cannot take over easily. In the past, the policy focus was on the provision of education, today it is on outcomes, shifting from looking upwards in the hierarchy towards looking outwards to the next teacher, the next school. The past was about delivered wisdom, the challenge now is to foster user-generated wisdom among teachers and school leaders in the front line. In the past, different students were taught in

similar ways; today teachers are expected to embrace diversity with differentiated pedagogical practices. The goal of the past was standardization and conformity, today it is about being ingenious, about personalizing educational experiences; the past was curriculum centered, the present is learner centered, which means that education systems increasingly need to identify how individuals learn differently and foster new forms of educational provision that take learning to the learner and allow individuals to learn in the ways that are most conducive to their progress.

In short, the kind of education needed today requires teachers to be high-level knowledge workers who constantly advance their own professional knowledge as well as that of their profession. Teachers need to be agents of innovation not least because innovation is critically important for generating new sources of growth through improved efficiency and productivity.[3] This is also true in the education sector, where innovation applied to both curricula and teaching methods can help to improve learning outcomes and prepare students for the rapidly changing demands of the 21st-century labor market. While innovative teaching is recognized in both school evaluations and teacher-appraisal systems in many countries, it is sobering to learn that three out of four teachers responding to the OECD Teaching and Learning International Survey (TALIS) in 2008[4] reported that they would not be rewarded for being more innovative in their teaching.[5] The incentives for encouraging innovation appear to be missing.

Box 2.2 Singapore's TE21 Model of Teacher Education

Singapore's National Institute for Education as a university-based teacher education institution seeks to provide the theoretical foundation to produce the "thinking teacher" whilst concurrently having strong partnerships with key stakeholders and the schools to ensure strong clinical practice and realities of professionalism in teacher development. Its new TE21 Model seeks to enhance key elements of teacher education, including the underpinning philosophy, curriculum, desired outcomes for our teachers, and academic pathways. These are considered essential prerequisites in meeting the challenges of the 21st-century classroom. The model (see figure below) focuses on three value paradigms: Learner-centered, Teacher Identity and Service to the Profession and Community. Learner-centered values puts the learner at the center of teachers' work by being aware of learner development and diversity, believing that all youths can learn, caring for the learner, striving for scholarship in content teaching, knowing how people learn best, and learning to design the best learning environment possible. Teacher identity values refer to having high standards and strong drive to learn in view of the rapid changes in the education milieu, to be responsive to student needs. The values of service to the profession and community focuses on teachers' commitment to their profession through active collaborations and striving to become better practitioners to benefit the teaching community. The model also underscores the requisite knowledge and skills that teachers must possess in light of the latest global trends, and to improve student outcomes.

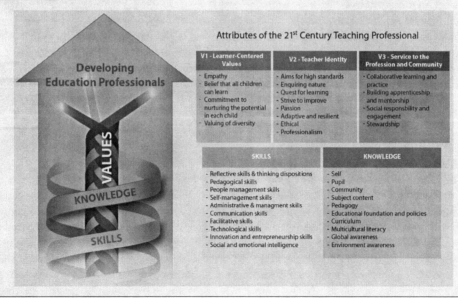

Source: www.nie.edu.sg/files/spcs/TE21_Executive%20Summary_101109.pdf.

Figure 2.1

Consequences of teacher performance as reported by teachers

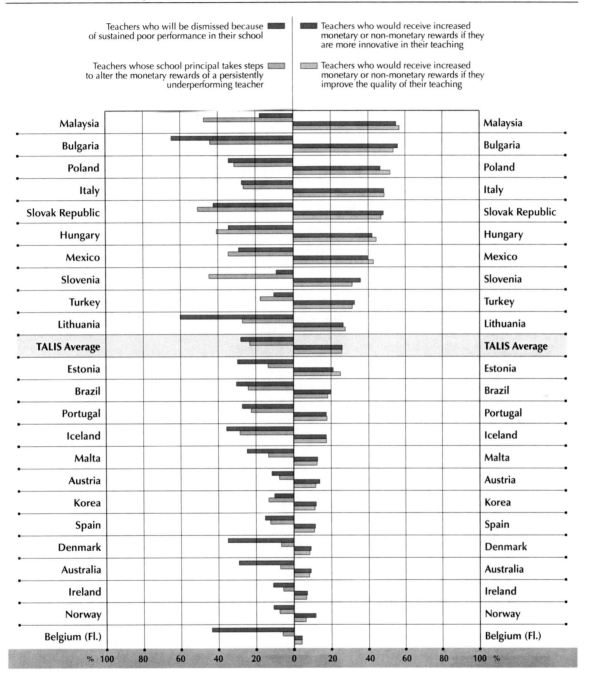

Countries are ranked in descending order of the percentage of teachers reporting to receive increased monetary or non-monetary rewards for an improvement in the quality of their teaching.

Source: OECD (2009a), Table 5.9.

What can teacher preparation programs do to prepare graduates who are ready to teach well in a 21st-century classroom? Education systems generally struggle with finding answers to this question and there is no agreement across countries on how success should be measured and quality assured. However, there seems considerable agreement across countries regarding important attributes that 21st-century learning environments should provide.

For example, the OECD's comparative review of innovative learning environments[6] concludes that, in order to be most effective, learning environments should:

- make learning central, encourage engagement, and be the place where students come to understand themselves as learners;

- ensure that learning is social and often collaborative;

- be highly attuned to students' motivations and the importance of emotions;

- be acutely sensitive to individual differences, including in prior knowledge;

- be demanding of every student, without overloading students;

- use assessments that emphasize formative feedback; and

- promote connections across activities and subjects, both in and out of school.

Taken together, these principles form a demanding framework on which teachers' professionalism is based. In addition to developing such individual skills, teachers also need to be able and have opportunities to work collaboratively with others in designing learning environments, addressing the learning needs of particular groups of students, developing themselves professionally, and teaching with others in team approaches. The OECD's comparative review of innovative learning environments concludes:

- Teachers need to be well-versed in the subjects they teach in order to be adept at using different methods and, if necessary, changing their approaches to optimize learning. This includes content-specific strategies and methods to teach specific content.

- They need a rich repertoire of teaching strategies, the ability to combine approaches, and the knowledge of how and when to use certain methods and strategies.

- The strategies used should include direct, whole-group teaching, guided discovery, group work, and the facilitation of self-study and individual discovery. They should also include personalized feedback.

- Teachers need to have a deep understanding of how learning happens, in general, and of individual students' motivations, emotions and lives outside the classroom, in particular.

- Teachers need to be able to work in highly collaborative ways, working with other teachers, professionals and para-professionals within the same organization, or with individuals in other organizations, networks of professional communities and different partnership arrangements, which may include mentoring teachers.

- Teachers need to acquire strong skills in technology and the use of technology as an effective teaching tool, to both optimize the use of digital resources in their teaching and use information-management systems to track student learning.

- Teachers need to develop the capacity to help design, lead, manage and plan learning environments in collaboration with others.

- Last but not least, teachers need to reflect on their practices in order to learn from their experience.

These all imply extensive and intensive teacher learning. Some countries approach this with innovative materials and approaches to teaching in order to change entrenched perceptions about and attitudes toward learning. Innovative approaches also recognize that teacher learning will take place in the company of other teachers, not as a solitary exercise – an acknowledgement of the effectiveness of collaborative learning as part of a professional continuum (see Box 2.3).

The level of need for such teacher learning is significant. Data from TALIS 2008 suggests that teachers need development in key areas, including instructional practice. Indeed, more than half of the teachers surveyed reported that they wanted more professional development than they had received during the 18-month survey period. The extent of unsatisfied demand is sizeable in every country, ranging from 31% in the Flemish Community of Belgium to over 80% in Brazil, Malaysia and Mexico.[7]

Box 2.3 Teacher education in Finland

Teacher education in Finland has at least four distinguishing qualities:

- Research based. Teacher candidates are not only expected to become familiar with the knowledge base in education and human development, but they are required to write a research-based dissertation as the final requirement for the masters degree. Upper grade teachers typically pick a topic in their subject area; primary grade teachers typically study some aspect of pedagogy. The rationale for requiring a research-based dissertation is that teachers are expected to engage in disciplined inquiry in the classroom throughout their teaching career.

- Strong focus on developing pedagogical content knowledge. Traditional teacher preparation programs too often treat good pedagogy as generic, assuming that good questioning skills, for example, are equally applicable to all subjects. Because teacher education in Finland is a shared responsibility between the teacher education faculty and the academic subject faculty, there is substantial attention to subject-specific pedagogy for prospective primary as well as upper-grade teachers.

- Good training for all Finnish teachers in diagnosing students with learning difficulties and in adapting their instruction to the varying learning needs and styles of their students.

- A very strong clinical component. Teachers' preparation includes both extensive course work on how to teach – with a strong emphasis on using research based on state-of-the-art practice – and at least a full year of clinical experience in a school associated with the university. These model schools are intended to develop and model innovative practices, as well as to foster research on learning and teaching.

Within these model schools, student teachers participate in problem-solving groups, a common feature in Finnish schools. The problem-solving groups engage in a cycle of planning, action, and reflection/evaluation that is reinforced throughout the teacher education program and is, in fact, a model for what teachers will plan for their own students, who are expected to use similar kinds of research and inquiry in their own studies. The entire system is intended to improve through continual reflection, evaluation, and problem-solving, at the level of the classroom, school, municipality, and nation.

Source: OECD (2011a).

UNDERSTANDING LEARNING TO IMPROVE TEACHING PRACTICES

A central foundation for improving teaching is an understanding of learning. The body of evidence on how children learn has grown greatly over the past years. However, this knowledge base has not always had a profound impact on teacher practice in the classroom. Research shows that teachers, like most people, interpret new ideas through their past experiences[8] and their established beliefs about learning and teaching. As a result, innovative ideas are often simply absorbed into traditional classroom practices.

Interestingly, teachers' beliefs about teaching practice are remarkably consistent across countries. TALIS 2008 revealed that, on average, teachers in all but one of the 23 participating countries endorsed a constructivist view of teaching, which focuses on students as active participants in the process of acquiring knowledge, more strongly than they embraced a belief in the direct transmission of knowledge. However, countries did differ in the strength of their teachers' endorsements of each of the two approaches. Teachers in Australia, Korea, north-western Europe and Scandinavia show a stronger preference for a constructivist view than teachers in Malaysia, South America and southern Europe. Teachers in eastern European countries fall somewhere in between.[9]

While changing entrenched beliefs is a challenge in itself, broadening teachers' repertoires is not just about assisting teachers with change; it is also about developing and continually updating a base of professional knowledge about teaching practices.

There are several dimensions that OECD's comparative review of innovative learning environments suggests hold significant promise which are examined in this report.

Inquiry-based teaching and learning

Inquiry-based teaching and learning – which includes a family of approaches such as design-based learning and problem-based learning (for an example see Box 2.4) – can be effective when used with small groups of students, particularly when guided by a curriculum that establishes clearly defined goals and when students are regularly assessed.[10] Consequently, professional development for teachers needs to include assessing student work. The design of assessments is also critical. Specifically, if only traditional learning outcomes are assessed, then inquiry-based and traditional methods of instruction appear to yield similar results. The additional benefits from inquiry learning – namely that it nurtures communication, collaboration, creativity and deep thinking - become apparent when the assessments try to determine how well the knowledge that has been acquired is applied and when they measure the quality of reasoning.

At the same time, the pedagogies required to implement inquiry-based approaches are more complex than the direct transmission of knowledge to students via textbooks or lectures. These pedagogies tend to be highly dependent on the knowledge and skills of the teachers involved.[11] Teachers who don't understand how these student-centered approaches work are more likely to consider them "unstructured", as they may not appreciate the need for constant assessment and revision of the approach, if necessary, as the lessons unfold.

Classroom research[12] has shown that simply providing students with a rich source of information and an interesting problem is not enough to develop a successful inquiry-based approach. Students need help in understanding the problem, applying the knowledge they already have or are acquiring, evaluating their designs, explaining failures, and revising, if necessary. They usually need some explicit instruction in using resources, finding information, organizing and communicating ideas, setting goals and assessing their progress. Teachers must encourage student self-assessment, the use of evidence, and collaboration for these approaches to work effectively.

The available evidence suggests that the prevailing teaching practices around the world have yet to embrace these approaches. In TALIS 2008, teachers reported using more traditionally structured teaching practices in the classroom, and using student-oriented practices and enhanced teaching activities relatively less frequently. The size of the reported differences varies greatly among countries, but the pattern is the same across all TALIS countries, suggesting that more use should be made of student-oriented and enhanced activities, as these may promote inquiry-based learning.[13]

Box 2.4 **Teach less, learn more**

In 2004, Prime Minister Lee Hsien Loong introduced the idea of "Teach Less, Learn More" as the next step under the Thinking Schools, Learning Nation umbrella. Its aim was to open up more "white space" in the curriculum to engage students more deeply in learning. Despite the system's widely-recognised successes, learners were still seen as too passive, overloaded with content, driven to perform, but not necessarily inspired. Teach Less, Learn More aims to "touch the hearts and engage the minds of learners by promoting a different learning paradigm in which there is less dependence on rote learning, repetitive tests and instruction, and more on engaged learning, discovery through experiences, differentiated teaching, learning of lifelong skills, and the building of character through innovative and effective teaching approaches and strategies." (Ho Peng interview). Further moves in this direction were made in 2008 with an envisioning exercise that led to Curriculum 2015. According to Ho Peng, Director General of Education in the Singapore Ministry of Education, this review asserted that the Singapore education system had strong holding power and important strengths in literacy, mathematics and science, and that these should remain. However, it needed to do better on the soft skills that enable future learning. In addition, "the overload of information has put a premium on the ability to do critical analysis. Working across cultures will require language skills and a larger world view".

Source: OECD (2011a).

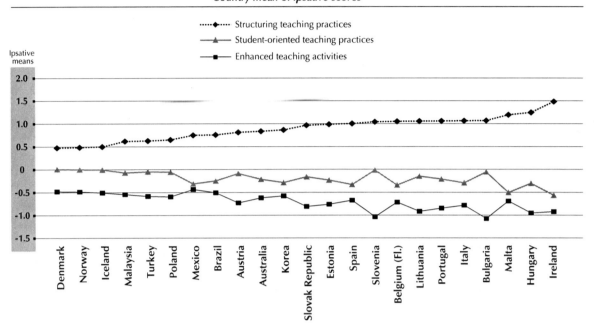

Figure 2.2

Approaches to teaching
Country mean of ipsative scores

Countries are ranked by the relative frequency with which they engage in structuring teaching practices, student-oriented teaching practices and enhanced activities. So, teachers in Denmark adopt the different practices to a fairly similar degree, while teachers in Ireland use structuring teaching practices much more than they do either student-oriented practices and enhanced activities.
Source: OECD, *TALIS Database*.

Incorporating assessment into teaching

The OECD considers an effective learning environment as one that encourages students to be engaged as learners and is well-regulated. If, for example, learning is not happening as intended, then adjustments need to be made in the methods used, in the sequence of information presented, or both. Intervention by teachers or other professionals can occur at any time during the teaching process: before lessons begin, during the lessons, or later, for example, when a teacher sees that a certain pedagogical method works better with one group of students and then applies that method to other groups. Intervention also occurs when teachers encourage students to consult with and support each other during the learning process.

Student assessments are a crucial element of effective learning environments. At the same time, assessments that just offer feedback about students' current achievements are of limited benefit in the long run. While the approaches and methods that countries use for assessment vary widely, there is broad agreement among countries on key features that 21st-century assessments need to possess: For example, they should be multi-layered, extending from classrooms to schools to regional to national levels. They should also be aligned with the development of significant 21st-century learning goals, standards and instructional systems; be adaptable and responsive to new developments; be largely performance-based; add value for teaching and learning by providing information that can be acted on by students, teachers, and administrators; and, of course, meet the general criteria for good assessments (i.e. be fair, technically sound; valid for purpose, and part of a comprehensive and well-aligned system of assessments at all levels of education). In addition, to improve student learning, assessments should also involve: encouraging pupils to be involved in their own learning; adjusting teaching practices to take account of the results of assessments; recognizing the profound influence assessment has on students' motivation and self-esteem, both of which are crucial influences on learning; and fostering students' ability to assess their own work and understand how to improve.[14]

There are many promising initiatives underway in these areas (for examples, see Box 2.5). And yet, a significant share of teachers are not confident about their abilities to assess students effectively. For example, TALIS 2008 shows that in countries such as Italy, Lithuania and Malaysia, one quarter or more of lower secondary teachers report a great need for professional development in this area.[15]

Box 2.5 Curriculum-embedded assessments: Scotland and Sweden

Curriculum-embedded assessments address several of the challenges of developing assessments that are instructionally useful. Curriculum-embedded assessments avoid problems of generalisability and reliability associated with teacher-designed assessments. Well-designed curriculum embedded or on-demand assessments may also improve the validity of teachers' assessments – helping to ensure that teachers are able to make appropriate inferences about student learning in relation to learning goals – while providing information in a timely manner.

Sweden has developed "on-demand" assessments. Teachers may decide when students are ready to take a test in a particular subject or skill area, drawing from a central bank of assessment tasks. Control over timing of tests means that teachers are able to provide students with feedback when it is relevant to the learning unit.

In Scotland, assessment of progress and development needs for pupils is based on the experiences and outcomes for Curriculum for Excellence. Teachers assess progress across the breadth of learning, in challenging aspects and the ability to apply learning in different contexts. Quality assurance and moderation practice in conjunction with guidance and an on-line National Assessment Resource, which provides a wide range of examples of assessment practice, supports teachers in having a shared understanding of standards and expectations and applying these consistently.

Source: Janet W. Looney (2011).

Collaborative learning

When students engage with each other during learning, classrooms become vital, creative environments not only for acquiring knowledge, but also for learning the communication skills required in today's society and economy[16] (see Boxes 2.6 and 2.7). The widespread use of information and communication technologies, and the breakneck speed at which these technologies are evolving, are changing the nature of co-operative learning for the 21st century.

Research on collaborative learning[17] provides evidence of its positive impact on academic achievement. However, research also suggests that it would not be wise to abandon individual learning. Co-operative learning and individual learning are not mutually exclusive; rather, they can and should complement each other.

Many teachers claim that they use co-operative learning techniques regularly, but observational studies find that these techniques are mostly used informally and do not incorporate the group goals and individual accountability that research has identified as essential to this type of learning. Co-operative learning is relatively inexpensive to support and easily adopted. Yet, despite evidence of its effectiveness, it remains at the fringe of school policy and practice.

Box 2.6 A Learning Community, CEIP Andalucía, Seville, Spain

This is a pre-primary and primary state school with all learners at risk of exclusion. The teachers fostered the change and considered *learning communities* to be a key concept in providing quality education and to break the circle of poverty and social exclusion. These are realised through such activities and approaches as: weekly tutorship; students' representative meetings; discussion on the subjects for project work; the monthly family assembly; and the assessment tool elaborated by staff together with the Regional Administration for Education which comprises indicators of achievements and obstacles while also guiding improvements. A key feature are the interactive groups based on co-operative learning. The learners split up into subgroups of 5 or 6 students each; lesson time is divided in periods of 15-20 minutes, each devoted to a different activity but all subject related, with subgroup dynamics coordinated by volunteers from families, the university, and collaborating associations. Project work in a single class or in a grade or group of different grades aims to overcome curriculum fragmentation around four stages: planning, searching, organizing, and assessing.

Source: Country case for the OECD "Innovative Learning Environments" project.

Box 2.7 Student Team Learning (STL) group work methods

The majority of all experimental studies of practical co-operative learning methods involve *Student Team Learning* (STL) methods. All co-operative learning methods share the idea that students work together and are responsible for one another's learning as well as their own. STL also emphasises team goals and collective definitions of success, which can only be achieved if all members of the team learn the objectives being taught. That is, the important thing is not to *do* something together but to *learn* something as a team. Three concepts are central to all such methods: *i)* team rewards, *ii)* individual accountability, and *iii)* equal opportunities for success.

Student Teams-Achievement Divisions (STAD) has been used in a wide variety of subjects, and is most appropriate for teaching well-defined objectives, such as mathematical computations and applications, language usage and mechanics, geography and map skills, and science facts and concepts. Students typically work in 4-member heterogeneous teams to help each other master academic content and teachers follow a schedule of teaching, team work and individual assessment. The teams receive certificates and other recognition based on the average scores of all team members on weekly quizzes. Numerous studies of STAD have found positive effects of the program on traditional learning outcomes in mathematics, language arts, science, and other subjects.

Teams-Games-Tournament (TGT) uses the same teacher presentations and teamwork as in STAD, but replaces the quizzes with weekly tournaments. In these, students compete with members of other teams to contribute points to their team score. The winner at each tournament table brings the same number of points to his or her team, regardless of which table it is; this means that low achievers (competing with other low achievers) and high achievers (competing with other high achievers) have equal opportunity for success.

Source: OECD (2010b), Chapter 7.

Advanced technology in the classroom

It is essential for teachers to understand how young people learn, play and socialize outside the classroom and there are many efforts to provide opportunities for this (see Boxes 2.8-2.12). Digital media have the potential to transform learning environments and empower learners to become active in shaping their own education.[18] Yet young students and teachers in traditional learning environments often do not have access to or are discouraged from using computers and other information and communication technologies in the classroom. Evidence from PISA also finds that the use of computers at school varies substantially across different countries and economies.[19]

Box 2.8 Teacher collaboration in cyberspace

In the Netherlands, a 2008 report on open educational resources spurred interest in developing a way for teachers across the country to collaborate on educational materials and practices. The result is *Wikiwijs*, literally "Wikiwise", an Internet-based platform where teachers can find, download, develop and share educational resources. Developed by the Open Universiteit Nederland and Kennisnet at the request of the ministry of education, the platform is based on open-source software, open content and open standards. The *Wikiwijs* platform was launched in December 2009; then, after eight months of testing, a revised version was launched in September 2010.

Teachers can freely use anything they find in the *Wikiwijs* database in their classrooms. While the scope of *Wikiwijs* covers the entire Dutch education system, from primary schools to universities, during this trial phase, the only school subjects examined on the platform are mathematics and the Dutch language. All documentation on *Wikiwijs* is in Dutch.

Source: *http://www.wikiwijs.nl/task/international.psml.*

Using technology should not be confused with taking a technology-driven approach. The problem with the latter is that it often fails to take the student into account, and assumes that students and teachers will adapt to the requirements of the new technology and not vice versa.[20] The use of new technologies should be adapted to fit the needs of students and teachers; it should not be an end in itself. In TALIS 2008, lower secondary teachers reported a great need for professional development in information and communication technologies. More than one in three teachers in Brazil, Ireland, Lithuania and Malaysia reported high levels of need for development in this area.[21]

Box 2.9 The Le@rning Federation, Australia and New Zealand

A joint venture called The Le@rning Federation, was developed as a major digital content project for Australian and New Zealand schools. The Le@rning Federation developed learning objects for schools as well as learning and content management systems. Some initiatives involved the development of content to meet the curriculum, professional development, and other educational priorities of education systems.

The Le@rning Federation began as a major digital content project for Australian and New Zealand schools. It developed specifications for educational soundness and new delivery systems such as web portals, learning management systems, and content management systems. A number of schools implemented major software packages to support these functions. The Le@rning Federation also developed a "Basic E-Learning Tool Set" to provide schools with the basic functionality for managing learning objectives, until comprehensive learning content management systems could be implemented within jurisdictions. State and territory education authorities also operated various initiatives for providing their schools with digital content.

Source: OECD (2010d), Chapter 10.

Box 2.10 1:1 Initiatives - one student, one digital device

Handhelds (more affordable than notebooks) opened the door to 1:1 in education. Over the last decade, more and more public and private stakeholders across the world have been supporting 1:1 initiatives in education. In the United States, the state of Maine was the first to equip every 7th and 8th grade student and every 7th through 12th grade teacher state-wide with personal access to learning technology. The One Laptop per Child initiative (OLPC) initiative may have inspired the development of a new category of low-cost devices, netbooks, which, together with smartphones, seem to be the technological drivers of contemporary initiatives.

The decreasing cost of ICT devices, combined with the lighter weight of laptops and increasing availability of wireless connectivity, have been the main enablers of the rapid spread of such initiatives and their implementation at a broad scale. Despite the limitations of available evidence, research supports the positive impacts of 1:1 initiatives in writing and ICT skills.

Source: Oscar Valiente (2010).

Box 2.11 Courtenay Gardens Primary School, Victoria, Australia

This is a primary school (students age 5-12) in a low-socio-economic area which intensively uses multimedia facilities and research-based personalized learning frameworks. Students have access to a multimedia television studio and a radio broadcasting station, which foster students' development of organizational skills, social behavior, literacy and numeracy, and connect them with the community. There is a performing arts center and outdoor fitness stations. Classrooms are technology-rich and purpose-built with shared learning spaces for team teaching and group work. Teacher teams meet weekly for planning, evaluation and peer support and the staff engages in regular, research-based instructional coaching activities. Student progress is registered in an electronic school-wide data tracker that allows evaluation against whole class and year performance. Parents can follow a training program to provide assistance in the classroom.

Source: Country case submitted to the OECD "Innovative Learning Environments" project.

Box 2.12 Community Learning Campus, Olds, Alberta Canada

The Community Learning Campus (CLC) is an innovative approach to high school, post-secondary and community education, sharing resources and working jointly with a variety of community groups and agencies. It focuses on providing an active, constructive, and holistic educational environment that brings together high school and post-secondary education in one place (which may be virtual), seeking to create a seamless transition for students wishing to enter the workforce, apprenticeship, college, or university. The CLC is both a virtual and a physical learning space in four multi-use facilities: 1) core high school; 2) fine arts and multi-media center; 3) health and wellness center; and 4) the Bell eLearning Center. Delivery is either seminar-based or class-based, both of which are constructivist and organized around project work. Programs are organized around four pillars – personal, knowledge, community, and global – and navigation relies on the CLC Learner Map, which is both a framework for individual learner pathway decisions and a graphic enabling community access.

Source: Country case submitted to the OECD "Innovative Learning Environments" project.

No single best method

One of the professional skills of a teacher is to know how to use all of these different approaches and when to apply them. There is no single best way of teaching and that is even more true in the 21st century than in the past. Teachers today need to know how to combine "guided discovery" with "direct instruction" methods, depending on the individual students, the context of instruction and the aims of the teaching. One extensive review[22] concludes that innovative learning environments are characterized by a good balance between discovery and personal exploration on the one hand, and systematic instruction and guidance on the other, all the while bearing in mind individual differences in students' abilities, needs and motivation. It also finds that the balance between external regulation by the teacher and self-regulation by the student will vary during the student's education: as the student's own competence increases, the share of self-regulation can also grow while explicit instructional support can diminish.

Research finds that most of the preferred methods and approaches result in positive learning outcomes when they are done well. This means that teachers must have a good understanding of how particular approaches are used and must be flexible enough to adapt and apply them to different situations or students. The drive to enlarge teachers' repertoires is, then, less a matter of encouraging innovation than of improving student learning.

DESIGNING ECOSYSTEMS FOR A 21ST-CENTURY TEACHING PROFESSION

Consider what would happen if you were on an airplane and the pilot came on the intercom as you were starting your descent and said, "I've always wanted to try this without the flaps." Or if your surgeon said to you in your pre-surgical conference, "you know, I'd really like to do it this way. I originally learned how to do it in 1978." Would you be a willing participant in this?[23]

One of the key challenges for the teaching profession is to strengthen the "technical core" of its professional practices. What does it take to improve the use and dissemination of proved and promising teaching practices? How do we generate and share cumulative knowledge in education? This requires the development of educational ecosystems that support the creation, accumulation and diffusion of this professional knowledge.

Turning teaching into an even more knowledge-intensive profession implies a re-consideration of how knowledge is generated and applied within education. An ecosystem conducive to innovation and constant improvement is based on the attitudes and prevailing culture of the various players in the sector, the development and transmission of knowledge, and initiative and calculated risk-taking. Such ecosystems need to draw on four sources: innovation and knowledge inspired by science (research and evaluation); innovation inspired by firms (entrepreneurial development of new products and services); innovation and knowledge inspired by practitioners (teachers, school heads); and innovation inspired by users (students, parents, communities) (see Box 2.13).

Box 2.13 Funding innovation – The UK's Sinnott Fellowship

The UK's Department for Children, Schools and Families introduced the Sinnott Fellowship in 2009 to fund the work of outstanding teachers who create innovative links between the school and the outer community with the aim of improving student aspirations and outcomes. The Fellowship, named after educator and trade unionist Steve Sinnot, selected 15 talented secondary-school practitioners and allows them to spend two days a week, over two terms, creating a program of outward-facing activities for their school. The Fellowship offered support to these individual projects through a network of contacts and resources. These projects, in turn, were expected to include all or some of the following components: activities for children/young people; community and voluntary groups; the world of work and business links; parental engagement; further and higher education and adult learning; international understanding; and access to statutory support and services. In the end, these projects aimed to anchor schools at the heart of their communities.

Dozens of projects had been developed and implemented since the program began. One, developed by the head of the physical education faculty at a London high school, involved training a group of students in basketball coaching so that those students would then train younger students in the game. With a Paralympian champion engaged as mentor, the project improved students' abilities in planning, budgeting and marketing, helped to boost students' self-confidence and enhanced the students' leadership qualities.

In another project, created by the enrichment leader in a disadvantaged school in Nottingham, the school developed links with national and international businesses with the aim of demonstrating to students why education is important in today's labor market. A representative from a construction company explained how part of the local university was constructed and took students on a tour of the building; a lawyer from a European legal firm explained England's justice system and led a mock trial; and a representative from a national energy company explained the relevance of science study to the company's work. All discussed career opportunities in their field. As part of the program, a national department store chain offered students an interview skills day, running a series of mock job interviews to show students what to expect when they try to enter the world of work.

A third project was designed by the head of the creative arts faculty at a disadvantaged secondary school in Great Yarmouth. The school, which specializes in mathematics and computing and suffered from financial and personnel problems, teamed with a private boarding school to provide mutually beneficial opportunities to both sets of students. A scholarship award was created to allow one student from the disadvantaged school to study at the private boarding school. Meanwhile, students from the more advantaged school act as literacy and numeracy mentors to students from the disadvantaged school and provide technical assistance for theatrical productions, while the disadvantaged school's expertise in information technologies helps the private school develop its own information infrastructure.

The UK government's evaluation of the Sinnott Fellowship program is available at the Fellowship website.

Source: *http://www.outwardfacingschools.org.uk/the-sinnott-fellowship/*.

The ecosystem for a knowledge-intensive teaching profession includes research and development; education systems; school organization; mobilizing general-purpose technology, particularly information and communication technologies; and measuring innovation and improvement in education.

Research and development

In most sectors, public and private research and development (R&D) expenditure is a good indicator of the breadth and depth of innovation and knowledge acquired. Part of the knowledge applied by teachers is developed by scientists. For example, teachers' practice must be informed by the latest discoveries about dyslexia and dyscalculia so that they can diagnose these conditions and develop appropriate teaching and learning strategies for affected students (see Box 2.14).

But research and development should not be limited to public research. In the health sector, for example, it is not only the doctors, surgeons and other professionals who innovate; they also use the procedures and administer the medication developed by the pharmaceutical and medical-imaging industries. In education, too, businesses could develop products and services that improve both the effectiveness and efficiency of education systems, and transform the latest knowledge into equipment that teachers can use in classrooms.

It is striking that there is generally little public funding for educational research. Private businesses do not seem to invest heavily in knowledge that can be applied to the formal education sector, and policy makers do not seem to have a clear strategy for stimulating business investment in education R&D. In 2008, the public R&D budget for education stood at 1.8%, on average, of the total public-research budget in the 26 countries for which this information was available. In contrast, the public R&D budget for health stood at 8.6% of the total public-research budget. On average, OECD countries allocated 15.5 times more of their public budgets to health research than to education research, but only 1.2 times more of their public expenditure to education than to health.

Box 2.14 Best Evidence Synthesis Program, New Zealand

The Iterative Best Evidence Synthesis Program is a government brokerage agency through which effective R&D has enabled educational practice to make a much bigger positive difference for diverse learners. The magnitude of positive impact for, the responsiveness of, the sector ownership gained, and the futures orientation of the most effective R&D are compelling.

Often such R&D has gone through many iterations to create the kind of educational development that can work powerfully for diverse learners. As an initial step, through funding educational researchers and the collaborative and iterative processes necessary to undertake first iteration BES developments, BES is seeking to build the capability of the national research community to transform relevant but fragmented research knowledge into a more useful tool for both policy makers and practitioners. BES is also seeking to steer the research community towards a greater focus on informing educational development through R&D.

Source: OECD (2007), Chapter 5.

School organization

The importance of turning schools into learning organizations where teachers can improve and learn from each other's accumulated knowledge has long been acknowledged. There are many examples of such policies and practices (see Boxes 2.15- 2.18) but there is little empirical evidence available yet to support the argument that such schools are associated with better performance and more innovation.

Teachers can do more, and should be encouraged to do more, to share their expertise and experience systematically in ways that go beyond the mere exchange of information. OECD data show that teachers report relatively infrequent collaboration with colleagues within the school, beyond a mere exchange of information and ideas; direct professional collaboration to enhance student learning is more rare.[24]

Understanding that collaboration takes time, some countries are providing teachers with some scheduled time to encourage them to engage in such co-operation. Data from TALIS[25] show that teachers who exchange ideas and information and co-ordinate their practices with other teachers report more positive teacher-student relations at their school. Thus, it may be reasonable to encourage teachers' co-operation in conjunction with improving teacher-student relations, as these are two sides of a positive school culture. Positive teacher-student relations are not only associated with student achievement, they are also closely related to individual teachers' job satisfaction (see Figure 2.3). This finding emphasizes the role of teachers' positive evaluations of the school environment for effective education and teacher well-being. Efforts to improve school organization are particularly important in larger public schools attended by students with mainly low to average ability. Several of the East Asian countries provide interesting models for building on professional teacher collaboration to make the most of their top-performing teachers (Box 2.15).

Box 2.15 Preparing teachers to lead improvement in Japan and China

In Japan, all teachers participate in regular lesson studies in their schools.

The Japanese tradition of lesson studies in which groups of teachers review their lessons and how to improve them, in part through analysis of student errors, provides one of the most effective mechanisms for teachers' self-reflection as well as being a tool for continuous improvement. Observers of Japanese elementary school classrooms have long noted the consistency and thoroughness with which a mathmatics concept is taught and the way in which the teacher leads a discussion of mathematical ideas, both correct and incorrect, so that students gain a firm grasp on the concept. This school-by-school lesson study often culminates in large public research lessons. For example, when a new subject is added to the national curriculum, groups of teachers and researchers review research and curriculum materials and refine their ideas in pilot classrooms over a year before holding a public research lesson, which can be viewed electronically by hundreds of teachers, researchers and policymakers.

The tradition of lesson study in Japan also means that Japanese teachers are not alone. They work together in a disciplined way to improve the quality of the lessons they teach. That means that teachers whose practice lags behind that of the leaders can see what good practice is. Because their colleagues know who the poor performers are and discuss them, the poor performers have both the incentive and the means to improve their performance. Since the structure of the East Asian teaching workforce includes opportunities to become a master teacher and move up a ladder of increasing prestige and responsibility, it also pays for the good teacher to become even better.

In Shanghai, China, teachers are trained to be action researchers in effective practice, with the best teachers going on to support new teachers and helping to improve lesson quality.

The authorities in the Shanghai province of China emphasize giving prospective teachers the skills they will need for action research, and their method for improving their education system over time relies on research performed by teachers. As in Finland (Box 1.3), all students in Shanghai are expected to perform at high levels and teachers are expected to make sure that no student, literally, will be allowed to fall behind. This makes it essential that teachers identify students who are just beginning to flounder, diagnose the problem, and have the skills and knowledge needed to create a large and constantly updated reservoir of solutions for the student performance problems they have diagnosed.

During the course of their careers, teachers in Shanghai are involved in subject-based "teaching-study groups" to improve teaching at the grassroots level on a day-to-day basis. There are timetabled sessions when the study group meets, often with related personnel, such as laboratory assistants, to draw up very detailed lesson schemes for a particular topic for the following week. The lesson plan serves not only as a guide for the teacher during the lesson, but also as documentation of the teacher's professional performance. During actual teaching, teachers may observe each other or may be observed by peers. For example, when a change in curriculum introduces a new teaching topic, teachers may be observed by new teachers, so these can learn from more experienced colleagues; by senior teachers, for mentoring purposes; or by the school principal, for monitoring or to provide constructive development assistance. Sometimes, teachers are expected to teach demonstration lessons, called public lessons, for a large number of other teachers to observe and comment upon.

This structured organization of teaching in Shanghai is not only a means for administration; it is also a major platform for professional enhancement. Teachers in Shanghai are classified into four grades that indicate their professional status. Promotion from one grade to the next often requires the capacity to give demonstration lessons, contribute to the induction of new teachers, publish in journals or magazines about education or teaching, and so forth. The provincial office often identifies the best teachers emerging from evaluation processes and relieves them of some or all of their teaching duties so that they can give lectures to their peers, provide demonstrations, and coach other teachers on a district, provincial and even national level.

...

Carefully picked schools are often asked to pilot new programs or policies before they are scaled-up, and the best teachers in those schools are enlisted as co-researchers to evaluate the effectiveness of the new practices.

The practices described here for Shanghai are similar in other East Asian countries. The East Asian countries taking part in PISA all provide interesting models for building on professional teacher collaboration to make the most of their top-performing teachers.

Source: OECD (2011a).

Figure 2.3
Student-teacher relationships and student performance

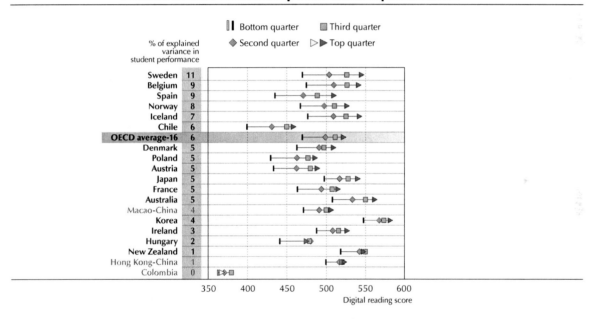

Note: Countries in which differences between the top and bottom quarters of this index are statistically significant are marked in a darker tone.
Countries are ranked in descending order of the percentage of explained variance in student performance.
Source: OECD, *PISA 2009 Database*, Table VI.4.9.

With its famous "lesson studies" or "teaching research sessions" (*jugyokenkyuu*), Japan provides a good illustration of the fact that certain distinctive characteristics of work organization in the education sector can help to establish a culture of ongoing development and allow for an intense exchange of knowledge. Other organizational routines or models based on "communities of practice" have the same aim, namely to create a web of professional relations that will generate a continual dynamic of learning and improvement within establishments.

Too many policies have focused on individual teachers and leaders instead of trying to improve and change how teachers work. A lot of time can be wasted "waiting for superman", when small changes that put improvement, professional discussions and collegiality at the center of the schools are actually achievable. In Ontario, for example, improvement has been based on a change in teachers' working conditions and school routines.

It is important to identify the conditions in which different types of learning organizations can emerge and how teachers can share the knowledge that they have accumulated during their working lives. Some policy programs have managed to influence work organization in the business sector. In education, which is predominantly public in all OECD countries, there is no reason why public authorities should not try to do so.

Box 2.16 The Pedagogy and Content Routine (PCR) – a "Kernel Routine"

There is growing interest in different organizational "routines" designed to ensure that learning is center stage in schools, through social practices that help to create strong learning communities and reinforce teachers' knowledge, professionalism, and their ability to act on what they learn. "Kernel routines" start with a basic process that can then be extended and adapted over time.

An example of such a routine – the Pedagogy and Content Routine (PCR) – has been developed by the University of Pittsburgh. This routine involves highly participatory training for teachers specific to the demanding programs they must teach, practiced in a continuous cycle of observation and professional learning. It meets six criteria critical to such routines. First, it is centered on the technical core of teaching and learning. Second, it is anchored in the official curriculum of the school *and* the enacted curriculum of the classroom. Third, it uses principles of learning and disciplinary literacy, and model lessons that are all based on research. Fourth, it builds trust and mutual access among staff and provides safe venues for educators to work with new practices. Fifth, it provides a route by which new knowledge can enter a school's practice through training, observation and discussion. Sixth, it can be tailored by school staff and transformed over time – the "kernelling" aspect.

Source: OECD (2010b), Chapter 12.

Box 2.17 Open Access College, South Australia

Those who are not able to attend regular schooling are given the opportunity to continue their education in the Open Access College. This innovative distance education alternative features mixed-aged grouping, effective use of ICT, and collaborative and individualized learning. All learning within the program is personally tailored to meet the diverse needs of individual students. Individual learning plans are developed for all students, and ongoing contact occurs between teachers and individual students, interdisciplinary themes are developed based on student interests and resources are accessible for each student online to access in their own time. Both quantitative and qualitative data reveal improved student engagement and attendance.

Source: Country case of the OECD "Innovative Learning Environments" project.

Box 2.18 Culture Path, Kuopio Finland

The Culture Path Program is targeted at students aged 7-16. It aims at enhancing the social, emotional, and physical well-being of the children through culture and art, by ensuring that every student has access to the city's cultural services. This is realized with practical tools for teachers to implement goal-oriented cultural education, and by strengthening the cooperation between schools and cultural institutions, supporting the development of schools as cultural communities. The program is divided into nine "paths" related to art, libraries, theatre etc., which are designed for the needs and curriculum objectives of a particular grade level, within and across different subjects. As part of the paths, students visit at least one local cultural institution outside the school environment every year. After eight years on the Culture Path, 9th graders can use the city's cultural services for free.

Source: Country case of the OECD "Innovative Learning Environments" project.

Box 2.19 Projektschule Impuls, Rorschach, Switzerland

Projektschule Impuls is a school characterized by mixed-age groupings, with a student parliament, and high learner responsibility and co-determination of directions. There is a particular organization of the typical school day beginning in a circle and (for grades 3-6) foreign language learning, before working on the "weekly plan" and then project groups. One feature is the 25 minutes of "sand glass" time, when the students work in total silence. All students write a diary on a daily basis, which is also intended to improve written abilities. The teaching is organized in teams, and the teachers spend part of their time in the school and the rest of their time in the teacher education college.

Source: Country case for the OECD "Innovative Learning Environments" project.

Designing expert systems for teachers

Effective teachers work collaboratively with their colleagues and are continually learning and growing in ways that improve their teaching practice and enhance student learning. To support this, education authorities need to invest in creating learning communities that design and implement professional development and assess its impact on teacher practice. By defining the content and design of a professional development program, teachers can ensure that their professional learning and classroom practice are connected, which in turn strengthens student learning.

One way to change the culture of the teaching profession is to use data analysis more widely (Box 2.19). Using information and communication technologies in education is most often perceived as using new technological equipment – digital boards, computers, laptops, handheld devices – in the course of instruction. Another way to look at the transformative power of these technologies is through the design of "expert" or "knowledge-management" systems, like the ones that support the professional activity of doctors.

Longitudinal information systems in education systematically collect information on students and schools. These systems were initially designed to provide information about student and school performance at the system level. A new generation of systems aims to give immediate feedback to teachers, schools and students, allowing them to benchmark their performance in "real time" and to use also large-scale data collections in a formative way.

Technology also makes it possible to build a new generation of longitudinal information systems that go beyond performance data and can contribute to the development of a professional culture of continuous improvement and innovation in education systems. Those systems allow for better empirical assessment of practices, rapid diagnoses of the problems encountered by students or schools, better informed decision-making, and wider dissemination of knowledge. The quick feedback given to teachers, parents and students on students' performance can, in turn, help inform the design of remedial strategies for students who are falling behind. These systems can bring in a more personalized culture of teaching, with individualized reports on students and incentives to use evaluation in formative ways. They could thus help to put continuous improvement at the center of the teaching culture.

These systems can also be used as knowledge-management platforms where instructional materials, including course materials, tests, quizzes, diagnostic tools, videos and other resources that support both teachers and students, are shared. A good policy in open educational resources could make them even more effective. Thanks to social-network technology, the platforms can connect teachers facing similar difficulties and create a more collaborative culture of teaching, which, in turn, could foster innovation and acquisition of knowledge. With good visualization tools, these systems will allow teachers in different schools to compare the performance of, say, underprivileged students, with the ultimate aim of improving teaching practices to reach these students.

Last but not least, such systems can enhance the precision of education research and allow for more systematic evaluations of teaching practices and innovative or experimental programs. Generating evidence on the outcomes of a new method or product is a key step towards wider dissemination and use in education systems.

CONCLUSIONS

Many nations around the world have undertaken a wide range of reforms of curriculum, instruction, and assessments with the intention of better preparing all children for the higher educational demands of life and work in the 21st century. Various frameworks have been developed to systematize the skills that young people need to be successful in this rapidly changing world and to identify the competencies which teachers need, in turn, to effectively teach those skills to their students. The demands placed on teachers in the 21st century are high: Teachers need to be well-versed in the subjects they teach in order to be adept at using different methods and, if necessary, changing their approaches to optimize learning. They need a rich repertoire of teaching strategies, the ability to combine approaches, and the knowledge of how and when to use certain methods and strategies. Such strategies should include direct, whole-group teaching, guided discovery, group work, and the facilitation of self-study and individual discovery. They should also include personalized feedback. Importantly, teachers also need to have a deep understanding of how learning happens, in general, and of individual students' motivations, emotions and lives outside the classroom, in particular. Teachers need to be able to work in highly collaborative ways, working with other teachers, professionals and para-professionals within the same organization, or with individuals in other organizations, networks of professional communities and different partnership arrangements, which may include mentoring teachers. Last but not least, teachers need to acquire strong skills in technology and the use of technology as an effective teaching tool, to both optimize the use of digital resources in their teaching and use information-management systems to track student learning.

This leads to the question: What teacher preparation programs are needed to prepare graduates who are ready to teach well in a 21st-century classroom? One of the key challenges for the teaching profession is to strengthen the "technical core" of its professional practices which requires the development of educational ecosystems that support the creation, accumulation and diffusion of this professional knowledge. Such ecosystems need to draw on four sources: innovation and knowledge inspired by science (research and evaluation); innovation inspired by firms (entrepreneurial development of new products and services); innovation and knowledge inspired by practitioners (teachers, school heads); and innovation inspired by users (students, parents, communities). While the evidence base in this area is only emerging, this chapter has identified a range of promising practices in these areas.

Notes

1. Trilling, B. and C. Fadel (2009).

2. Charles Fadel is the founder and chairman of the Center for Curriculum Redesign, *http://curriculumredesign.org* and co-author with Bernie Trilling of *21st Century Skills* (Wiley, 2009), *www.21stcenturyskillsbook.com/index.php*.

3. OECD (2010a).

4. TALIS (implemented in 2007-08) focused on lower secondary education (level 2 of the 1997 revision of the International Standard Classification of Education, ISCED 97) teachers and the principals of their schools and seeks to provide data relevant to policy on the role and functioning of school leadership; how teachers' work is appraised and the feedback they receive; teachers' professional development; and teachers' beliefs and attitudes about teaching and their pedagogical practices. TALIS is a collaborative effort by member and partner countries of the OECD. Twenty-three countries participated in TALIS 2008: Australia, Austria, Belgium (Fl.), Brazil, Bulgaria, Denmark, Estonia, Hungary, Iceland, Ireland, Italy, Republic of Korea, Lithuania, Malaysia, Malta, Mexico, Norway, Poland, Portugal, Slovak Republic, Slovenia, Spain and Turkey. TALIS 2008 was also conducted in the Netherlands but as the required sampling standards were not achieved, their data are not included in the international comparisons.

5. For data, see OECD (2009).

6. OECD (2010b).

7. For data, see OECD (2009).

8. Remillard (2005).

9. For data, see OECD (2009).

10. Barron and Darling-Hammond (2010).

11. Good and Brophy (1986).

12. Barron, et al. (1998); Gertzman and Kolodner (1996); Puntambeckar and Kolodner (2005).

13. For data, see OECD (2009).

14. Wiliam (2010).

15. For data, see OECD (2009).

16. Slavin (2010).

17. Lehtinen (2003); Salomon (1993); van der Linden, et al. (2000).

18. Mayer (2010).

19. OECD (2010c).

20. Norman (1993).

21. For data, see OECD (2009).

22. Mayer (2004).

23. Elmore, R. (2002).

24. For data, see OECD (2009).

25. For data, see OECD (2009).

References

Barron, B.J.S., et al. (1998), "Doing with understanding: Lessons from research on problem- and project-based learning", *Journal of the Learning Sciences,* Vol. 7 (3-4), pp. 271-311.

Barron, B., and **L. Darling-Hammond** (2010), "Prospects and Challenges for Inquiry-based Approaches to Learning" in OECD (2010), *The Nature of Learning: Using Research to Inspire Practice,* OECD Publishing.

Elmore, R. (2002), "The limits of change", *Harvard Education Letter,* January-February.

Gertzman, A. and **J.L. Kolodner** (1996), "A case study of problem-based learning in middle-school science class: Lessons learned", in the proceedings of the Second Annual Conference on the Learning Sciences, Evanston, Illinois, pp. 91-98.

Good, T.L. and **J.E. Brophy** (1986), *Educational Psychology* (3rd ed.), Longman, New York.

Lehtinen, E. (2003), "Computer-supported collaborative learning: An approach to powerful learning environments", in E. De Corte, L. Verschaffel, N. Entwistle and J. van Merriënboer (Eds.), *Powerful Learning Environments: Unravelling Basic Components and Dimensions,* Advances in Learning and Instruction Series, Elsevier Science Ltd., Oxford, pp. 35-53.

Looney, J.W. (2011), "Integrating Formative and Summative Assessment: Progress Toward a Seamless System?", *OECD Education Working Papers,* No. 58, OECD Publishing.

Mayer, R.E. (2004), "Should there be a three-strikes rule against pure discovery learning?" *American Psychologist,* Vol. 59 (1), pp. 14-19.

Mayer, R.E. (2010), "Learning with Technology?" in OECD, *The Nature of Learning: Using Research to Inspire Practice,* OECD Publishing.

Norman, D.A. (1993), *Things That Make Us Smart: Defending Human Attributes in the Age of the Machine,* Addison-Wesley Longman Publishing Co., Boston, Massachusettes.

OECD (2007), *Evidence in Education: Linking Policy and Research,* OECD Publishing.

OECD (2009), *Creating Effective Teaching and Learning Environments: First Results from TALIS,* OECD Publishing.

OECD (2010a) *Innovation Strategy A Head Start on Tomorrow,* OECD Publishing.

OECD (2010b), *The Nature of Learning: Using Research to Inspire Practice,* OECD Publishing.

OECD (2010c), *Innovative Workplaces: Making Better Use of Skills within Organisations,* OECD Publishing.

OECD (2010d), *Inspired by Technology, Driven by Pedagogy,* OECD Publishing.

OECD (2011a), *Strong Performers and Successful Reformers in Education: Lessons from PISA for the United States,* OECD Publishing.

Puntambekar, S. and **J.L. Kolodner** (2005), "Toward implementing distributed scaffolding: Helping students learn science from design", *Journal of Research in Science Teaching,* Vol. 42 (2), pp. 185–217.

Remillard, J.T. (2005), "Examining Key Concepts in Research on Teachers' Use of Mathematics Curricula", *Review of Educational Research,* Vol. 75, No. 2, pp. 211-246.

Salomon, G. (Ed.), (1993), *Distributed Cognition: Psychological and Educational Considerations,* Cambridge University Press, Cambridge.

Slavin, R.E. (2010), "Co-operative Learning: What Makes Groupwork Work?", in OECD, *The Nature of Learning: Using Research to Inspire Practice,* OECD Publishing.

Trilling, B. and **C. Fadel** (2009), *21st Century Skills – Learning for Life in our Times,* Wiley.

Valiente, O. (2010), "1-1 in Education: Current Practice, International Comparative Research Evidence and Policy Implications", *OECD Education Working Papers,* No. 44, OECD Publishing.

van der Linden, J., et al. (2000) "Collaborative learning", in R.J. Simons, J. van der Linden and T. Duffy (Eds.), *New Learning,* Kluwer Academic Publishers, Dordrecht, The Netherlands, pp. 37-54.

Wiliam, D. (2010), "The Role of Formative Assessment in Effective Learning Environments" in OECD, *The Nature of Learning: Using Research to Inspire Practice,* OECD Publishing.

Chapter 3

MATCHING TEACHER DEMAND AND SUPPLY

Many education systems face a daunting challenge in recruiting high-quality graduates as teachers, particularly in shortage areas, and retaining them once they are hired. How have countries succeeded in matching their supply of high-quality teachers to their needs? How have they prepared teachers for priority subjects or locations? Competitive compensation and other incentives, career prospects and diversity, and giving teachers responsibility as professionals are important parts of strategies to attract the most talented teaches to the most challenging classrooms. Active recruitment campaigns can emphasize the fulfilling nature of teaching as a profession, and seek to draw in groups that might not otherwise have considered teaching. Where teaching is seen as an attractive profession, its status can further be enhanced through selective recruitment that makes teachers feel that they will be going into a career sought after by accomplished professionals. All this demands that initial education prepares new teachers to play an active role in designing and delivery of education, rather than just following standardized practices.

THE CHALLENGE OF TEACHER SHORTAGES

Recruiting high-quality graduates as teachers, especially in shortage areas, and retaining them once they are hired is a challenging task for education systems. In the PISA 2009 assessment, an average of close to 20% of 15-year-olds were enrolled in schools whose leaders reported that a lack of qualified mathematics or science teachers was hindering instruction in their schools. In some countries over half of school leaders reported that this was a problem (see Figure 3.1).

Figure 3.1

Perceived shortage of mathematics and science teachers

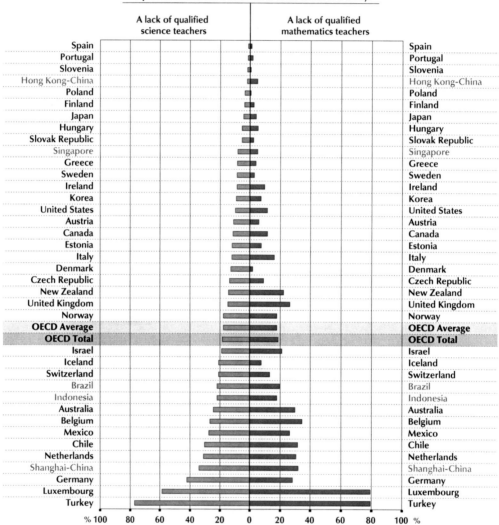

Source: OECD, *PISA 2009 Database.*

A shortage of teachers can imply that teachers are overloaded with instructional and administrative work, unable to meet student needs, and sometimes required to teach subjects outside their expertise. School systems often respond to teacher shortages in the short-term by some combination of lowering qualification requirements for entry to the profession; assigning teachers to teach in subject areas in which they are not fully qualified; increasing the number of classes that teachers are allocated; or increasing class sizes.[1] Such responses, even if they ensure that classrooms are not left without a teacher, raise concerns about the quality of teaching and learning.

56

Figure 3.2

Relationship between school average socio-economic background and school resources

Disadvantaged schools are more likely to have more or better resources, in **bold** if relationship is statistically different from the OECD average
Advantaged schools are more likely to have more or better resources, in **bold** if relationship is statistically different from the OECD average
Within country correlation is not statistically significant

	Simple correlation between the school mean socio-economic background and:					
	Percentage of full-time teachers	Percentage of certified teachers among all full-time teachers	Percentage of teachers with university-level degree (ISCED 5A) among all full-time teachers	Index of quality of school's educational resources	Computer/student ratio	Student/teacher ratio[1]
Australia	-0.21	-0.05	0.02	**0.31**	0.01	-0.07
Austria	-0.13	0.21	**0.64**	0.03	-0.05	-0.07
Belgium	-0.18	0.05	**0.58**	0.02	**-0.23**	**0.66**
Canada	0.01	0.14	0.03	0.18	-0.05	0.09
Chile	-0.04	-0.01	**0.25**	**0.35**	**0.32**	-0.05
Czech Republic	**-0.32**	**0.29**	**0.37**	0.00	0.15	0.08
Denmark	0.01	-0.17	0.16	0.04	-0.08	**0.27**
Estonia	0.14	0.00	0.00	0.10	-0.09	**0.43**
Finland	**0.17**	-0.01	-0.01	0.13	-0.01	0.08
France	w	w	w	w	w	w
Germany	-0.15	-0.02	-0.02	0.06	-0.18	**0.28**
Greece	-0.11	0.06	0.24	0.16	-0.12	0.25
Hungary	**-0.33**	0.07	0.07	0.11	**-0.20**	0.02
Iceland	**0.20**	**0.39**	**0.30**	**0.06**	**-0.41**	**0.40**
Ireland	0.12	-0.10	-0.08	0.16	-0.03	**0.49**
Israel	-0.08	-0.06	0.20	0.25	0.08	**-0.20**
Italy	-0.06	**0.16**	0.13	0.15	-0.19	**0.50**
Japan	-0.14	0.04	0.20	0.17	**-0.34**	**0.38**
Korea	-0.14	0.00	-0.03	-0.04	**-0.53**	**0.30**
Luxembourg	**-0.16**	-0.01	**0.39**	0.13	-0.13	**0.28**
Mexico	-0.09	**-0.13**	-0.04	**0.59**	0.14	0.03
Netherlands	**-0.34**	**-0.12**	**0.62**	0.06	-0.16	**0.38**
New Zealand	-0.04	0.08	0.07	0.16	-0.02	0.11
Norway	-0.05	0.04	0.15	0.14	-0.02	0.19
Poland	-0.02	0.03	-0.05	0.06	-0.16	0.01
Portugal	**0.14**	-0.05	0.04	0.24	-0.02	**0.39**
Slovak Republic	-0.09	**0.28**	**-0.21**	-0.05	-0.06	0.00
Slovenia	**0.46**	**0.32**	**0.55**	0.13	**-0.21**	**-0.25**
Spain	**-0.29**	m	m	0.10	-0.16	**0.45**
Sweden	0.05	0.01	-0.04	0.26	**0.13**	0.12
Switzerland	-0.11	-0.07	0.24	0.10	0.03	0.06
Turkey	0.12	-0.04	0.04	0.04	-0.06	**-0.26**
United Kingdom	**-0.36**	0.05	-0.03	0.00	0.01	-0.10
United States	**-0.42**	**-0.24**	0.10	0.22	0.06	**-0.17**
OECD average	-0.07	0.04	0.15	0.13	-0.08	0.15
Albania	**-0.25**	0.00	**0.38**	**0.44**	**0.24**	0.15
Argentina	0.13	0.13	0.22	**0.51**	**0.21**	-0.02
Azerbaijan	0.05	-0.06	**0.44**	0.19	0.17	0.23
Brazil	-0.03	0.10	0.03	**0.52**	**0.25**	**-0.20**
Bulgaria	-0.08	**0.17**	0.17	0.09	-0.17	0.21
Colombia	**-0.24**	**-0.16**	-0.08	**0.53**	0.19	-0.14
Croatia	0.09	0.02	**0.28**	0.09	0.17	0.32
Dubai (UAE)	**0.32**	**0.61**	-0.01	**0.34**	**0.47**	**-0.27**
Hong Kong-China	-0.19	-0.06	0.12	0.06	0.04	0.02
Indonesia	**0.24**	**0.27**	0.16	**0.44**	0.14	**-0.16**
Jordan	-0.04	0.00	-0.02	0.26	0.05	0.06
Kazakhstan	**0.23**	0.04	**0.34**	0.21	-0.12	**0.44**
Kyrgyzstan	**0.17**	0.08	**0.35**	0.27	**0.13**	0.27
Latvia	**0.19**	-0.03	0.19	0.14	0.00	**0.38**
Liechtenstein	-0.15	0.02	**0.57**	**-0.91**	**0.79**	**0.70**
Lithuania	**0.21**	0.09	0.19	-0.02	**-0.49**	0.21
Macao-China	**0.11**	0.05	-0.18	0.26	**0.22**	**0.17**
Montenegro	0.07	**0.32**	**0.38**	-0.11	-0.19	**0.33**
Panama	**-0.51**	**-0.47**	-0.13	**0.68**	**0.38**	0.03
Peru	-0.21	0.08	**0.48**	**0.53**	**0.46**	-0.02
Qatar	**0.03**	-0.04	-0.07	**0.23**	**0.19**	**0.11**
Romania	0.05	0.10	0.11	0.20	-0.07	-0.02
Russian Federation	**0.18**	0.08	**0.31**	**0.26**	0.02	**0.29**
Serbia	0.10	0.06	0.06	-0.01	0.00	0.11
Shanghai-China	**0.14**	0.13	**0.32**	0.16	-0.10	**-0.13**
Singapore	-0.13	0.00	**0.22**	0.10	**-0.18**	**-0.14**
Chinese Taipei	0.12	**0.34**	0.29	0.19	-0.04	-0.07
Thailand	0.07	0.06	0.16	**0.39**	0.00	-0.02
Trinidad and Tobago	**-0.19**	0.09	**0.56**	0.12	0.08	**0.38**
Tunisia	-0.06	0.00	**0.20**	0.13	0.15	-0.02
Uruguay	-0.01	**0.27**	0.08	**0.33**	**0.30**	0.13

1. In contrast to the other columns, negative correlations indicate more favorable characteristics for advantaged students.
Source: OECD, *PISA 2009 Database*, Table II.2.2.

Looking at the ways in which teachers are distributed among socio-economically more disadvantaged and advantaged schools provides another perspective on the issue of teacher shortages. With the exception of Turkey, Slovenia, Israel and the United States – students in disadvantaged schools tend to have better access to full-time teachers as mirrored in more favorable student/teacher ratios (Column 1 in Figure 3.2). At the same time disadvantaged schools tend to have fewer teachers with advanced university qualifications than socio-economically advantaged schools (Column 3 in Figure 3.2) indicating real differences in quality of teaching in more disadvantaged schools

All in all, teacher shortage is a significant problem in many of the summit countries, although its levels vary significantly across educational levels, subjects and schools. An analysis of teacher preferences for schools also shows that the least favored schools are schools in remote settings and schools with higher proportions of disadvantaged children and children from ethnic and minority language backgrounds.[2] A higher concentration of lesser qualified or novice teachers in schools serving disadvantaged students can have a negative impact on student performance, further diminishing their chances of success. In short, while the impact of effective teaching on students with lower performance levels tends to be greatest, these are often the least likely to receive it.[3] Matching teacher demand is therefore particularly important for students in disadvantaged schools who find themselves in classes with the least experienced and least qualified teachers.

The issue of teacher demand and supply is both complex and multi-dimensional, as it reflects several challenges: how to expand the pool of qualified teachers, how to address shortages in specific subjects, how to recruit teachers to the places where they are most needed, how to distribute teachers in equitable and efficient ways, and how to retain qualified teachers over time.[4] Common to most education systems that demonstrate high performance and very low between-school variation in performance in PISA is that they attract teachers equitably across the school system, including to hard-to-staff schools. This chapter examines policies pursued to achieve this.

MAKING TEACHING AN ATTRACTIVE CAREER CHOICE

PISA shows that the best-performing education systems provide most of their students with the kind and quality of education that average performers offer only to a small elite. This implies that these systems provide excellent teaching for all students. In order to achieve this, school systems often aim to recruit their teachers from the same pool from which all their top professionals are recruited. But people who see themselves as candidates for the professions, and are attracted to the working conditions enjoyed by professionals, may not find what they're looking for in schools organized in prescriptive work environments that use bureaucratic management to direct their work.

Many education systems have therefore transformed the work organization in their schools by replacing administrative forms of management with professional norms that provide the status, pay, professional autonomy and accountability, and the high-quality training and responsibility that go with professional work. They also tend to provide effective systems of social dialogue, and appealing forms of employment that balance flexibility with job security, and grant sufficient authority for schools to manage and deploy their human resources. In many education systems, these aspects tend to be the focus of explicit national or regional policies.

Even where recruiting the most highly qualified graduates remains a challenge, policy makers tend to acknowledge that teaching quality is strongly affected by the pool of talent from which teachers are chosen. People are attracted to certain professions by some combination of the occupational status, work environment, sense of personal contribution and the financial rewards associated with a given profession. Teacher policy needs to examine these aspects closely, particularly in light of teacher shortages that many advanced economies already face and that will grow in the near future as large numbers of teachers reach retirement age.[5] And, as noted before, even where general teacher supply and demand are in balance, many countries face shortages of specialist teachers and shortages in schools serving disadvantaged or isolated communities, most notably in the fields of mathematics and science.

Policy responses are needed at two levels. The first concerns the nature of the teaching profession itself and teachers' work environment. These policies seek to improve the profession's general status and competitive position in the job market and are the focus of this paper. The second involves more targeted responses and incentives for particular types of teacher shortage, which recognizes that that there is not a single labor market for teachers, but a set of them, distinguished by school type and characteristics, such as subject specialization. An important consideration here is that the responsiveness to incentives depends on the characteristics of individuals. For example, individuals

in certain academic disciplines, such as science, and teachers with higher academic credentials are less likely to be attracted to teaching in the first place, and are less likely to return to teaching once they leave. Women often value the potential flexibility that teaching can offer, so improved leave provisions, opportunities for part-time employment and career breaks, and child care are likely to be particularly important to their career choices.[6] Surveys of what teachers themselves value about their work also provide important insights into what needs to be emphasized in recruitment: the social relevance of teaching; working with young people; creativity; autonomy; and collaboration with colleagues.

It is important to note that the status of the teaching profession is not just a static attribute of culture but has, in some countries, changed significantly. As shown in the boxes on Singapore (Box 3.1) and Finland (Box 3.2), vigorous intervention that directly addresses the attractiveness of teaching compared to other graduate professions can make a big difference. Interesting approaches towards recruitment pursued by some countries include:

- promotional programs targeted at groups that are "non-traditional" entrants to teaching;

- reinventing selection criteria for new teachers, with the aim of identifying applicants with the greatest potential, including through interviews, by preparing lesson plans, and by demonstrating teaching skills;

- changing the role of seniority in determining teacher assignments and creating incentives to attract experienced teachers to hard to staff schools, in order to avoid situations where new teachers are assigned to the more difficult and unpopular schools, further disadvantaging students there as well as potentially damaging teachers' career development; and

- for desirable teaching jobs, giving greater weight to qualities that are harder to measure, such as enthusiasm, commitment and sensitivity to students' needs, where these are seen to be more directly related to the quality of teaching and learning than the traditional emphases on qualifications and years of experience.

Box 3.1 Throughout Singapore, teaching talent is identified and nurtured rather than being left to chance

Singapore is notable for its comprehensive approach to identifying and nurturing teaching talent. It has developed a comprehensive system for selecting, training, compensating and developing teachers and principals, thereby creating tremendous capacity at the point of education delivery.

- *Recruitment:* Prospective teachers are carefully selected from the top one-third of the secondary school graduating class, by panels that include current principals. Strong academic ability is essential, as is commitment to the profession and to serving diverse student bodies. Prospective teachers receive a monthly stipend that is competitive with the monthly salary for fresh graduates in other fields. They must commit to teaching for at least three years. Interest in teaching is seeded early through teaching internships for high school students; there is also a system for mid-career entry, which is a way of bringing real-world experience to students.

- *Training:* All teachers receive training in the Singapore curriculum at the National Institute of Education (NIE) at Nanyang Technological University. They take either a diploma or a degree course depending on their level of education at entry. There is a close working relationship between NIE and the schools, where all new teachers are mentored for the first few years. As NIE's primary purpose is training all Singapore teachers, there are no divisions between arts and sciences and education faculties. Thus, according to Lee Sing Kong, the conflicting priorities that plague many Western teacher education programs are less significant and there is a stronger focus on pedagogical content. NIE has put in place a matrix organizational structure whereby program offices (e.g. Office for Teacher Education) liaise with individual academic groups in drawing up initial teacher training programs. This means that these programs are designed with the teacher in mind, rather than to suit the interests of the various academic departments. As such, there is a stronger focus on pedagogical content and greater synergies among modules within each program.

...

- **Compensation:** The Ministry of Education keeps a close watch on occupational starting salaries and adjusts the salaries for new teachers to ensure that teaching is seen as being as equally attractive as other occupations for new graduates. In effect, the country wants its most qualified candidates to regard teaching as just as attractively compensated as other professions. This is in line with findings from PISA where relative levels of teacher pay tends to be associated with higher system-level performance, other factors held equal.[7] Teacher salaries do not increase as much over time as those in private sector jobs, but there are many other career opportunities within education for teachers. Teaching is also regarded as a 12-month position. There are retention bonuses and high-performing teachers can also earn significant amounts in performance bonuses.

- **Professional development:** In recognizing the need for teachers to keep up with the rapid changes occurring in the world and to be able to constantly improve their practice, they are entitled to 100 hours of professional development per year. This may be undertaken in several ways. Courses at the National Institute of Education focus on subject matter and pedagogical knowledge and lead towards higher degrees or advanced diplomas. Much professional development is school-based, led by staff developers. Their job is to identify teaching-based problems in a school, for example, with a group's mathematics performance; or to introduce new practices such as project-based learning or new uses of ICT. Each school also has a fund through which it can support teacher growth, including developing fresh perspectives by going abroad to learn about aspects of education in other countries. Teacher networks and professional learning communities encourage peer-to-peer learning and the Academy of Singapore Teachers, was opened in September 2010 to further encourage teachers to continuously share best practices.

- **Performance appraisal:** Like every other profession in Singapore, teachers' performance is appraised annually by a number of people and against 16 different competencies. Included in this Enhanced Performance Management System is teachers' contribution to the academic and character development of the students in their charge, their collaboration with parents and community groups, and their contribution to their colleagues and the school as a whole. Teachers who do outstanding work receive a bonus from the school's bonus pool. This individual appraisal system sits within the context of great attention to the school's overall plan for educational excellence, since all students in Singapore have multiple teachers, even in primary school.

- **Career development:** Throughout Singapore, talent is identified and nurtured rather than being left to chance. After three years of teaching, teachers are assessed annually to see which of three career paths would best suit them – master teacher, specialist in curriculum or research or school leader. Each path has salary increments. Teachers with potential as school leaders are moved to middle management teams and receive training to prepare them for their new roles. Middle managers' performance is assessed for their potential to become vice principals, and later, principals. Each stage involves a range of experience and training to prepare candidates for school leadership and innovation.

- **Leadership selection and training:** Singapore has a clear understanding that high-quality teaching and strong school performance require effective leaders. Singapore's approach to leadership is modeled on that found in large corporations. The key is not just the training program, but the whole approach to identifying and developing talent. This differs from the US or UK approach, for example, in which a teacher can apply to train as a principal or school head, and then apply for a position in a school. In Singapore, young teachers are continuously assessed for their leadership potential and given opportunities to demonstrate and learn, for example, by serving on committees, then being promoted to head of department at a relatively young age. Some are transferred to the ministry for a period. After these experiences are monitored, potential principals are selected for interviews and go through leadership situational exercises. If they pass these, then they go to NIE for six months of executive leadership training, with their salaries paid. The process is comprehensive and intensive and includes an international study trip and a project on school innovation. Only 35 people per year are selected for the executive leadership training. Asked why Singapore uses the "select then train" rather than the "train then select" model, Professor Lee Sing Kong said that while the US/UK approach is feasible, it carries a higher risk. Singapore is very confident that they consistently have the best possible leaders for their schools and that there is a wide range of inputs into their selection. Principals are transferred between schools periodically as part of Singapore's continuous improvement strategy.

Source: OECD (2011a).

Research shows that people who have close contact with schools – such as parents who assist in classrooms, or employers who have students in workplace learning programs – often have much more positive attitudes towards teachers than people with little direct contact. This suggests that building stronger links between the schools and the community can also help to enhance the status of teaching. Teachers and school leaders can play a key role in strengthening connections with families and communities as part of effective learning. This can involve eliciting greater support from stakeholders with traditional expectations about teaching by communicating current knowledge about what makes learning effective. Personalized relationships with learners and their families can be part of this process, as can after-school and extra-curricular programs, support for families as learning environments, and making more explicit the links between formal learning and life after schooling.

Employers increasingly recognize the need to provide workers with a good work-life balance and opportunities to combine work with family responsibilities and other activities. Some countries allow part-time teaching or opportunities throughout the career to gain experience outside schools through sabbatical leave, extended leave without pay, and job exchanges with industry. Although all such initiatives involve costs, those costs need to be set against the benefits of lower staff turnover, improved morale, and introducing new knowledge and skills into schools.

The essence of professional work can be seen as the acknowledgement that it is the professional, and not the supervisor, who has the knowledge needed to make the important decisions as to what services are needed and how they are to be provided. Organizations dominated by professionals are those in which there are fewer layers of management, workers are consulted on all matters of consequence, and workers have considerable discretion with respect to diagnosing client needs and deciding which services are appropriate to address those needs. Indeed, in many professions, and for many professionals, the worker is also the manager and, in many cases, the owner as well.

In education, too, policy makers have often concluded that top-down initiatives alone were insufficient to achieve deep and lasting changes in practice because reforms focused on aspects that were too distant from the instructional core of teaching and learning; because reforms assumed that teachers would know how to do things they actually didn't know how to do; because too many conflicting reforms asked teachers to do too many things simultaneously; or because teachers and schools did not buy into the reform strategy. Over the past decade, many education systems have granted significantly more discretion to school heads and school faculties,[8] something that teachers often refer to as a factor contributing to the attractiveness of the teaching profession, and something that PISA shows to be closely related to school performance, when combined with appropriate accountability arrangements.[9] Finland (see Box 3.2) and Ontario provide examples of how formerly centralized systems have shifted emphasis towards:

- improving the act of teaching;

- giving careful and detailed attention to implementation, along with opportunities for teachers to practice new ideas and learn from their colleagues;

- developing an integrated strategy and set of expectations for both teachers and students; and

- securing support from teachers and unions for the reforms.

In some countries, great discretion is given to the faculty, as a whole, and to its individual members. In others, more discretion is given to schools that are doing well and less to those that might be struggling. In some countries, the school leader is little more than the lead teacher; in others, the authorities continue to look to the school leader to set the direction and manage the faculty.

Results from PISA suggest that an emphasis on professional responsibility at the frontline does not conflict with the establishment of centralized standards and assessments; rather, these go hand-in-hand.[10]

Countries are also trying to attract different types of people into teaching, not just to overcome shortages, but also to broaden the range of teachers' backgrounds and experiences. This includes promoting the benefits of a teaching career to groups who are often under-represented among teacher ranks, such as men and those from minority backgrounds.

Box 3.2 Teachers and schools assume responsibility for reform in Finland

Finland has made teaching a sought-after occupation by raising entry standards and giving teachers a high degree of responsibility, including as "action researchers" to find effective educational solutions. Finland has raised the social status of its teachers to a level where there are few occupations with higher status. University professors are among the most highly regarded of all professionals, and even the word for teacher is the same for school teachers as for university professors. In 2010, over 6 600 applicants competed for 660 available slots in primary school preparation programs in the eight universities that educate teachers, making teaching one of the most sought-after professions.[11] As a result of this competitive climate, teaching is now a highly selective occupation in Finland, with highly skilled, well-trained teachers spread throughout the country.

While teachers in Finland have always enjoyed respect in society, a combination of raising the bar for entry and granting teachers greater autonomy over their classrooms and working conditions than their peers enjoy elsewhere has helped to raise the status of the profession. Finnish teachers have earned the trust of parents and the wider society by their demonstrated capacity to use professional discretion and judgment in the way they manage their classrooms and respond to the challenge of helping virtually all students become successful learners.

Since the 1980s, the Finnish system of accountability has been redeveloped entirely from the bottom up. Teacher candidates are selected, in part, according to their capacity to convey their belief in the core mission of public education in Finland, which is deeply humanistic as well as civic and economic. The preparation they receive is designed to build a powerful sense of individual responsibility for the learning and well-being of all the students in their care. During their careers, they must combine the roles of researcher and practitioner. Finnish teachers are not only expected to become familiar with the knowledge base in education and human development, but are also required to write a research-based thesis as the final requirement for the master's degree.

Source: OECD (2011a).

The following are some examples of interesting techniques various countries use to broaden the background of their teaching force:

- Opening the teaching profession to individuals with relevant experience outside education, not just in vocational programs (whose teachers are required to have industrial experience in some countries);

- Recognizing the skills and experience gained outside education and reflecting those in starting salaries;

- Enabling appropriately qualified entrants, including mature student teacher trainees, to start working or enter apprenticeship programs and earn a salary before acquiring teacher education qualifications; and

- Offering more flexible approaches to teacher education that provide opportunities for part-time study and distance learning, and that give credits for relevant qualifications and experience. Such alternative pathways into teaching can be particularly appealing to under-represented groups, such as men and those from minority backgrounds.

COMPENSATION SCHEMES TO MATCH TEACHER SUPPLY AND DEMAND

Teachers' salaries increased in real terms between 2000 and 2009 in virtually all OECD countries, but tend to remain below those of other graduates (see Figure 3.3). Statutory salaries for teachers with 15 years of experience are, on average, around 80% of full-time earnings for 25-64 year-olds with tertiary education, and 60% or below in the Czech Republic, Hungary, Iceland and the Slovak Republic.[12] Cross-country comparisons using PISA data show that relative pay-levels of teachers are related to average student performance in education systems, after other system-level factors have been accounted for.[13] At the same time, other aspects of teachers' employment conditions, such as vacations, relative job security and pensions, are often more generous than in other occupations.

OECD research suggests that where teachers' salaries are low relative to professions requiring similar qualifications, teacher supply appears to be quite price-elastic: for a given percentage increase in teachers' relative salaries, the supply of potential teachers increases by a greater percentage. In countries where teachers' salaries are already relatively high, teacher supply tends to be less elastic: a given percentage increase in salary produces a lower percentage increase in supply.[14]

Figure 3.3

Teachers' salaries relative to those of workers with college degrees

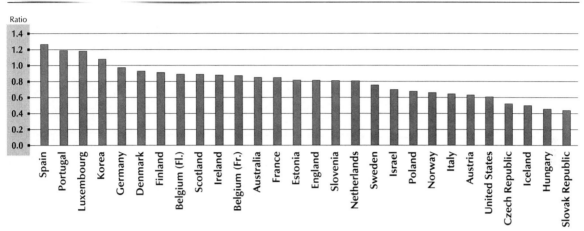

Countries are ranked in descending order of the ratio of salary after 15 years of experience/minimum training to earnings for full-time, full-year workers with tertiary education aged 25 to 64 (latest available year).
Source: OECD (2011b), Table D3.2.

Nevertheless, the large size of the teaching workforce means that to raise salaries across-the-board by even a few percentage points is very costly. Furthermore, the teacher labor market is diverse, and teacher recruitment difficulties vary by type of school, subject specialization, and region. Also, in many countries the problems of teacher shortages and high turnover of staff are felt most acutely in schools that are already disadvantaged. Some countries are therefore targeting larger salary increases to schools with particular needs or teacher groups in short supply or have developed greater local flexibility in salary schemes. For example, some targeted policy initiatives aim to attract teachers in subjects such as mathematics, science, technology and vocational subjects.

Fee waivers, scholarships and forgivable loans are some of the financial incentives being provided to attract such people into teacher education; and additional payments and recognition of work experience are provided for those who already have the types of qualifications that are in short supply.

In efforts to recruit teachers for specific subjects or geographic areas, many OECD countries have experience with financial incentive packages. Indeed, targeted financial incentives for teachers – salary increases and other types of financial additional payments – are often cited as important for dealing with unattractive working conditions in particular sets of schools. They can also be perceived by teachers as a reward for the more challenging work they undertake in these schools or offset changes in demand in competing occupations by making the teaching profession more attractive. Many countries provide substantial salary allowances for teaching in difficult areas, transportation assistance for teachers in remote areas, or additional payments for teachers with skills in short supply to help ensure that all schools are staffed with teachers of similar quality (see Figure 3.4). This type of mechanism can be more cost efficient than across-the-board salary incentives and can serve better the purpose, if they are well designed.

Additional payments can take different forms: in Chile, Denmark, England, Estonia, Finland, France, Ireland, Israel, Mexico, the Netherlands, Sweden, Turkey and the United States, additional payments typically have an impact on the teacher's base salary scale. In Australia, Denmark, England, Estonia, Finland, France, Greece, Hungary, Ireland, Israel, Italy, Japan, the Netherlands, Portugal, Slovak Republic and Switzerland they tend to take the form of extra payments that can be yearly or a one-time additional payment. In some cases, teachers can also receive additional payments to offset the high cost of living in certain areas.[15]

Figure 3.4 (1/2)

Decisions on payments for teachers in public institutions (2009)

Criteria for base salary and additional payments awarded to teachers in public institutions

	Experience — Years of experience as a teacher	Management responsibilities in addition to teaching duties	Teaching more classes or hours than required by full-time contract	Special tasks (career guidance or counseling)	Teaching in a disadvantaged, remote or high cost area (location allowance)	Special activities (e.g. sports and drama clubs, homework clubs, summer school, etc.)	Teaching students with special educational needs (in regular schools)	Teaching courses in a particular field
OECD								
Australia	–	–				▲	▲	
Austria	– ▲	▲	▲	▲			△	
Belgium (Fl.)	–		△					
Belgium (Fr.)	–			△				
Canada	m m m	m m m	m m m	m m m	m m m	m m m	m m m	m m m
Chile	–				–			
Czech Republic	–	▲ △	– ▲ △	▲ △		▲ △	– ▲ △	
Denmark	– ▲ △	▲ △	▲ △	▲	– ▲ △	▲ △	▲ ▲	▲ △
England	– ▲ △	– ▲ △	▲ △		– ▲ △	▲ △	▲ △	– ▲ △
Estonia	–	▲ △	▲ △	– ▲	– ▲	▲ △	▲ △	
Finland	▲	–		▲ △		▲	▲ △	△
France	–	▲ △	▲ △	▲ △	– ▲		△ –	
Germany	–	–		△				
Greece	–	▲		△	▲	▲		
Hungary	–	▲	▲	▲	▲	▲	▲	
Iceland	– ▲ △	– ▲ △	▲ △	– ▲ △		▲ △	– ▲ △	
Ireland	– ▲ △	– ▲			– ▲			
Israel	–	– ▲	– ▲	– ▲		▲	– ▲	
Italy	–	△		△	△	▲	△	
Japan	–	▲	▲		▲	△	▲	
Korea	–	▲		△	△		▲	▲
Luxembourg	–		△	△		–		
Mexico	– ▲ △	– ▲	– ▲	– ▲	– ▲			– ▲
Netherlands	– ▲ △	– ▲ △	– ▲	– ▲ △	– ▲ △	– ▲ △	– ▲ △	– ▲ △
New Zealand	m m m	m m m	m m m	m m m	m m m	m m m	m m m	m m m
Norway	–	▲		△	– ▲ △	▲	▲ △	
Poland	– △		▲		▲	▲	▲	
Portugal	–	▲		△	▲		–	
Scotland	–					▲		
Slovak Republic	–	▲ △		▲ △	▲ △	▲ △	▲ △	
Slovenia	–	–		△	△		△	△
Spain	–	▲			▲			
Sweden	–	–		△	–			–
Switzerland	–	–		△	△		△ –	
Turkey	–		▲	▲	–	▲		
United States	–	▲			– ▲	▲		▲
Other G20								
Argentina	m m m	m m m	m m m	m m m	m m m	m m m	m m m	m m m
Brazil	m m m	m m m	m m m	m m m	m m m	m m m	m m m	m m m
China	m m m	m m m	m m m	m m m	m m m	m m m	m m m	m m m
India	m m m	m m m	m m m	m m m	m m m	m m m	m m m	m m m
Indonesia	m m m	m m m	m m m	m m m	m m m	m m m	m m m	m m m
Russian Federation	–	–	–		–	▲	–	▲
Saudi Arabia	m m m	m m m	m m m	m m m	m m m	m m m	m m m	m m m
South Africa	m m m	m m m	m m m	m m m	m m m	m m m	m m m	m m m

Criteria for:

– : Decisions on position in base salary scale

▲ : Decisions on supplemental payments which are paid every year

△ : Decisions on supplemental incidental payments

Source: OECD (2011b).

Please refer to the Reader's Guide in Education at a Glance 2011: OECD Indicators (*www.oecd.org/edu/eag2011*) *for information concerning the symbols replacing missing data.*

Figure 3.4 (2/2)

Decisions on payments for teachers in public institutions (2009)

Criteria for base salary and additional payments awarded to teachers in public institutions

| | Criteria related to teachers' qualifications, training and performance | | | | | | Criteria based on demography | | |
	Holding an initial educational qualification higher than the minimum qualification required to enter the teaching profession	Holding a higher than minimum level of teacher certification or training obtained during professional life	Outstanding performance in teaching	Successful completion of professional development activities	Reaching high scores in the qualification examination	Holding an educational qualification in multiple subjects	Family status (married, number of children)	Age (independent of years of teaching experience)	Other
OECD									
Australia	−	−					▲		
Austria			△				▲		▲
Belgium (Fl.)	−	▲							▲
Belgium (Fr.)	−	−							▲ △
Canada	m m m	m m m	m m m	m m m	m m m	m m m	m m m	m m m	m m m
Chile		−	△	−		▲			−
Czech Republic			− ▲ △					− △	
Denmark	− ▲ △	− ▲ △	▲ △	− ▲ △		− ▲ △			
England	− ▲ △		− ▲ △						
Estonia	−	−	▲ △	−		▲ △			
Finland	−	− ▲	▲	▲		−			
France				−			▲		
Germany							−	−	
Greece	−	▲					▲		−
Hungary	−	−		△ −		▲			▲
Iceland	− ▲ △	− ▲ △		▲ △	△	△		− ▲	
Ireland	− ▲	− ▲							
Israel	−	−			▲		− ▲	− ▲	
Italy							−		
Japan							▲		▲
Korea				△			△	▲	
Luxembourg		−		−			▲	−	
Mexico	− ▲	− ▲	− ▲	− ▲	− ▲				
Netherlands	− ▲ △	− ▲ △	− ▲ △	− ▲ △	− ▲ △	− ▲ △			
New Zealand	m m m	m m m	m m m	m m m	m m m	m m m	m m m	m m m	m m m
Norway	− ▲	▲	▲	▲	▲	▲		▲	
Poland	− ▲ △		▲ △	−		△			▲ △
Portugal	−	−		−	−		▲		
Scotland		−							
Slovak Republic			▲ △	− ▲				△	
Slovenia	▲	▲		△	−				△
Spain		▲		−					
Sweden	−	−	−	−					
Switzerland							▲		▲
Turkey	−	▲	−	△		▲	▲		▲
United States	− ▲	− ▲		△	− ▲				
Other G20									
Argentina	m m m	m m m	m m m	m m m	m m m	m m m	m m m	m m m	m m m
Brazil	m m m	m m m	m m m	m m m	m m m	m m m	m m m	m m m	m m m
China	m m m	m m m	m m m	m m m	m m m	m m m	m m m	m m m	m m m
India	m m m	m m m	m m m	m m m	m m m	m m m	m m m	m m m	m m m
Indonesia	m m m	m m m	m m m	m m m	m m m	m m m	m m m	m m m	m m m
Russian Federation	−	−	▲	−	−				
Saudi Arabia	m m m	m m m	m m m	m m m	m m m	m m m	m m m	m m m	m m m
South Africa	m m m	m m m	m m m	m m m	m m m	m m m	m m m	m m m	m m m

Criteria for:

− : Decisions on position in base salary scale

▲ : Decisions on supplemental payments which are paid every year

△ : Decisions on supplemental incidental payments

Source: OECD (2011b).

Please refer to the Reader's Guide in Education at a Glance 2011: OECD Indicators (*www.oecd.org/edu/eag2011*) *for information concerning the symbols replacing missing data.*

Incentives need to be large enough to make a difference. For instance in some cases, disadvantaged schools would need to pay 20% or even 50% than more advantaged schools to prevent teachers from leaving.[16] At the same time, such mechanisms need to be well designed in order to avoid labeling certain schools as "difficult" which may discourage students, teachers and parents.[17]

To ensure that teachers stay in disadvantaged schools, working there can be valued formally in the teacher career path (Box 3.3). Also, if certain schools are far less appealing for teachers and in order not only to attract but also to retain teachers, incentives can be integrated in the salary scale rather than be awarded as a one-time additional payment.

Denmark, England, Finland, Korea, Mexico, the Netherland, Sweden and the United States offer additional payments for teachers who teach in certain fields in which there are teacher shortages, which are usually given on an annual basis. Their effectiveness depends partly on the level of teachers' salaries relative to other professions.

Box 3.3 Multiple incentives to attract excellent teachers to disadvantaged schools in Korea and in North Carolina

In **Korea**, all teachers are held to high standards, which contribute to the country's high levels of performance and equitable distribution of teachers. Other elements contributing to the high calibre of the teaching force are the highly respected status of teachers, job stability, high pay, and positive working conditions, including high levels of teacher collaboration. Low socio-economic status students in Korea are actually more likely than high socio-economic status' students to be taught by high quality mathematics teachers, as measured by characteristics such as: full certification, mathematics or mathematic education major and at least three years of experience. Multiple incentives are offered to candidates who work in high need schools. Incentives include additional salary, smaller class size, less instructional time, additional credit towards future promotion to administrative positions, and the ability to choose the next school where one works.

In the United States, **North Carolina** enacted teaching quality improvement plans with five key features: increased initial certification requirements for teachers, increased salaries tied to meeting performance standards, new teacher mentoring, ongoing professional development for all teachers, and scholarships and loan "forgiveness" programs targeted to recruit high quality candidates to teach in disadvantaged schools. The state also offers incentives to attract higher quality candidates and improve the effectiveness of new and continuing teachers, through rigorous initial training, mentoring and ongoing development. North Carolina offered a retention bonus (USD 1 800) for certified mathematics, science and special education teachers in high-poverty and low-performing schools. Overall, the bonus program reduced teacher turnover by 17%, a cost saving of approximately USD 36 000 for each teacher who chooses not to or delays leaving or moving schools. Before the bonus was implemented, a third of teachers in these subjects were uncertified and many were concentrated in disadvantaged schools.

Source: OECD (2012).

Some countries have responded to teacher supply issues with systems of individual pay. In Sweden, for example, the government only sets a minimum starting salary and pay is negotiated between the school leader and the teacher (see Box 3.4).

Also worthy of attention are non-salary strategies, such as less class-contact time or smaller classes, for schools in difficult areas or that have particular education needs.

Last but not least, working conditions and teacher satisfaction and retention are closely related.[18] Inversely, the lack of a positive work environment contributes to the high attrition rates in certain schools, especially in the case of disadvantaged schools.[19] School leader support, collaboration with colleagues and adequate resources play a significant role in teachers' decisions to stay in disadvantaged schools (see Box 3.5).

All this said, policies to encourage more people to enter teaching are unlikely to pay off if high-quality candidates find it hard to gain teaching posts. The best candidates, who are likely to have good job prospects outside teaching, may not be willing to wait in a lengthy queue or endure a succession of short-term teaching assignments in difficult schools. Well-structured and -resourced selection processes and programs of induction that ensure that the best candidates get the available jobs are therefore critical. Reducing the weight given to seniority in ranking applicants for teaching vacancies can also help reduce the risk that new teachers will be disproportionately assigned to difficult schools.

Box 3.4 Individual pay in Sweden

In Sweden, pay is now negotiated between the principal and the teacher.

One of the most radical approaches to compensation systems has been implemented in Sweden, where the federal government establishes minimum starting salaries and leaves the decisions about individual teachers' salaries to be negotiated annually by the principal and the teacher. If the teacher requests assistance, the teachers' union can participate in the negotiation. In Sweden, the centrally bargained fixed-pay scheme for teachers was abolished in 1995 as part of a package designed to enhance local autonomy and flexibility in the school system. The government committed itself to raising teachers' salaries substantially over a five-year period, but on the condition that not all teachers received the same raise. This means that there is no fixed upper limit and only a minimum basic salary is centrally negotiated, along with the aggregate rise in the teacher-salary bill. Salaries are negotiated when a teacher is hired, and teacher and employer agree on the salary to be paid at the beginning of the term of employment. The individual negotiation involves: (1) teachers' qualification areas: teachers in upper secondary schools have higher salaries than teachers in compulsory schools or teachers in pre-schools; (2) the labor market situation: in regions where teacher shortages are more acute, teachers get higher salaries; the same occurs for certain subjects like mathematics or science; (3) the performance of the teacher: the collective central agreement requires that pay raises be linked to improved performance, allowing schools to differentiate the pay of teachers with similar tasks; and (4) the range of responsibilities of teachers: principals can reward teachers if they work harder and take up more tasks than generally expected.

There is now much greater variety in teachers' pay in Sweden, with those teachers in areas of shortage and with higher demonstrated performance able to negotiate a higher salary. The scheme is underpinned by a system of central government grants to ensure that low-income municipalities are able to compete effectively for teachers and other staff in the service sectors of the municipality. Sweden, with its individual teacher pay system introduced in 1995, provides an interesting example of a country that has attempted to combine a strong tradition of teacher unionism and consultative processes with opportunities for flexible responses and non-standardized working conditions at the school level. The system was at first strongly contested by unions and teacher organizations, but now enjoys an over 70% approval rate among unionized teachers.

Source: National Advisory Committee for the Ministry of Education and Science (2003).

Box 3.5 Additional support in school for teachers in England

In 2003, England developed a program, Raising Standards and Tackling Workload – a National Agreement to improve working conditions for teachers. In a PricewaterhouseCoopers survey, teachers had said that two-thirds of their time was spent on non-teaching activities. Since teacher workload was given as a major reason for teacher retirements and attrition, the new program reduced workloads by reducing the overall hours in the teacher contract, providing guaranteed planning time, reducing paperwork requirements and adding support staff to provide routine administrative services and help teachers and support students. Support staff including bursars, administrative, technical and classroom support staff were recognised as important members of the school team, and the program created new career paths in three areas: pedagogical, behavioral/guidance, and administrative/organizational. Studies reported that the addition of support staff had a positive impact on teaching, teachers' job satisfaction, stress and workload, and student learning and behavior. The purpose of the program was to ensure better learning environments for students and a better working environment for teachers.

Teachers in England and Wales responded very favorably to the 2003 Raising Standards and Tackling Workload agreement. This agreement reduced the amount of administrative/ clerical duties assigned to teachers by adding support staff and providing them with better training to assume those responsibilities. It also phased in guaranteed, additional planning, preparation and assessment time for teachers. Over 97% of teachers surveyed for the Department of Education and Skills in 2004 responded that teaching and learning had improved because of the agreement, and about half reported that teacher workloads had decreased overall.

Source: OECD (2009b).

ESTABLISHING EFFECTIVE EMPLOYMENT CONDITIONS

The predominant model for teacher employment in OECD countries is "career-based" public service in which entry is competitive, career development is extensively regulated and lifetime employment is largely guaranteed.[20] Where teachers are not commonly removed for unsatisfactory performance, the quality of teachers depends mainly on setting high standards of entering teacher-preparation programs, on the quality of their initial preparation, and on the attention given to the quality of their preparation following their initial induction. Under career-based systems, the risk is that the quality of the teaching force depends excessively on getting initial recruitment and teacher education right, and that any improvement over time will take many years to affect most serving teachers. Moreover, career advancement can become heavily dependent on adhering to organizational norms, which helps to ensure uniformity and predictability of service and a strong group ethos, but can make systems inflexible to change and ill-equipped to serve diverse needs in different settings.

In some countries, public servants are required to apply for specific positions by showing that their competencies match specific job requirements, rather than having a guaranteed career. However, this can increase recruitment and management costs, and make it harder to develop shared values and provide consistent service. Another approach has been to introduce more contract or temporary employment positions in parallel with career-based systems. This opens up possibilities for external recruitment, provides local managers with more scope for personnel decisions, and institutes management by objectives. However, the general experience in OECD countries is that it is not easy to graft features from a markedly different system onto a well-established employment model. Those in career-based systems who have met demanding entrance criteria and accepted relatively low starting salaries can feel threatened by a less predictable future. Those accustomed to professional status and autonomy derived from their specialist skills may feel threatened by moves to institute system-wide standards. The OECD's *Teachers Matter* study, PISA and the annual data collection conducted for *Education at a Glance* identify a number of trends in country reforms that are highlighted below.

Successful enterprises often report that personnel selection is the most important set of decisions that they make. In the case of teaching, the evidence suggests that all too often the selection process follows rules about qualifications and seniority that bear little relationship to the qualities needed to be an effective teacher. The sheer size of school systems in many countries means that the process of teacher selection is often highly impersonal, and it is hard for teachers to build a sense of commitment to the schools to which they are appointed – or for the schools to build a sense of commitment to them. Data from PISA suggest that many of the high-performing education systems have responded by giving schools more responsibility – and accountability – for teacher selection, working conditions and development (see Figure 1.b).

The OECD's *Teachers Matter* study describes how school leaders in many of the best-performing education systems actively seek out and develop the best possible teachers and, with personal interviews and visits to schools by candidates, seek to optimize the match between applicants and school needs. The study suggests that such approaches work best where parallel steps are taken to ensure that accountability, efficiency and equity are not jeopardized, for example by developing school leaders' skills in personnel management, providing disadvantaged schools with greater resources with which to recruit effective teachers, making information more accessible in the teacher labor market, and monitoring the outcomes of a more decentralized approach and adjusting accordingly. However, successful decentralization of personnel management, and of school decision-making more generally, require that central and regional authorities help to ensure that teachers are adequately and equitably distributed throughout the country. It is also important to have independent appeals procedures to ensure fairness and protect teachers' rights.

A desire for increased flexibility in the labor market, including to accommodate maternity/paternity leave, has led to increased part-time employment across many sectors of the economy, teaching among them. On average across OECD countries, about one in six teachers works on a part-time basis in public institutions at primary and lower secondary levels of education.[21] In some countries, part-time work is common among teachers: between one in five and one in three teachers in Australia, the Flemish Community of Belgium, Iceland, and New Zealand work part time, as do more than one-third of teachers in Norway and Sweden, and nearly half the teachers in Germany (primary education) and the Netherlands.

In the majority of OECD countries, part-time employment opportunities depend upon a decision taken at the school level or by local authorities/government; in five of the countries with the largest proportions of part-time employment, the decision is taken at the school level. Schools recognize that their teaching and school organization requirements change; and these countries have some flexibility in their teacher workforce that reflects these changing requirements.

There is considerable evidence that some new teachers, no matter how well prepared and supported, struggle to perform well on the job, or find that the job does not meet their expectations. This could be due to several factors at the teacher, classroom and school levels. On average for all countries who participated in the TALIS 2008 survey,[22] new teachers reported spending 5% more time (13% for experienced teachers compared with 18% for new teachers) on keeping order in the classroom. In one-third of the countries new teachers said that they spend up to 20% of their time on classroom management and discipline. Obviously, this reduces the time spent on actual teaching and learning. New teachers spend 73% of their time on teaching, while experienced teachers said they spend 79% of their time on this core task. In addition, new teachers surveyed in TALIS 2008 reported significantly lower levels of self-efficacy than more experienced teachers. On average, this difference was statistically significant both across TALIS 2008 countries and in the Flemish Community of Belgium, Denmark, Estonia, Iceland, Ireland, Korea, Malaysia, Malta, Norway, Poland, the Slovak Republic and Turkey. Often, these differences were not quantitatively large, but they are important, given that they highlight differences in teachers' beliefs about their effectiveness in the classroom.[23]

In a number of countries, a formal probationary process, combined with adequate teacher support, provides an opportunity for both new teachers and their employers to assess whether teaching is the right career for them. In some countries, the successful completion of probation is acknowledged as a major step in the teaching career. The OECD's *Education at a Glance* found that, among 26 countries with comparable data, 16 countries have a mandatory probation period for teachers. This period usually lasts for one year, but in some countries (Greece, Luxembourg) it lasts for two years, and in Germany it can even be extended to three years. In seven OECD countries, teachers receive job tenure after completing their probationary period. In some countries, such as Austria, six years are necessary to achieve job tenure, whereas there is only a one-month probation period. In other countries a period of time is necessary to get tenure, even if there is no probation period. For example, in Mexico, a teacher needs six months to get tenure without any probation period, two years to achieve tenure in Iceland, and three years in the Flemish Community of Belgium.

Limited mobility of teachers between schools, and between teaching and other occupations, can restrict the spread of new ideas and approaches, and result in teachers having few opportunities for diverse career experiences. It can also lead to an inequitable distribution of teachers, where teachers do not move from the most favored schools. In some cases the lack of mobility means that some regions of the country might have teacher shortages while others have an oversupply of teachers. In some countries, providing incentives for greater mobility and removing barriers are important policy responses. In countries with different education jurisdictions, such as federal systems, the mutual recognition of teaching qualifications is crucial, as it ensures that entitlements to leave and retirement benefits move with the teacher. Recognizing the skills and experience gained outside education is also an important means of encouraging greater career mobility among teachers, as is providing flexible re-entry pathways to the profession. International mobility of teachers is also a growing phenomenon, raising issues of recognition of qualifications, certifications and procedures for recruitment and induction.[24]

Given the large number of teachers and applicants involved in most school systems, it is often difficult and costly for employers to use extensive information when selecting candidates. It can be just as difficult for candidates for teaching positions to have precise information about the schools to which they apply, or even about broad trends in the labor market and the available vacancies. Such information gaps and limitations mean that many application and selection decisions are sub-optimal. The development of transparent and prompt systems to close the information gaps between teachers and schools is essential for an effectively functioning teacher labor market, especially where schools are more directly involved in teacher recruitment and selection. Some countries require all teaching vacancies to be posted, and create websites where the information is centralized or establish a network of agencies to co-ordinate and foster recruitment activities. Since imbalances in the teacher labor market can take a long time to be rectified, tools for monitoring and projecting teacher demand and supply under different scenarios can also help.

ENSURING HIGH-QUALITY INITIAL TEACHER EDUCATION
Though perhaps not as central to matching teacher demand and supply, initial teacher education is another important part of the equation to ensure the supply of a high-quality teaching force in the longer term. OECD research has identified some principles that are worth noting:[25]

- *Education systems benefit from clear and concise profiles of what teachers are expected to know and be able to do in specific subject areas.* This includes both subject-matter knowledge as well as knowledge of how to teach it. Such profiles can guide initial teacher education, teacher certification, teachers' on-going evaluation, professional development and career advancement, and also help to assess the extent to which these different elements are effective. The profiles can reflect the school's learning objectives and profession-wide understanding of what counts as accomplished teaching.

- Many countries have moved their initial teacher-education programs towards a ***model based less on academic preparation and more on preparing professionals in school settings, with an appropriate balance between theory and practice and collaboration among teachers as a key aspect.*** In these programs, teachers get into classrooms earlier, spend more time there and get more and better support in the process. This can include both extensive course work on how to teach – with a strong emphasis on using research based on state-of-the-art practice – and more than a year teaching in a designated school, associated with the university, during which time the teacher is expected to develop and pilot innovative practices and undertake research on learning and teaching, in partnership with other teachers and under the guidance of accomplished teachers. The Finnish University Training is a prominent example for the effective implementation of such an approach.

- ***More flexible structures of initial teacher education can be effective in opening up new routes into the teaching career, without compromising the rigor of traditional routes.*** The stages of initial teacher education, induction and professional development need to be interconnected to create a lifelong learning framework for teachers. In many countries, teacher education is not just providing sound basic training in subject-matter knowledge, pedagogy related to subjects, and general pedagogical knowledge; it also seeks to develop the skills for reflective practice and on-the-job research. Increasingly, initial teacher education tends to emphasize developing the capacity of teachers in training to diagnose student problems swiftly and accurately and to draw from a wide repertoire of possible solutions to find those that are appropriate to the diagnosis. Some countries provide teachers with the research skills needed to enable them to improve their practice in systematic ways. For example, in Finland, the Shanghai province of China and many parts of the United States, teachers are trained to be action researchers in practice, with the ability to work out ways of ensuring that any student starting to fall behind is helped effectively.

- In addition, some countries have moved from a system in which teachers are recruited into a larger number of specialized colleges of teacher education, with relatively low entrance standards, to a relatively smaller number of university-based teacher-education colleges with relatively high entrance standards and relatively high status in the university.

PROVIDING FOR ATTRACTIVE CAREERS

Matching teacher demand and supply also relies on an environment that facilitates success and encourages effective teachers to continue in teaching. There is concern in a number of countries that the rates at which teachers are leaving the profession are compounding school staffing problems and leading to a loss of teaching expertise. As alluded to earlier, teacher attrition rates tend to be higher in the first few years of teaching, while they decline the longer that teachers are in the profession, before they increase again as teachers approach retirement.[26] This implies that large private and social costs are incurred in preparing some people for a profession that they soon find does not meet their expectations, that is insufficiently rewarding, or too difficult, or some combination of these factors. It underlines the importance for new teachers to participate in structured induction programs involving a reduced teaching load, trained mentor teachers in schools, and close partnerships with teacher-education institutions, and for school systems to ensure that the criteria and processes used to allocate teachers to schools are designed such that new teachers are not concentrated in the more difficult and unpopular locations.

Although attractive salaries are clearly important for making teaching more appealing and retaining effective teachers, the OECD's *Teachers Matter* study concludes that policy needs to address more than pay:

Teachers place considerable emphasis on the quality of their relations with students and colleagues, on feeling supported by school leaders, on good working conditions, and on opportunities to develop their skills. Some countries are therefore placing greater emphasis on teacher evaluations to support improvements in teaching practice. While these evaluations are designed mainly to enhance classroom practice, they provide opportunities for teachers' work to be recognized and celebrated, and help both teachers and schools to identify professional development priorities. They can also provide a basis for rewarding teachers for exemplary performance.

Teaching careers can benefit from greater diversification, which can help meet school needs and also provide more opportunities and recognition for teachers. In most countries, opportunities for promotion and new responsibilities are generally limited for teachers who want to stay in the classroom. Promotions generally involve teachers spending less time in classrooms, and thus reduce one of the major sources of job satisfaction. Even for those who would like to take on more roles outside the classroom, in many countries those opportunities are limited. Some countries are moving to open more career opportunities for teachers, spurred, in part, by the greater variety of school roles

that have been delegated significant decision-making responsibilities. Examples from OECD countries (see Box 3.6) suggest that greater career diversity can be achieved by creating new positions associated with specific tasks and roles in addition to classroom teaching, which leads to greater horizontal differentiation; and through a competency-based teaching career ladder that recognizes extra responsibilities, and that leads to greater vertical differentiation. In the latter, each stage is more demanding than the prior stage, involving more responsibilities, and is open to fewer people, but is accompanied by a significant rise in status and, often, compensation. The recognition that schools and teachers need to perform a greater range of tasks and assume more responsibility also calls for the creation of new roles, such as mentors of new and trainee teachers, co-coordinators of in-service education, and school project co-coordinators.

Greater emphasis on school leadership can help address the need for teachers to feel valued and supported in their work. In addition, well-trained professional and administrative staff can help reduce the burden on teachers, better facilities for staff preparation and planning would help build collegiality, and more flexible working conditions, especially for more experienced teachers, would prevent career burnout and retain important skills in schools.

Providing support for new teachers should move beyond simply providing administrative and planning support, however. New teachers in many countries feel that they do not receive support and feedback on the most important element of their role as a teacher: their teaching practice. TALIS 2008 asked teachers about the frequency with which they received appraisal and feedback and from which source: the school leader; other teachers or members of the school management team; or an individual or body external to the school. Most new teachers reported receiving some form of appraisal and feedback from both the school leader and other teachers. However, in most countries, except for Korea, Mexico and Turkey, more than half of new teachers never received appraisal or feedback from an external individual. More than 19% of new teachers had never received appraisal or feedback on their work. In some countries, the percentage of new teachers who had not received appraisal and feedback is considerably higher. For example, in Italy 60% of new teachers had not received appraisal and feedback. This is the only country where over half of new teachers had not received any such feedback on their work. However, this figure is also high in Spain and Portugal, where 32% of new teachers reported never having received appraisal and feedback, and Iceland (24%).

As mentioned earlier, many countries offer mentoring and induction programs to help teachers in the early years of their profession. Indeed, approximately three-quarters of new teachers surveyed in TALIS 2008 work in schools that have formal mentoring or induction programs. But, perhaps surprisingly, new teachers who work in schools with induction or mentoring programs were not significantly more likely to receive more frequent appraisal and feedback than other new teachers. In fact, whether or not a school had induction or mentoring programs had little impact on the appraisal and feedback new teachers in that school received.[27]

As noted before, teachers are largely employed as public servants, and in a number of countries this is associated with tenured employment. While some may consider security of employment as an incentive to become a teacher, there may not be sufficient incentives or support systems for all teachers to continuously review their skills and improve their practice, especially where there are only limited mechanisms for teacher appraisal and accountability. Tenured employment can also make it difficult to adjust teacher numbers when enrolments decline or curricula change, and may mean that the burden of adjustment falls on those who lack tenure, commonly those near the beginning of their careers. To avoid this, it is important that emphasis be placed on the licensing aspect of teaching and that high quality robust evaluation systems and professional development are deployed to ensure that all teachers are engaged in professional practice that promotes student learning.

In some countries teachers need to renew their teaching certificates after a period of time, and often have to demonstrate that they have participated in on-going professional development and coursework to increase, deepen, and strengthen their knowledge. The basis for renewal can be as simple as an attestation that the teacher is continuing to meet standards of performance that are agreed throughout the teaching profession. Such systems must ensure an open, fair and transparent system of teacher appraisal, involving teaching peers, school leaders and external experts who are properly trained and resourced for these tasks – and who are themselves evaluated on a regular basis. Underpinning these models is the view that the interests of students will be better served where teachers achieve employment security by continuing to do a good job, rather than by regulation that effectively guarantees their employment. Periodic reviews also provide the opportunity to recognize and acknowledge quality teaching. Some countries also have fair but speedy mechanisms to address ineffective teaching. Teachers in these countries have the opportunity and support to improve but, if they do not, they can be moved either into other roles or out of the school system.

Box 3.6 Providing greater career diversity in Australia, England and Wales, Ireland and Québec (Canada)

In *Australia*, teachers typically have access to a career structure that involves two to four stages, with annual salary increments within each stage. The stages normally range from beginning teacher to experienced teacher, to experienced teacher with responsibility (leading teacher) or learning area or grade-level co-coordinator, assistant principal, principal, and regional/district office positions. Advancement from one stage to the next, especially at the higher levels, usually requires applying for widely advertised vacancies. As they move up the scale, teachers are expected to have deeper levels of knowledge, demonstrate more sophisticated and effective teaching, take on responsibility for co-curricular aspects of the school, assist colleagues and so on. By "leading teacher" stage, they are expected to demonstrate exemplary teaching, educational leadership, and the ability to initiate and manage change.

In *England and Wales*, the new career grade of Advanced Skills Teacher (AST), introduced in 1998, is designed to provide an alternative route for career development for teachers who wish to stay in the classroom. Their role is to provide pedagogic leadership within their own and other schools. Typically, they will spend 20% of their time in an "outreach" role supporting professional development of their colleagues, and teach in class for the remaining time. Teachers can take up an AST post at any point in their career, but in order to do so they must pass the AST assessment. They prepare a portfolio that shows how they meet the prescribed standards for the grade, which is evaluated by an external assessor. The assessor also interviews the applicants and observes their professional practice. In July 2004, some 5 000 teachers had passed the AST assessment. The intention is that the grade will ultimately form between 3% and 5% of the workforce.

Ireland has introduced four categories of promotion posts: principal, deputy principal, assistant principal, and special duties teacher. Each has special management duties and receives both salary and time allowances. In addition to classroom teaching, assistant principals and special duties teachers have special responsibility for academic, administrative and pastoral matters, including timetabling arrangements, liaison with parents' associations, supervising the maintenance and availability of school equipment, and so on. They are selected by a panel that consists of a principal, chair of the management board, and an independent external assessor. Over the course of their careers, about 50% of teachers can expect to receive one of these positions.

In *Québec*, experienced teachers can work as mentors for student teachers. Experienced teachers coach and guide the student teachers and undertake specific training. They receive either additional pay or a reduction in classroom teaching responsibilities. About 12 000 teachers participate in the mentor program. Some of these experienced teachers also have an opportunity to become co-researchers with university staff and to participate in collaborative studies on subjects such as teaching, learning, classroom management and student success or failure. In addition, experienced teachers may be released from some of their normal duties to provide support for less-experienced colleagues.

Source: OECD (2005).

MEETING THE NEED FOR ONGOING PROFESSIONAL DEVELOPMENT TO ADDRESS ISSUES OF TEACHER SUPPLY

Recruiting and selecting promising graduates is crucial for meeting the demand for teachers, but it is only one part of managing human resources in education and it is noteworthy that far from all high-performing education systems recruit their teachers from the top-third of graduates. Successful reform cannot wait for a new generation of teachers; it requires investment in the present teaching force, providing quality professional development, adequate career structures and diversification, and enlisting the commitment of teachers to reform. The ILO/UNESCO Committee of Experts on the Application of the Recommendations concerning Teaching Personnel notes in its 2009 report that "Teaching career structures…are evolving to encourage better teaching practices and incentives for teachers to remain in teaching, but much more needs to be done to link teacher education and professional development, evaluation and career progression. Evidence from international surveys…point to a general lack of professional development support adapted to the needs of teachers and learners."[28]

The following analysis looks at how the individual development of teachers can be improved and how greater collaboration among teachers can improve teaching quality.

In many countries, the role and functioning of schools are changing – as is what is expected of teachers. They are asked to teach in increasingly multicultural classrooms. They must place greater emphasis on integrating students with special learning needs, both special difficulties and special talents, in their classes. They need to make more effective use of information and communication technologies for teaching. They are required to engage more in planning within evaluative and accountability frameworks. And they are asked to do more to involve parents in schools. No matter how good the pre-service education for teachers is, it cannot be expected to prepare teachers for all the challenges they will face throughout their careers.

Given the complexity of teaching and learning, high quality professional development is necessary to ensure that all teachers are able to meet the needs of diverse student populations, effectively use data to guide reform, engage parents, and become active agents of their own professional growth. The development of teachers beyond their initial education can serve a range of purposes, including to:

- update individuals' knowledge of a subject in light of recent advances in the area;
- update individuals' skills and approaches in light of the development of new teaching techniques and objectives, new circumstances, and new educational research;
- enable individuals to apply changes made to curricula or other aspects of teaching practice;
- enable schools to develop and apply new strategies concerning the curriculum and other aspects of teaching practice;
- exchange information and expertise among teachers and others, e.g. academics and industrialists; and/or
- help weaker teachers become more effective.

Issues of professional development are not just relevant to the overall supply of quality teachers, but also to address specific issues of teacher shortages. Across the 18 OECD countries participating in TALIS, the aspect of teachers' work most frequently rated by teachers as an area of need for development was "Teaching special learning needs students". This can be especially challenging in the case of disadvantaged schools, as students in these schools often have a wider range of abilities and needs. It is also worth highlighting that one out of five teachers across countries – and more than one out of three in Korea, Austria, Slovenia and Hungary - indicated that he or she needs professional development in student discipline and behavioral issues. Again, that is particularly relevant for teachers in disadvantaged schools as PISA shows such schools to typically have a poorer disciplinary climate. Last but not least, 13 % of teachers – and 25 % in Italy and in Ireland – reported that they do not feel prepared to teach in a multicultural setting. At the same time, there are many examples of efforts to address these issues.

In seeking to meet teachers' professional development requirements, policy makers and practitioners need to consider both how to support and encourage participation and how to ensure that opportunities match teachers' needs. This needs to be balanced with the cost in terms of both finance and teachers' time. OECD research identifies several aspects as central to successfully bridging the gap between the ideal learning environment and day-to-day practice:[29]

- Well-structured and -resourced induction programs can support new teachers in their transition to full teaching responsibilities before they obtain all the rights and responsibilities of full-time professional teachers. In some countries, once teachers have completed their pre-service education and begun their teaching, they begin one or two years of heavily supervised teaching. During this period, the new teacher typically receives a reduced workload, mentoring by master teachers, and continued formal instruction.
- Effective professional development needs to be ongoing, include training, practice and feedback, and provide adequate time and follow-up support. Successful programs involve teachers in learning activities that are similar to those they will use with their students, and encourage the development of teachers' learning communities.
- Teacher development needs to be linked with wider goals of school and system development, and with appraisal and feedback practices and school evaluation.
- There is often a need to re-examine structures and practices that inhibit inter-disciplinary practice and to provide more room for teachers to take time to learn deeply, and employ inquiry- and group-based approaches, especially in the core areas of curriculum and assessment.

Box 3.7 Professional development for teaching minority students in New Zealand

Recent research in New Zealand reveals that Culturally Responsive Teaching (CRT) may be an effective part of a comprehensive professional development program. In New Zealand, a comprehensive professional development program for teaching Māori students, *Te Kotahitanga*, led to improved achievement of Māori students and higher overall student achievement in participating schools. The program is unique because it was developed based on interviews with year 9 and 10 Māori students about what they believed they needed to be successful. Since Māori students, on average, have lower levels of academic performance and graduation rates than their peers *Te Kotahitanga* was designed to improve Māori student achievement in New Zealand by improving teacher-student relationships using Culturally Responsive Teaching and improving teacher effectiveness with comprehensive instructional support.

Te Kotahitanga includes direction by lead facilitators, workshops, classroom observations and feedback, facilitator-led teacher collaboration and problem-solving based on observational and student outcomes data, and shadow-coaching for individual teachers.

Thus, the program includes both professional development and other supports that can assist teachers in being more effective with students. Māori students who attended schools that engaged in the program scored significantly higher in mathematics, physics and science, and no differently in English and history when compared to matched schools without *Te Kotahitanga*. In addition, overall student performance increased at twice the rate of the average national gain, as measured by the percentage of Year 9 entrants attaining NCEA Level 1 in Year 11. The number of students attaining NCEA Level 1 in year 11 indicates that students are on-time to graduate. These findings indicate that the program has positive effects not only for Māori students but for all students at participating schools.

Source : OECD (2010b).

Box 3.8 Innovative teacher-preparation programs in the United States

The Boston Teacher Residency (BTR), established in 2003, is a teacher-preparation program that recruits high-performing college graduates and professionals and prepares them to teach in Boston schools. The program focuses on mastering the skills that teachers will need to be effective in the public schools in which teachers will work, emphasizing clinical training and pairing residents with experienced classroom teachers. Residents begin the program with a two-month summer institute, and then spend their first year in a classroom four days a week, alongside a master teacher, spending the fifth day attending courses and seminars. This approach allows residents to master both the theory and practice of teaching simultaneously. After their first year, residents receive an initial teacher license and a master's degree in education, and continue to receive support from BTR in the form of induction coaching, courses and seminars, and placement in collaborative clusters within schools. Early indicators of success include a rigorous recruitment and selection process in which only 13% of applicants are admitted, three-year retention rates of 85% (far above the U.S. average for urban schools), growth of the program's outputs to fill 60% of Boston's annual need for math and science teachers, and highly favorable reviews from school principals, with 96% of principals saying they would recommend hiring a BTR graduate to another principal. A study of the program's impact on student achievement concluded that BTR math completers were less effective in the first two years of teaching and English completers were comparable to other teachers. The study also found that BTR candidates would surpass their peers in improving student achievement after the first couple of years. Given that these candidates are retained at higher rates and eventually have higher student achievement rates, the authors found that BTR graduates may be the better investment for the district. BTR recently received a USD 5 million "development" grant under the U.S. Department of Education's Investing in Innovation Fund, which seeks to identify and scale-up promising and proven practices in teacher education and other priority areas.

Source: *www.bostonteacherresidency.org.*

In some countries, ongoing professional development already plays an important role. In the Chinese province of Shanghai, each teacher is expected to engage in 240 hours of professional development within five years of being hired. Singapore provides teachers with an entitlement of 100 hours of professional development per year to keep up with the rapid changes occurring in the world and to be able to improve their practice. More generally, results from TALIS show that, across countries, almost 90% of teachers participated in some form of professional development over an 18-month period and, on average, spent just under one day per month in professional development[30] (see also Figures 3.5 and 3.6). However, there is considerable variation in the incidence and intensity of teacher participation in professional development both across and within countries;[31] older teachers tend to engage in less professional development than younger ones. The types of development undertaken by teachers explain some of these variations. Countries in which a high percentage of teachers take part in "qualification programs" or "individual and collaborative research" tend to have a higher average number of days of development, but only a small minority of teachers tends to participate in these activities.

Teachers consider better and more targeted professional development as an important lever towards improvement. TALIS data show that teachers' participation in professional development goes hand-in-hand with their mastery of a wider array of methods to use in the classroom, even if it is not clear to what extent professional development triggers or responds to the adoption of new techniques. TALIS data also identify close associations between professional development and a positive school climate, teaching beliefs, co-operation among teachers and teachers' job satisfaction.

However, schools and systems need to better match the costs and benefits of, and supply and demand for, professional development. Results from TALIS show that, across countries, relatively few teachers participate in the kinds of professional development that they believe has the largest impact on their work, namely qualification programs and individual and collaborative research, even if those who do commit considerable time and money to these courses consider them effective. Conversely, the types of activities that teachers consider less effective, namely one-off education conferences and seminars, show comparatively high participation rates. This being said, research on how the incidence and intensity of different types of professional development activities influences learning outcomes is still limited.

Figure 3.5
Comparison of impact and participation by types of development activity

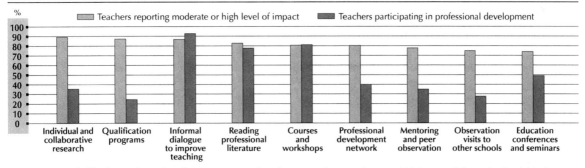

Activities are ranked in descending order of the percentage of teachers reporting a moderate or high impact of the professional development they look.
Source: OECD (2009a), Table 3.2 and 3.8.

Figure 3.6
Reasons for not taking more professional development
Among those teachers who wanted more development than they received (international averages)

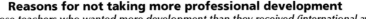
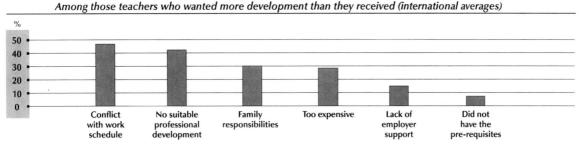

Reasons are ranked in descending order of frequency with which the barrier was reported by teachers.
Source: OECD (2009a), Table 3.7.

Despite high levels of participation in development activities, the professional development needs of a significant proportion of teachers are often not fully met. The TALIS survey found that:

- Some 55% of the teachers surveyed reported that they wanted more professional development than they received during the 18-month survey period. The extent of unsatisfied demand is sizeable in every country, ranging from 31% to over 80%.
- Across countries, teachers who were more likely to report unsatisfied demand were in public schools, women, and under 40 years of age.
- Across countries, the aspects of teachers' work with greatest need for development are "teaching special-needs students", followed by "information and communication technology teaching skills" and "student discipline and behavior".

What prevents teachers from undertaking as much professional development as they would like? The most common reason, cited by nearly half of teachers in TALIS, was conflict with their work schedule (Figure 3.6). However, almost as many cited the lack of suitable opportunities for professional development, and these teachers also generally engaged in less development activity.

But it is not just a question of producing more of the same professional development. Teachers consistently reported that their greatest need for professional development was in learning how to handle differences in student learning styles and backgrounds, using information and communication technologies effectively, and improving student behavior (see Figure 3.7). These responses provide some direction on where future efforts should focus, and suggest that a sound assessment of provision and support of development is important.

Of course, a certain level of unsatisfied demand is to be expected; it is only natural that a proportion of teachers will, at some time, not feel fully equipped to carry out their work effectively. Nonetheless, the extent of unsatisfied demand appears large, and in some countries the great majority of teachers report that they need more professional development than they receive. The extent to which this undermines the effectiveness of these teachers is difficult to assess; but it is equally difficult to imagine that such deficits are not to some extent detrimental to effective teaching and learning. The cost of providing additional professional development needs to be seen in relation to the cost of not providing it, in terms of lost opportunities for students to learn.

Figure 3.7

Areas of greatest need for teacher professional development
International average of percentage of teachers reporting a high level of need

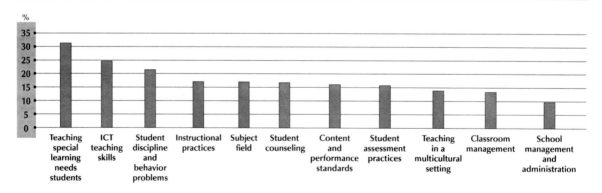

Areas are ranked in descending order of the international average where teachers report a high level of need for development.
Source: OECD (2009a), Table 3.4.

Even if there is no country in which the professional development of teachers is completely free, TALIS data indicate that teachers in most countries feel that the level of support they receive, in terms of finance and scheduled time specifically devoted to development activities, is significant. An average of around two-thirds of teachers in participating countries pay nothing for these activities, and a similar proportion receives allocated time. Schools and public authorities clearly make a significant investment in teachers' professional development.

The fact that a sizeable proportion of teachers underwrite the cost of their professional development is evidence that many teachers contribute to the cost of advancing their career if they cannot find free programs of adequate quality. In fact, the data show that when teachers pay for their own professional development, they tend to participate in more of it: those who paid the full cost took over twice as many teacher-education courses as those who received them for free. This partly reflects the fact that courses that are paid for tend to lead to professional qualifications and are more time-consuming. This suggests that providing programs for free is not necessarily the only way to stimulate participation, at least when teachers are seeking to further their careers and their earnings prospects, such as when they prepare for becoming head teachers, inspectors or teachers at a superior level of education.

There is a growing amount of research on the most effective forms of professional development which has implications for its provision and organization at school and system level. The English Government's paper, the "Case for Change", (Department for Education, 2010), noted "convincing evidence that collaborative professional development is more strongly associated with improvements in teaching and learning…(and)…appears more likely to produce changes in teacher practice, attitudes or beliefs and in pupil outcomes." These findings were a result of research reviews initiated by the National Union of Teachers for England and Wales in preparation for establishing its professional development program and were carried out by Cordingley, et al. (2003, 2005a, 2005b, and 2007) for the EPPI Centre at the Social Science Research Centre, Institute of Education, University of London.

CONCLUSIONS

Many education systems face a daunting challenge in recruiting high-quality graduates as teachers, particularly in shortage areas, and retaining them once they are hired. And yet, this chapter has shown a range of cases that successfully match teacher demand and supply even in difficult contexts. In fact, common to most education systems that demonstrate high performance and low between-school variation in performance in PISA is that they attract high quality teachers equitably across the school system, including to hard-to-staff schools.

The issue of teacher demand and supply is both complex and multi-dimensional, as it reflects several challenges: how to expand the pool of qualified teachers, how to address shortages in specific subjects, how to recruit teachers to the places where they are most needed, how distribute teachers in equitable and efficient ways, and how to retain qualified teachers over time.

Policy responses are needed at two levels. The first concerns the nature of the teaching profession itself and teachers' work environment. Such policies seek to improve the profession's general status and competitive position in the job market and are the focus of this paper. The second involves more targeted responses and incentives for particular types of teacher shortage, which recognizes that that there is not a single labor market for teachers, but a set of them, distinguished by school type and characteristics, such as subject specialization.

Competitive compensation and other incentives, career prospects and diversity, and giving teachers responsibility as professionals are important parts of strategies to attract the most talented teaches to the most challenging classrooms. Active recruitment campaigns can emphasize the fulfilling nature of teaching as a profession, and seek to draw in groups that might not otherwise have considered teaching. Where teaching is seen as an attractive profession, its status can further be enhanced through selective recruitment that makes teachers feel that they will be going into a career sought after by accomplished professionals. Initial teacher education is another important part of the equation to ensure the supply of high-quality teaching force in the longer term.

Last but not least, no matter how good the pre-service education for teachers is, it cannot be expected to prepare teachers for all the challenges they will face throughout their careers. High quality professional continuing development is necessary to ensure that all teachers are able to meet the demands of diverse student populations, effectively use data to guide reform, engage parents, and become active agents of their own professional growth.

Notes

1. OECD (2005).

2. OECD (2012).

3. OECD (2012).

4. OECD (2012).

5. For an analysis of teacher demographics, see Indicator D8 in the 2003 edition of OECD's *Education at a Glance*. For updated data on the same topic, see the OECD online database at *www.oecd.org/education/eag2011*.

6. For details, see OECD (2005).

7. For data, see OECD (2010a).

8. For data, see OECD (2010a).

9. It should be noted that autonomy of schools in managing their resources is positively related to school performance in PISA 2009 only in conjunction with established accountability arrangements. In the absence of accountability arrangements, school autonomy is related negatively to school performance (for data, see OECD [2010a]).

10. For data, see OECD (2010a).

11. The admissions process occurs in two stages. The initial paper screening is based on the applicant's matriculation exam score, upper secondary school record, and out-of-school accomplishments. Those who pass that screening must then take a written exam, be observed in a teaching-like activity in which their interaction and communication skills can be assessed, and be interviewed to assess, among other things, the strength of their motivation to teach (for details see OECD [2011a]).

12. In 2009, teachers' salaries at the primary level amount to, on average, 77% of full-time, full-year earnings for 25-64 year-olds with tertiary education, 81% of those earnings at lower secondary level, and 85% of those earnings at upper secondary level. The lowest relative teachers' salaries, compared to the salaries of other professionals with comparable education, are found in the Slovak Republic at all levels of education, and in Hungary and Iceland for primary and lower secondary school teachers, where statutory salaries for teachers with 15 years of experience are 50% or less of what a full-time, full-year worker with a tertiary education earns, on average. Relative salaries for teachers in primary and lower secondary education are highest in Korea, Portugal and Spain, where teachers earn more than the average salary of a worker with a tertiary education. In upper secondary education, teachers' salaries are at least 10% higher than those of comparably educated workers in Belgium, Luxembourg and Portugal, and up to 32% higher in Spain (for data, see the OECD's 2011 edition of *Education at a Glance*, Table D3.2).

13. For data, see OECD (2010a).

14. See OECD (2005).

15. Salaries in London for example exceed those in the rest of England by about 12% (Ladd, 2007).

16. Field, S., M. Kuczera and B. Pont (2007).

17. In North Carolina for example, labeling schools as "low-performing" made it harder to recruit and retain qualified teachers. Both experienced and novice teachers were about 25% more likely, to leave schools labelled low-performing compared to teachers in schools with similar student performance that were not so labelled. There is evidence of the same phenomenon for France.

18. OECD (2009a).

19. OECD (2012).

20. For data, see Figure IV.3.3a in OECD (2010a).

21. For data, see Indicator D3 in the 2007 edition of OECD's *Education at a Glance*.

22. Twenty-three countries participated in TALIS 2008: Australia, Austria, Belgium (Fl.), Brazil, Bulgaria, Denmark, Estonia, Hungary, Iceland, Ireland, Italy, Republic of Korea, Lithuania, Malaysia, Malta, Mexico, Norway, Poland, Portugal, Slovak Republic, Slovenia, Spain and Turkey. TALIS 2008 was also conducted in the Netherlands but as the required sampling standards were not achieved, their data are not included in the international comparisons.

23. See OECD (2011c).

24. See, for example, the Commonwealth Teachers Recruitment Protocol of 2004, developed at the request of the 15th Conference of Commonwealth Education Ministers, Edinburgh, UK 2003.

25. See OECD (2011a).

26. For an analysis, see OECD (2005).

27. See OECD (2011c).

28. See page 4 of the Joint ILO/UNESCO Committee of Experts on the Application of the Recommendations concerning Teaching Personnel (CEART), Paris, October 2009.

29. See OECD (2005).

30. TALIS asked teachers about their professional development activities during the 18 months prior to the survey. This period of time was chosen in order to cover activities over almost two school years in order to give a more representative picture and lessen possible distortions due to unusually busy or lean periods of development, and to ensure a manageable period for teachers' recall. Teachers were first asked to indicate whether or not they had participated in each of the following activities: (1) courses/workshops (e.g. on subject matter or methods and/or other education-related topics); (2) education conferences or seminars (at which teachers and/or researchers present their research results and discuss education problems); (3) qualification program (e.g. a degree program); (4) observation visits to other schools; (5) participation in a network of teachers formed specifically for the professional development of teachers; (6) individual or collaborative research on a topic of professional interest; and (7) mentoring and/or peer observation and coaching, as part of a formal school arrangement. Teachers were able to indicate participation in multiple activities. TALIS then asked teachers how many days of professional development they had attended in the 18 months prior to the survey and how many of these days were compulsory (for details, see OECD [2009a]).

31. The intensity of teacher participation in professional development varies considerably across countries, with Korea and Mexico seeing teachers participating, on average, over 30 days in 18 months, twice the average rate. Within-country variation in the intensity of professional development can also be high, most notably in Italy, Mexico, Korea, Poland and Spain (for data see OECD [2009a]).

References

Cordingley, P. et al. (2003), "The impact of collaborative CPD on classroom teaching and learning", *Research Evidence in Education Library*, EPPI-Centre, Social Science Research Unit, Institute of Education, University of London, London.

Cordingley, P. et al. (2005a), "The impact of collaborative CPD on classroom teaching and learning. What do teacher impact data tell us about collaborative CPD?", *Research Evidence in Education Library*, EPPI-Centre, Social Science Research Unit, Institute of Education, University of London, London.

Cordingley, P. et al. (2005b), "The impact of collaborative continuing professional development (CPD) on classroom teaching and learning. How do collaborative and sustained CPD and sustained but not collaborative CPD affect teaching and learning?", *Research Evidence in Education Library*, EPPI-Centre, Social Science Research Unit, Institute of Education, University of London, London.

Cordingley, P. et al. (2007), "Evidence for Policy and Practice Information and Co-ordinating Centre. What do specialists do in CPD programmes for which there is evidence of positive outcomes for pupils and teachers?", *Research Evidence in Education Library*, EPPI-Centre, Social Science Research Unit, Institute of Education, University of London, London.

Department for Education (2010), *The Case for Change*, Department for Education, United Kingdom.

Field, S., M. Kuczera and **B. Pont** (2007), *No More Failures: Ten Steps to Equity in Education, Education and Training Policy*, OECD Publishing.

National Advisory Committee for the Ministry of Education and Science (2003), *Attracting, Developing and Retaining Effective Teachers: Country Background Report for Sweden*, Ministry of Education and Science, Stockholm.

OECD (2003), *Education at a Glance 2003: OECD Indicators*, OECD Publishing.

OECD (2005), *Teachers Matter: Attracting, Developing and Retaining Effective Teachers*, OECD Publishing.

OECD (2007), *Education at a Glance 2007: OECD Indicators*, OECD Publishing.

OECD (2009a), *Creating Effective Teaching and Learning Environments: First Results from TALIS*, OECD Publishing.

OECD (2009b), *Evaluating and Rewarding the Quality of Teachers: International Practices*, OECD Publishing.

OECD (2010a), *PISA 2009 Results: What Makes a School Successful? Resources, Policies and Practices* (Volume IV), PISA, OECD Publishing.

OECD (2011a), *Strong Performers and Successful Reformers in Education: Lessons from PISA for the United States*, OECD Publishing.

OECD (2010b), *Educating Teachers for Diversity: Meeting the Challenge*, OECD Publishing.

OECD (2011b), *Education at a Glance 2011: OECD Indicators*, OECD Publishing.

OECD (2011c), *The Experience of New Teachers: Results from TALIS 2008*, OECD Publishing.

OECD (2012), *Equity and Quality in Education: Supporting Disadvantaged Schools and Students*, OECD Publishing.

Reflections on the 2012 International Summit on the Teaching Profession

Ministers, union leaders and teacher leaders from 23 of the 25 highest-performing and most rapidly improving education systems on PISA accepted an invitation from U.S. Education Secretary Arne Duncan, the OECD and Education International to discuss how to prepare teachers and develop school leaders for the 21st century. It was an unprecedented turnout of those in education who can make change happen. They met because they realize the urgency of raising the status of the education profession, because they know that governments and the profession are in this together, and no doubt also because they were convened by an education secretary who has demonstrated that bold reform can be successfully implemented even in the most challenging times.

It was striking to see how much education – traditionally inward-looking, siloed and at times provincial – has become internationalized, with success no longer measured by national standards alone but by what the best-performing education systems show can be achieved. Secretary Duncan may have surprised delegates when he explained how much of his reform agenda builds on the experience of the most successful educational systems and the outcomes from last year's Summit. But no less so did Zhang Minxuan, mastermind of Shanghai's school reform that helped to propel the province to the top of rankings on the most recent PISA assessment, when he recounted how he and his colleagues had toured the world in the 1990s to find out how countries as different as the United States and Switzerland were successfully addressing the policy challenges his province had faced at that time. The idea was not to copy what they were doing, but to learn from them and put together a design for Shanghai that would be superior to anything that they had seen anywhere. Though one can always question whether policies that are successful in one place will succeed in another – and surely no country can simply adopt another nation's system or policies – comparative data and analysis seem to rapidly expand the scope for learning from the successes and failures of education policies and practices around the world.

Where important things are happening in schools, there are people that make these things happen. A consistent thread throughout discussions at the Summit was the central role of leadership in high-performing education systems. This was all about supporting, evaluating and developing teacher quality; about vision for results, equity and accountability and a culture of commitment rather than compliance; and about aligning pedagogical goals with strategic resource management.

I also took away from the discussions how important it is to have a system-wide perspective and connect school leaders so that their work is coherently aligned with the larger goals of the systems. Ministers and union leaders stressed the need to distribute leadership effectively so that school leaders can take on this larger system-level role. As the Swedish Minister Jan Björklund put it, if there are too few people involved in leadership, things will simply not change because there are so few people promoting change and so many against it. Or, in the words of the Slovenian Minister Žiga Turk, in the age of Twitter, your effectiveness as a leader depends much less on your administrative powers than on your capacity to attract followers. But it became equally clear that there can be competing demands between leadership and leaders, between structures and coherence, on the one hand, and visionary and entrepreneurial individuals, on the other – and between the need to pinpoint responsibilities in schools and avoid autocratic school leadership that undermines the profession and precludes the development of 21st-century teaching skills.

While everyone seemed to agree on what leadership in the 21st century needs to look like, there was much debate about how best to develop effective leaders. Some countries explained that they put the premium on professionalized recruitment, seeking to attract high-quality candidates and carefully selecting candidates with strong instructional

knowledge, a track record of improved learning outcomes, and leadership potential. Others underlined the central role of high-quality training, careful induction and ongoing development and appraisal in order to enable school leaders to set a strategic direction for their schools, remain responsive to local needs, enhance their role in teachers' professional development, and promote teamwork among teachers.

The success in leveraging the knowledge and skills of talented leaders for system-wide improvement and developing effective leaders at scale, as reported by high-performing countries as different as Canada, Finland or Singapore, seemed truly remarkable. These countries do not wait until teachers have reached the level of seniority to apply for leadership positions; they assess young teachers continuously for their leadership potential and give them ample opportunity to develop their leadership capacity. They put far-sighted succession planning in place and show that leaders are not just born but can be developed and supported. It was widely agreed that success will depend on school leaders defining and assuming their professional responsibilities or, as the Dutch Minister Marja van Bijsterveldt put it, governments will need to listen to the voices of principals and teachers to articulate what the standards of their professional practice should be.

The Summit then turned to how to prepare and enable teachers to deliver the skills that students will need to succeed in the 21st century. Everyone realizes that the skills that are easiest to teach and easiest to test are now also the skills that are easiest to automate, digitize and outsource. Of ever-growing importance, but so much harder to develop, are ways of thinking – creativity, critical thinking, problem-solving, decision-making and learning; ways of working – including communication and collaboration; and tools for working – including information and communications technologies. The Nordic countries, in particular, also highlighted the importance of skills as they relate to citizenship, life and career, and to personal and social responsibility.

That led Ministers and union leaders to debate the kind of learning environments that would be conducive to the development of such skills. It became clear that 21st-century learning environments must make learning central and encourage student engagement, ensure that learning is social and collaborative, be relevant and highly attuned to students' motivations, be acutely sensitive to individual differences and provide formative feedback, promote connections across activities and subjects, both in and out of school, and perhaps most important, be demanding of all students without overloading them. Hong Kong brought up the interesting question of where the spiral of equipping students for the 21st century, preparing teachers to teach those students, and creating the teacher training institutions that can develop those teachers ends. Nobody was able to provide an answer, but the list of demands participants placed on teachers in the 21st century seemed very long. They need to be well-versed in the subjects they teach, and that includes both content-specific strategies and teaching methods. They need a deep understanding of how learning occurs and mastery of a broad range of learning strategies. They need to work in highly collaborative ways with other teachers and professionals in networks of professional communities. They need to reflect on their practices in order to learn from their experience. And they need to master the skills in technology required both to optimize the use of digital resources in their teaching and to use information-management systems to track student learning.

While countries such as Singapore and Finland were acknowledged as being somewhat further advanced than others in the pursuit of these goals, every country seems to struggle with the widening gap between what modern societies demand and what today's school systems deliver. One thing became clear, however: many education systems are giving teachers mixed messages about the skills they know are needed, on the one hand, and what they make visible and thus value in the form of examinations and assessments, on the other. Unions brought this up and underlined the urgency for examinations and assessments to re-appraise trade-offs between validity gains and efficiency gains. Governments will need to deliver on this if they are serious about walking the walk when it comes to 21st-century skills.

Ministers and union leaders struggled equally hard with the third theme of the Summit: how to improve the match between teacher demand and supply. Even if some ministers stated that they had plenty of teachers, virtually all seemed to have difficulties in attracting the most talented teachers to the most challenging classrooms to ensure that every student benefits from high-quality teaching. In a number of countries, the challenge is compounded by aging teacher populations, frequently leading to an overload of instruction and administrative work for teachers and, at the system level, to lowered requirements for entry into the profession and teaching other subjects. In some countries, there was talk of a downward spiral – from lowered standards for entry, to lowered confidence in the profession, resulting in more prescriptive teaching and less personalization – that risked driving the most talented teachers out of the profession, thus further aggravating the mismatch between teacher supply and demand.

Not surprisingly, this was also the area where governments and unions seemed widest apart. Union leaders were right in emphasizing that, in many countries, teacher pay is not up to the pay in other professions requiring similar qualifications. As the Finnish union leader put it, if you pay peanuts you will get monkeys. But this discussion overlooked that many of the countries that are paying their teachers well are simply making more effective spending choices between teacher pay and professional development, on the one hand, and instruction time and class sizes, on the other. These countries often end up spending far less overall than countries that have tied up much of their spending in smaller class sizes, which unions also continue to push for. It has been easy to achieve more with more resources, but in these times of economic difficulties, governments and unions will need to take a hard look at how to achieve more with less.

Ministers and union leaders agreed, however, that making teaching a well-respected profession and a more attractive career choice, both intellectually and financially, investing in teacher development, and creating competitive employment conditions were all essential for achieving a better balance between teacher supply and demand. It was striking to see how high-performing education systems have generally transformed the work organization in their schools by replacing administrative forms of management with norms that provide the status, pay, autonomy and accountability, and the high-quality training, responsibility and collaborative work that are integral to all professions. These countries also tend to provide effective systems of social dialogue, and appealing forms of employment that balance flexibility with job security, and grant sufficient authority for schools to manage and deploy their human resources. Not least, they complement policies and practices to expand the pool of talented teachers with targeted responses to particular types of teacher shortages that offer incentives for teachers to work in tougher conditions.

Delegates also pointed out that matching teacher supply and demand relies on an environment that facilitates success and that encourages effective teachers to continue in teaching. Teacher leaders, in particular, emphasized that they place a premium on self-efficacy in an instructional environment where they are, on genuine career prospects, on the quality of their relations with students and colleagues, on feeling supported by their school leaders, and on adequate working conditions.

Last but not least, it became clear that education needs to become a social project. Partnerships and coalitions are necessary for strengthening and building the profession. Such coalitions demand trust and respect, and require all actors to move beyond their comfort zone. As several speakers noted, seeking short-term political gains by shaming teachers will not strengthen the profession but tear it apart.

As complex as the challenges are, and as much as one could be tempted to dwell on their complexity and despair, it was encouraging to see how ministers and union leaders took away important lessons for their own country in the concluding session of the Summit:

Belgium intends to conclude a pact with providers of education and trade unions on the teaching career.

China seeks to vigorously improve the pre-service education for teachers and expand early childhood education for all children. Denmark wants to make elevating the status of the teaching profession a top national priority and underlines that educational pathways from age 0 to 18 need to strike a careful balance between social and subject-matter skills.

Estonia aspires to a comprehensive reform of pre-service, in-service and co-operative professional development, following the model of the most advanced education systems.

Finland seeks to develop new collaborative models for school development and teacher-education development, a better alignment between curricular goals and educational assessment, and improved pedagogical use of social media.

Germany will bring its ministers and union leaders together to advance the dialogue among the social partners beyond rhetoric.

Hungary seeks to better align and reinforce the context, process, feedback and relationships among key players, aiming for genuine collaboration among stakeholders.

Japan will advance its holistic reform of preparation, recruitment and professional development.

Korea wants to strengthen collaboration between school leadership and local communities.

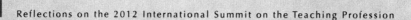

The Netherlands will introduce peer reviews for school leaders and teachers as the primary instrument for quality assurance.

New Zealand will further develop a systemic approach to making successful practice common practice.

Norway intends to work on career paths for teachers that can be combined with distributed and collaborative leadership, and focus on how to implement national reforms in the classroom.

Poland will place the premium on preparing teachers for 21st-century skills.

Singapore seeks to advance its whole-system approach to education reform to achieve impact and sustainability.

Sweden wants to do more to attract top students into the teaching profession and to create incentives to reward high-performing teachers throughout their careers.

Switzerland will seek new ways to create careers for teachers and integrate other professionals into teaching.

The United Kingdom seeks to promote an atmosphere that promotes trust in and respect for teachers.

The United States seeks to build a coherent and systemic process for engaging all actors in comprehensive, large-scale change, challenging every assumption, big or small.

Of course, none of these pronouncements implies a formal commitment on the part of governments or unions, but they underline the intention of ministers and union leaders to move the education agenda forward. The 2013 Summit will show how fast these visions turn into reality.

Andreas Schleicher
15 March 2012

Annex A
Selected comparative data on education from OECD sources

Figure A.1

Comparing countries' performance in reading

Statistically significantly **above** the OECD average
Not statistically significantly different from the OECD average
Statistically significantly **below** the OECD average

Mean	Comparison country	Countries whose mean score is NOT statistically significantly different from that of the comparison country
556	Shanghai-China	
539	Korea	Finland, Hong Kong-China
536	Finland	Korea, Hong Kong-China
533	Hong Kong-China	Korea, Finland
526	Singapore	Canada, New Zealand, Japan
524	Canada	Singapore, New Zealand, Japan
521	New Zealand	Singapore, Canada, Japan, Australia
520	Japan	Singapore, Canada, New Zealand, Australia, Netherlands
515	Australia	New Zealand, Japan, Netherlands
508	Netherlands	Japan, Australia, Belgium, Norway, Estonia, Switzerland, Poland, Iceland, United States, Liechtenstein, Sweden, Germany
506	Belgium	Netherlands, Norway, Estonia, Switzerland, Poland, United States, Liechtenstein
503	Norway	Netherlands, Belgium, Estonia, Switzerland, Poland, Iceland, United States, Liechtenstein, Sweden, Germany, Ireland, France
501	Estonia	Netherlands, Belgium, Norway, Switzerland, Poland, Iceland, United States, Liechtenstein, Sweden, Germany, Ireland, France, Chinese Taipei, Denmark, United Kingdom, Hungary
501	Switzerland	Netherlands, Belgium, Norway, Estonia, Poland, Iceland, United States, Liechtenstein, Sweden, Germany, Ireland, France, Chinese Taipei, Denmark, United Kingdom, Hungary
500	Poland	Netherlands, Belgium, Norway, Estonia, Switzerland, Iceland, United States, Liechtenstein, Sweden, Germany, Ireland, France, Chinese Taipei, Denmark, United Kingdom, Hungary
500	Iceland	Netherlands, Norway, Estonia, Switzerland, Poland, United States, Liechtenstein, Sweden, Germany, Ireland, France, Chinese Taipei, Hungary
500	United States	Netherlands, Belgium, Norway, Estonia, Switzerland, Poland, Iceland, Liechtenstein, Sweden, Germany, Ireland, France, Chinese Taipei, Denmark, United Kingdom, Hungary
499	Liechtenstein	Netherlands, Belgium, Norway, Estonia, Switzerland, Poland, Iceland, United States, Sweden, Germany, Ireland, France, Chinese Taipei, Denmark, United Kingdom, Hungary
497	Sweden	Netherlands, Norway, Estonia, Switzerland, Poland, Iceland, United States, Liechtenstein, Germany, Ireland, France, Chinese Taipei, Denmark, United Kingdom, Hungary, Portugal
497	Germany	Netherlands, Norway, Estonia, Switzerland, Poland, Iceland, United States, Liechtenstein, Sweden, Ireland, France, Chinese Taipei, Denmark, United Kingdom, Hungary
496	Ireland	Norway, Estonia, Switzerland, Poland, Iceland, United States, Liechtenstein, Sweden, Germany, France, Chinese Taipei, Denmark, United Kingdom, Hungary, Portugal
496	France	Norway, Estonia, Switzerland, Poland, Iceland, United States, Liechtenstein, Sweden, Germany, Ireland, Chinese Taipei, Denmark, United Kingdom, Hungary, Portugal
495	Chinese Taipei	Estonia, Switzerland, Poland, Iceland, United States, Liechtenstein, Sweden, Germany, Ireland, France, Denmark, United Kingdom, Hungary, Portugal
495	Denmark	Estonia, Switzerland, Poland, United States, Liechtenstein, Sweden, Germany, Ireland, France, Chinese Taipei, United Kingdom, Hungary, Portugal
494	United Kingdom	Estonia, Switzerland, Poland, United States, Liechtenstein, Sweden, Germany, Ireland, France, Chinese Taipei, Denmark, Hungary, Portugal
494	Hungary	Estonia, Switzerland, Poland, Iceland, United States, Liechtenstein, Sweden, Germany, Ireland, France, Chinese Taipei, Denmark, United Kingdom, Portugal
489	Portugal	Sweden, Ireland, France, Chinese Taipei, Denmark, United Kingdom, Hungary, Macao-China, Italy, Latvia, Slovenia, Greece
487	Macao-China	Portugal, Italy, Latvia, Greece
486	Italy	Portugal, Macao-China, Latvia, Slovenia, Greece, Spain
484	Latvia	Portugal, Macao-China, Italy, Slovenia, Greece, Spain, Czech Republic, Slovak Republic
483	Slovenia	Portugal, Italy, Latvia, Greece, Spain, Czech Republic
483	Greece	Portugal, Macao-China, Italy, Latvia, Slovenia, Spain, Czech Republic, Slovak Republic, Croatia, Israel
481	Spain	Italy, Latvia, Slovenia, Greece, Czech Republic, Slovak Republic, Croatia, Israel
478	Czech Republic	Latvia, Slovenia, Greece, Spain, Slovak Republic, Croatia, Israel, Luxembourg, Austria
477	Slovak Republic	Latvia, Greece, Spain, Czech Republic, Croatia, Israel, Luxembourg, Austria
476	Croatia	Greece, Spain, Czech Republic, Slovak Republic, Israel, Luxembourg, Austria, Lithuania
474	Israel	Greece, Spain, Czech Republic, Slovak Republic, Croatia, Luxembourg, Austria, Lithuania, Turkey
472	Luxembourg	Czech Republic, Slovak Republic, Croatia, Israel, Austria, Lithuania
470	Austria	Czech Republic, Slovak Republic, Croatia, Israel, Luxembourg, Lithuania, Turkey
468	Lithuania	Croatia, Israel, Luxembourg, Austria, Turkey
464	Turkey	Israel, Austria, Lithuania, Dubai (UAE), Russian Federation
459	Dubai (UAE)	Turkey, Russian Federation
459	Russian Federation	Turkey, Dubai (UAE)
449	Chile	Serbia
442	Serbia	Chile, Bulgaria
429	Bulgaria	Serbia, Uruguay, Mexico, Romania, Thailand, Trinidad and Tobago
426	Uruguay	Bulgaria, Mexico, Romania, Thailand
425	Mexico	Bulgaria, Uruguay, Romania, Thailand
424	Romania	Bulgaria, Uruguay, Mexico, Thailand, Trinidad and Tobago
421	Thailand	Bulgaria, Uruguay, Mexico, Romania, Trinidad and Tobago, Colombia
416	Trinidad and Tobago	Bulgaria, Romania, Thailand, Colombia, Brazil
413	Colombia	Thailand, Trinidad and Tobago, Brazil, Montenegro, Jordan
412	Brazil	Trinidad and Tobago, Colombia, Montenegro, Jordan
408	Montenegro	Colombia, Brazil, Jordan, Tunisia, Indonesia, Argentina
405	Jordan	Colombia, Brazil, Montenegro, Tunisia, Indonesia, Argentina
404	Tunisia	Montenegro, Jordan, Indonesia, Argentina
402	Indonesia	Montenegro, Jordan, Tunisia, Argentina
398	Argentina	Montenegro, Jordan, Tunisia, Indonesia, Kazakhstan
390	Kazakhstan	Argentina, Albania
385	Albania	Kazakhstan, Panama
372	Qatar	Panama, Peru
371	Panama	Albania, Qatar, Peru, Azerbaijan
370	Peru	Qatar, Panama, Azerbaijan
362	Azerbaijan	Panama, Peru
314	Kyrgyzstan	

Source: OECD, *PISA 2009 Database.*
StatLink ᔥᓀᓍ http://dx.doi.org/10.1787/888932343133

Figure A.2

Comparing countries' performance in mathematics

	Statistically significantly **above** the OECD average
	Not statistically significantly different from the OECD average
	Statistically significantly **below** the OECD average

Mean	Comparison country	Countries whose mean score is NOT statistically significantly different from that of the comparison country
600	Shanghai-China	
562	Singapore	
555	Hong Kong-China	Korea
546	Korea	Hong Kong-China, Chinese Taipei, Finland, Liechtenstein
543	Chinese Taipei	Korea, Finland, Liechtenstein, Switzerland
541	Finland	Korea, Chinese Taipei, Liechtenstein, Switzerland
536	Liechtenstein	Korea, Chinese Taipei, Finland, Switzerland, Japan, Netherlands
534	Switzerland	Chinese Taipei, Finland, Liechtenstein, Japan, Canada, Netherlands
529	Japan	Liechtenstein, Switzerland, Canada, Netherlands, Macao-China
527	Canada	Switzerland, Japan, Netherlands, Macao-China
526	Netherlands	Liechtenstein, Switzerland, Japan, Canada, Macao-China, New Zealand
525	Macao-China	Japan, Canada, Netherlands
519	New Zealand	Netherlands, Belgium, Australia, Germany
515	Belgium	New Zealand, Australia, Germany, Estonia
514	Australia	New Zealand, Belgium, Germany, Estonia
513	Germany	New Zealand, Belgium, Australia, Estonia, Iceland
512	Estonia	Belgium, Australia, Germany, Iceland
507	Iceland	Germany, Estonia, Denmark
503	Denmark	Iceland, Slovenia, Norway, France, Slovak Republic
501	Slovenia	Denmark, Norway, France, Slovak Republic, Austria
498	Norway	Denmark, Slovenia, France, Slovak Republic, Austria, Poland, Sweden, Czech Republic, United Kingdom, Hungary
497	France	Denmark, Slovenia, Norway, Slovak Republic, Austria, Poland, Sweden, Czech Republic, United Kingdom, Hungary
497	Slovak Republic	Denmark, Slovenia, Norway, France, Austria, Poland, Sweden, Czech Republic, United Kingdom, Hungary
496	Austria	Slovenia, Norway, France, Slovak Republic, Poland, Sweden, Czech Republic, United Kingdom, Hungary, United States
495	Poland	Norway, France, Slovak Republic, Austria, Sweden, Czech Republic, United Kingdom, Hungary, Luxembourg, United States, Portugal
494	Sweden	Norway, France, Slovak Republic, Austria, Poland, Czech Republic, United Kingdom, Hungary, Luxembourg, United States, Ireland, Portugal
493	Czech Republic	Norway, France, Slovak Republic, Austria, Poland, Sweden, United Kingdom, Hungary, Luxembourg, United States, Ireland, Portugal
492	United Kingdom	Norway, France, Slovak Republic, Austria, Poland, Sweden, Czech Republic, Hungary, Luxembourg, United States, Ireland, Portugal
490	Hungary	Norway, France, Slovak Republic, Austria, Poland, Sweden, Czech Republic, United Kingdom, Luxembourg, United States, Ireland, Portugal, Spain, Italy, Latvia
489	Luxembourg	Poland, Sweden, Czech Republic, United Kingdom, Hungary, United States, Ireland, Portugal
487	United States	Austria, Poland, Sweden, Czech Republic, United Kingdom, Hungary, Luxembourg, Ireland, Portugal, Spain, Italy, Latvia
487	Ireland	Sweden, Czech Republic, United Kingdom, Hungary, Luxembourg, United States, Portugal, Spain, Italy, Latvia
487	Portugal	Poland, Sweden, Czech Republic, United Kingdom, Hungary, Luxembourg, United States, Ireland, Spain, Italy, Latvia
483	Spain	Hungary, United States, Ireland, Portugal, Italy, Latvia
483	Italy	Hungary, United States, Ireland, Portugal, Spain, Latvia
482	Latvia	Hungary, United States, Ireland, Portugal, Spain, Italy, Lithuania
477	Lithuania	Latvia
468	Russian Federation	Greece, Croatia
466	Greece	Russian Federation, Croatia
460	Croatia	Russian Federation, Greece
453	Dubai (UAE)	Israel, Turkey
447	Israel	Dubai (UAE), Turkey, Serbia
445	Turkey	Dubai (UAE), Israel, Serbia
442	Serbia	Israel, Turkey
431	Azerbaijan	Bulgaria, Romania, Uruguay
428	Bulgaria	Azerbaijan, Romania, Uruguay, Chile, Thailand, Mexico
427	Romania	Azerbaijan, Bulgaria, Uruguay, Chile, Thailand
427	Uruguay	Azerbaijan, Bulgaria, Romania, Chile
421	Chile	Bulgaria, Romania, Uruguay, Thailand, Mexico
419	Thailand	Bulgaria, Romania, Chile, Mexico, Trinidad and Tobago
419	Mexico	Bulgaria, Chile, Thailand
414	Trinidad and Tobago	Thailand
405	Kazakhstan	Montenegro
403	Montenegro	Kazakhstan
388	Argentina	Jordan, Brazil, Colombia, Albania
387	Jordan	Argentina, Brazil, Colombia, Albania
386	Brazil	Argentina, Jordan, Colombia, Albania
381	Colombia	Argentina, Jordan, Brazil, Albania, Indonesia
377	Albania	Argentina, Jordan, Brazil, Colombia, Tunisia, Indonesia
371	Tunisia	Albania, Indonesia, Qatar, Peru, Panama
371	Indonesia	Colombia, Albania, Tunisia, Qatar, Peru, Panama
368	Qatar	Tunisia, Indonesia, Peru, Panama
365	Peru	Tunisia, Indonesia, Qatar, Panama
360	Panama	Tunisia, Indonesia, Qatar, Peru
331	Kyrgyzstan	

Source: OECD, *PISA 2009 Database*.
StatLink http://dx.doi.org/10.1787/888932343152

Figure A.3

Comparing countries' performance in science

	Statistically significantly **above** the OECD average
	Not statistically significantly different from the OECD average
	Statistically significantly **below** the OECD average

Mean	Comparison country	Countries whose mean score is NOT statistically significantly different from that comparison country
575	Shanghai-China	
554	Finland	Hong Kong-China
549	Hong Kong-China	Finland
542	Singapore	Japan, Korea
539	Japan	Singapore, Korea, New Zealand
538	Korea	Singapore, Japan, New Zealand
532	New Zealand	Japan, Korea, Canada, Estonia, Australia, Netherlands
529	Canada	New Zealand, Estonia, Australia, Netherlands
528	Estonia	New Zealand, Canada, Australia, Netherlands, Germany, Liechtenstein
527	Australia	New Zealand, Canada, Estonia, Netherlands, Chinese Taipei, Germany, Liechtenstein
522	Netherlands	New Zealand, Canada, Estonia, Australia, Chinese Taipei, Germany, Liechtenstein, Switzerland, United Kingdom, Slovenia
520	Chinese Taipei	Australia, Netherlands, Germany, Liechtenstein, Switzerland, United Kingdom
520	Germany	Estonia, Australia, Netherlands, Chinese Taipei, Liechtenstein, Switzerland, United Kingdom
520	Liechtenstein	Estonia, Australia, Netherlands, Chinese Taipei, Germany, Switzerland, United Kingdom
517	Switzerland	Netherlands, Chinese Taipei, Germany, Liechtenstein, United Kingdom, Slovenia, Macao-China
514	United Kingdom	Netherlands, Chinese Taipei, Germany, Liechtenstein, Switzerland, Slovenia, Macao-China, Poland, Ireland
512	Slovenia	Netherlands, Switzerland, United Kingdom, Macao-China, Poland, Ireland, Belgium
511	Macao-China	Switzerland, United Kingdom, Slovenia, Poland, Ireland, Belgium
508	Poland	United Kingdom, Slovenia, Macao-China, Ireland, Belgium, Hungary, United States
508	Ireland	United Kingdom, Slovenia, Macao-China, Poland, Belgium, Hungary, United States, Czech Republic, Norway
507	Belgium	Slovenia, Macao-China, Poland, Ireland, Hungary, United States, Czech Republic, Norway, France
503	Hungary	Poland, Ireland, Belgium, United States, Czech Republic, Norway, Denmark, France, Sweden, Austria
502	United States	Poland, Ireland, Belgium, Hungary, Czech Republic, Norway, Denmark, France, Iceland, Sweden, Austria, Latvia, Portugal
500	Czech Republic	Ireland, Belgium, Hungary, United States, Norway, Denmark, France, Iceland, Sweden, Austria, Latvia, Portugal
500	Norway	Ireland, Belgium, Hungary, United States, Czech Republic, Denmark, France, Iceland, Sweden, Austria, Latvia, Portugal
499	Denmark	Hungary, United States, Czech Republic, Norway, France, Iceland, Sweden, Austria, Latvia, Portugal
498	France	Belgium, Hungary, United States, Czech Republic, Norway, Denmark, Iceland, Sweden, Austria, Latvia, Portugal, Lithuania, Slovak Republic
496	Iceland	United States, Czech Republic, Norway, Denmark, France, Sweden, Austria, Latvia, Portugal, Lithuania, Slovak Republic
495	Sweden	Hungary, United States, Czech Republic, Norway, Denmark, France, Iceland, Austria, Latvia, Portugal, Lithuania, Slovak Republic, Italy
494	Austria	Hungary, United States, Czech Republic, Norway, Denmark, France, Iceland, Sweden, Latvia, Portugal, Lithuania, Slovak Republic, Italy, Spain, Croatia
494	Latvia	United States, Czech Republic, Norway, Denmark, France, Iceland, Sweden, Austria, Portugal, Lithuania, Slovak Republic, Italy, Spain, Croatia
493	Portugal	United States, Czech Republic, Norway, Denmark, France, Iceland, Sweden, Austria, Latvia, Lithuania, Slovak Republic, Italy, Spain, Croatia
491	Lithuania	France, Iceland, Sweden, Austria, Latvia, Portugal, Slovak Republic, Italy, Spain, Croatia
490	Slovak Republic	France, Iceland, Sweden, Austria, Latvia, Portugal, Lithuania, Italy, Spain, Croatia
489	Italy	Sweden, Austria, Latvia, Portugal, Lithuania, Slovak Republic, Spain, Croatia
488	Spain	Austria, Latvia, Portugal, Lithuania, Slovak Republic, Italy, Croatia, Luxembourg
486	Croatia	Austria, Latvia, Portugal, Lithuania, Slovak Republic, Italy, Spain, Luxembourg, Russian Federation
484	Luxembourg	Spain, Croatia, Russian Federation
478	Russian Federation	Croatia, Luxembourg, Greece
470	Greece	Russian Federation, Dubai (UAE)
466	Dubai (UAE)	Greece
455	Israel	Turkey, Chile
454	Turkey	Israel, Chile
447	Chile	Israel, Turkey, Serbia, Bulgaria
443	Serbia	Chile, Bulgaria
439	Bulgaria	Chile, Serbia, Romania, Uruguay
428	Romania	Bulgaria, Uruguay, Thailand
427	Uruguay	Bulgaria, Romania, Thailand
425	Thailand	Romania, Uruguay
416	Mexico	Jordan
415	Jordan	Mexico, Trinidad and Tobago
410	Trinidad and Tobago	Jordan, Brazil
405	Brazil	Trinidad and Tobago, Colombia, Montenegro, Argentina, Tunisia, Kazakhstan
402	Colombia	Brazil, Montenegro, Argentina, Tunisia, Kazakhstan
401	Montenegro	Brazil, Colombia, Argentina, Tunisia, Kazakhstan
401	Argentina	Brazil, Colombia, Montenegro, Tunisia, Kazakhstan, Albania
401	Tunisia	Brazil, Colombia, Montenegro, Argentina, Kazakhstan
400	Kazakhstan	Brazil, Colombia, Montenegro, Argentina, Tunisia, Albania
391	Albania	Argentina, Kazakhstan, Indonesia
383	Indonesia	Albania, Qatar, Panama, Azerbaijan
379	Qatar	Indonesia, Panama
376	Panama	Indonesia, Qatar, Azerbaijan, Peru
373	Azerbaijan	Indonesia, Panama, Peru
369	Peru	Panama, Azerbaijan
330	Kyrgyzstan	

Source: OECD, *PISA 2009 Database*.

StatLink ⟶ http://dx.doi.org/10.1787/888932343152

Figure A.4

Relationship between school average socio-economic background and school resources

Disadvantaged schools are more likely to have more or better resources, in **bold** if relationship is statistically different from the OECD average

Advantaged schools are more likely to have more or better resources, in **bold** if relationship is statistically different from the OECD average

Within country correlation is not statistically significant

| | Simple correlation between the school mean socio-economic background and: | | | | | |
	Percentage of full-time teachers	Percentage of certified teachers among all full-time teachers	Percentage of teachers with university-level (ISCED 5A) among all full-time teachers	Index of quality of school's educational resources	Computer/student ratio	Student/teacher ratio[1]
Australia	-0.21	-0.05	0.02	0.31	0.01	-0.07
Austria	-0.13	0.21	0.64	0.03	-0.05	-0.07
Belgium	-0.18	0.05	0.58	0.02	-0.23	0.66
Canada	0.01	0.14	0.03	0.18	-0.05	0.09
Chile	-0.04	-0.01	0.25	0.35	0.32	-0.05
Czech Republic	-0.32	0.29	0.37	0.00	0.15	0.08
Denmark	0.01	-0.17	0.16	0.04	-0.08	0.27
Estonia	0.14	0.00	0.00	0.10	-0.09	0.43
Finland	0.17	-0.01	-0.01	0.13	-0.01	0.08
France	c	c	c	c	c	c
Germany	-0.15	-0.02	-0.02	0.06	-0.18	0.28
Greece	-0.11	0.06	0.24	0.16	-0.12	0.25
Hungary	-0.33	0.07	0.07	0.11	-0.20	0.02
Iceland	0.20	0.39	0.30	0.06	-0.41	0.40
Ireland	0.12	-0.10	-0.08	0.16	-0.03	0.49
Israel	-0.08	-0.06	0.20	0.25	0.08	-0.20
Italy	-0.06	0.16	0.13	0.15	-0.19	0.50
Japan	-0.14	0.04	0.20	0.17	-0.34	0.38
Korea	-0.14	0.00	-0.03	-0.04	-0.53	0.30
Luxembourg	-0.16	-0.01	0.39	0.13	-0.13	0.28
Mexico	-0.09	-0.13	-0.04	0.59	0.14	0.03
Netherlands	-0.34	-0.12	0.62	0.06	-0.16	0.38
New Zealand	-0.04	0.08	0.07	0.16	-0.02	0.11
Norway	-0.05	0.04	0.15	0.14	-0.02	0.19
Poland	-0.02	0.03	-0.05	0.06	-0.16	0.01
Portugal	0.14	-0.05	0.04	0.24	-0.02	0.39
Slovak Republic	-0.09	0.28	-0.21	-0.05	-0.06	0.00
Slovenia	0.46	0.32	0.55	0.13	-0.21	-0.25
Spain	-0.29	c	c	0.10	-0.16	0.45
Sweden	0.05	0.01	-0.04	0.26	0.13	0.12
Switzerland	-0.11	-0.07	0.24	0.10	0.03	0.06
Turkey	0.12	-0.04	0.04	0.04	-0.06	-0.26
United Kingdom	-0.36	0.05	-0.03	0.00	0.01	-0.10
United States	-0.42	-0.24	0.10	0.22	0.06	-0.17
OECD average	-0.07	0.04	0.15	0.13	-0.08	0.15
Albania	-0.25	0.00	0.38	0.44	0.24	0.15
Argentina	0.13	0.13	0.22	0.51	0.21	-0.02
Azerbaijan	0.05	-0.06	0.44	0.19	0.17	0.23
Brazil	-0.03	0.10	0.03	0.52	0.25	-0.20
Bulgaria	-0.08	0.17	0.17	0.09	-0.17	0.21
Colombia	-0.24	-0.16	-0.08	0.53	0.19	-0.14
Croatia	0.09	0.02	0.28	0.09	0.17	0.32
Dubai (UAE)	0.32	0.61	-0.01	0.34	0.47	-0.27
Hong Kong-China	-0.19	-0.06	0.12	0.06	0.04	0.02
Indonesia	0.24	0.27	0.16	0.44	0.14	-0.16
Jordan	-0.04	0.00	-0.02	0.26	0.05	0.06
Kazakhstan	0.23	0.04	0.34	0.21	-0.12	0.44
Kyrgyzstan	0.17	0.08	0.35	0.27	0.13	0.27
Latvia	0.19	-0.03	0.19	0.14	0.00	0.38
Liechtenstein	-0.15	0.02	0.57	-0.91	0.79	0.70
Lithuania	0.21	0.09	0.19	-0.02	-0.49	0.21
Macao-China	0.11	0.05	-0.18	0.26	0.22	0.17
Montenegro	0.07	0.32	0.38	-0.11	-0.19	0.33
Panama	-0.51	-0.47	-0.13	0.68	0.38	0.03
Peru	-0.21	0.08	0.48	0.53	0.46	-0.02
Qatar	0.03	-0.04	-0.07	0.23	0.19	0.11
Romania	0.05	0.10	0.11	0.20	-0.07	-0.02
Russian Federation	0.18	0.08	0.31	0.26	0.02	0.29
Serbia	0.10	0.06	0.06	-0.01	0.00	0.11
Shanghai-China	0.14	0.13	0.32	0.16	-0.10	-0.13
Singapore	-0.13	0.00	0.22	0.10	-0.18	-0.14
Chinese Taipei	0.12	0.34	0.29	0.19	-0.04	-0.07
Thailand	0.07	0.06	0.16	0.39	0.00	-0.02
Trinidad and Tobago	-0.19	0.09	0.56	0.12	0.08	0.38
Tunisia	-0.06	0.00	0.20	0.13	0.15	-0.02
Uruguay	-0.01	0.27	0.08	0.33	0.30	0.13

1. In contrast to the other columns, negative correlations indicate more favorable characteristics for advantaged students.

Source: OECD, *PISA 2009 Database*, Table II.2.2.

StatLink http://dx.doi.org/10.1787/888932366636

89

Figure A.5

School principals' views of how teacher behavior affects students' learning

Index of teacher-related factors affecting school climate based on school principals' reports

- A Teachers' low expectations of students
- B Poor student-teacher relations
- C Teachers not meeting individual students' needs
- D Teacher absenteeism
- E Staff resisting change
- F Teachers being too strict with students
- G Students not being encouraged to achieve their full potential

	A	B	C	D	E	F	G		Variability in the index (S.D.)
OECD	Percentage of students in schools whose principals reported that the following phenomena hindered learning "not at all" or "very little"							Range between top and bottom quarter / Average index	
Australia	68	85	58	86	61	96	78		0.91
Austria	86	94	78	78	76	97	87		0.84
Belgium	87	96	76	75	71	96	84		0.86
Canada	86	89	75	88	62	94	86		0.82
Chile	51	92	62	69	60	86	57		1.00
Czech Republic	83	83	94	96	86	90	75		0.72
Denmark	95	97	88	89	91	98	93		0.82
Estonia	82	87	68	89	87	82	77		0.83
Finland	94	88	67	80	84	97	86		0.69
France	w	w	w	w	w	w	w		w
Germany	82	93	77	78	70	96	89		0.75
Greece	64	82	70	86	76	89	76		1.05
Hungary	94	96	94	94	90	89	69		0.86
Iceland	90	88	71	83	84	97	92		0.85
Ireland	78	92	76	88	82	89	84		0.87
Israel	73	86	67	71	80	90	80		0.86
Italy	74	73	73	91	48	85	67		0.84
Japan	76	85	71	97	63	81	61		0.87
Korea	66	90	67	99	66	84	83		0.79
Luxembourg	95	88	64	82	84	89	71		0.71
Mexico	65	81	69	78	59	80	60		1.01
Netherlands	66	90	44	62	61	86	45		0.67
New Zealand	63	83	57	95	73	95	82		0.79
Norway	80	90	52	75	79	98	77		0.71
Poland	90	98	89	77	85	98	91		0.86
Portugal	74	96	77	98	67	100	79		0.90
Slovak Republic	87	94	88	80	79	75	78		0.79
Slovenia	83	90	78	85	68	87	81		0.84
Spain	75	91	85	91	67	92	74		0.92
Sweden	77	93	64	87	67	99	75		0.83
Switzerland	94	91	81	96	74	97	89		0.73
Turkey	28	25	39	30	25	32	27		1.29
United Kingdom	79	97	77	87	83	98	92		0.80
United States	77	90	72	91	68	96	84		0.79
OECD average	78	88	72	83	72	90	77		0.84
Partners Albania	86	91	91	96	93	97	81		0.84
Argentina	70	88	73	51	62	87	55		1.09
Azerbaijan	67	67	80	82	81	91	76		1.09
Brazil	56	89	58	70	64	92	65		0.95
Bulgaria	73	84	70	73	87	88	72		1.13
Colombia	66	93	66	79	49	81	63		1.09
Croatia	79	90	75	94	58	90	72		0.82
Dubai (UAE)	86	89	80	86	77	87	92		1.23
Hong Kong-China	58	93	52	87	77	94	69		0.81
Indonesia	86	96	90	97	90	92	69		0.87
Jordan	60	62	64	58	61	86	69		1.08
Kazakhstan	43	60	55	60	66	60	58		1.38
Kyrgyzstan	54	71	69	66	64	65	59		1.37
Latvia	90	93	81	91	93	89	77		0.83
Liechtenstein	94	100	80	100	83	100	100		0.49
Lithuania	94	99	93	98	96	99	96		0.68
Macao-China	73	73	44	66	66	83	57		1.38
Montenegro	85	95	73	88	88	93	58		0.71
Panama	62	89	69	75	57	81	61		1.03
Peru	64	91	72	85	69	83	63		0.95
Qatar	77	80	82	88	84	88	85		1.07
Romania	84	90	89	99	69	91	83		0.80
Russian Federation	60	79	68	78	65	56	58		1.07
Serbia	71	94	70	93	59	84	61		0.78
Shanghai-China	58	59	45	71	60	73	47		1.33
Singapore	64	83	59	84	83	90	90		0.92
Chinese Taipei	52	57	54	70	56	67	52		1.42
Thailand	67	82	72	90	90	68	87		0.86
Trinidad and Tobago	45	66	34	41	54	91	71		0.94
Tunisia	33	83	69	40	73	83	74		0.86
Uruguay	53	92	68	35	57	94	33		1.03

-3.5   -2.5   -1.5   -0.5 0 0.5   1.5   2.5 Index points

Note: Higher values on the index indicate a positive teacher behavior.

Source: OECD, *PISA 2009 Database*, Table IV.4.5.

StatLink http://dx.doi.org/10.1787/888932366636

Figure A.6

School principals' views of how teacher behavior affects students' learning

Index of teacher-related factors affecting school climate based on school principals' reports

- A — Teachers' low expectations of students
- B — Poor student-teacher relations
- C — Teachers not meeting individual students' needs
- D — Teacher absenteeism
- E — Staff resisting change
- F — Teachers being too strict with students
- G — Students not being encouraged to achieve their full potential

		Percentage of students in schools whose principals reported that the following phenomena hindered learning "not at all" or "very little"							Range between top and bottom quarter ◆ Average index	Variability in the index (S.D.)
		A	B	C	D	E	F	G		
OECD	Australia	68	85	58	86	61	96	78		0.91
	Austria	86	94	78	78	76	97	87		0.84
	Belgium	87	96	76	75	71	96	84		0.86
	Canada	86	89	75	88	62	94	86		0.82
	Chile	51	92	62	69	60	86	57		1.00
	Czech Republic	83	83	94	96	86	90	75		0.72
	Denmark	95	97	88	89	91	98	93		0.82
	Estonia	82	87	68	89	87	82	77		0.83
	Finland	94	88	67	80	84	97	86		0.69
	France	w	w	w	w	w	w	w		w
	Germany	82	93	77	78	70	96	89		0.75
	Greece	64	82	70	86	76	89	76		1.05
	Hungary	94	96	94	94	90	89	69		0.86
	Iceland	90	88	71	83	84	97	92		0.85
	Ireland	78	92	76	88	82	89	84		0.87
	Israel	73	86	67	71	80	90	80		0.86
	Italy	74	73	73	91	48	85	67		0.84
	Japan	76	85	71	97	63	81	61		0.87
	Korea	66	90	67	99	66	84	83		0.79
	Luxembourg	95	88	64	82	84	89	71		0.71
	Mexico	65	81	69	78	59	80	60		1.01
	Netherlands	66	90	44	62	61	86	45		0.67
	New Zealand	63	83	57	95	73	95	82		0.79
	Norway	80	90	52	75	79	98	77		0.71
	Poland	90	98	89	77	85	98	91		0.86
	Portugal	74	96	77	98	67	100	79		0.90
	Slovak Republic	87	94	88	80	79	75	78		0.79
	Slovenia	83	90	78	85	68	87	81		0.84
	Spain	75	91	85	91	67	92	74		0.92
	Sweden	77	93	64	87	67	99	75		0.83
	Switzerland	94	91	81	96	74	97	89		0.73
	Turkey	28	25	39	30	25	32	27		1.29
	United Kingdom	79	97	77	87	83	98	92		0.80
	United States	77	90	72	91	68	96	84		0.79
	OECD average	78	88	72	83	72	90	77		0.84
Partners	Albania	86	91	91	96	93	97	81		0.84
	Argentina	70	88	73	51	62	87	55		1.09
	Azerbaijan	67	67	80	82	81	91	76		1.09
	Brazil	56	89	58	70	64	92	65		0.95
	Bulgaria	73	84	70	73	87	88	72		1.13
	Colombia	66	93	66	79	49	81	63		1.09
	Croatia	79	90	75	94	58	90	72		0.82
	Dubai (UAE)	86	89	80	86	77	87	92		1.23
	Hong Kong-China	58	93	52	87	77	94	69		0.81
	Indonesia	86	96	90	97	90	92	69		0.87
	Jordan	60	62	64	58	61	86	69		1.08
	Kazakhstan	43	60	55	60	66	60	58		1.38
	Kyrgyzstan	54	71	69	66	64	65	59		1.37
	Latvia	90	93	81	91	93	89	77		0.83
	Liechtenstein	94	100	80	100	83	100	100		0.49
	Lithuania	94	99	93	98	96	99	96		0.68
	Macao-China	73	73	44	66	66	83	57		1.38
	Montenegro	85	95	73	88	88	93	58		0.71
	Panama	62	89	69	75	57	81	61		1.03
	Peru	64	91	72	85	69	83	63		0.95
	Qatar	77	80	82	88	84	88	85		1.07
	Romania	84	90	89	99	69	91	83		0.80
	Russian Federation	60	79	68	78	65	56	58		1.07
	Serbia	71	94	70	93	59	84	61		0.78
	Shanghai-China	58	59	45	71	60	73	47		1.33
	Singapore	64	83	59	84	83	90	90		0.92
	Chinese Taipei	52	57	54	70	56	67	52		1.42
	Thailand	67	82	72	90	90	68	87		0.86
	Trinidad and Tobago	45	66	34	41	54	91	71		0.94
	Tunisia	33	83	69	40	73	83	74		0.86
	Uruguay	53	92	68	35	57	94	33		1.03

-3.5   -2.5   -1.5   -0.5 0 0.5   1.5   2.5 Index points

Note: Higher values on the index indicate a positive teacher behavior.
Source: OECD, *PISA 2009 Database*, Table IV.4.5.
StatLink ᴴᴴᴴᴴ http://dx.doi.org/10.1787/888932343418

Figure A.7

Compulsory and intended instruction time in public institutions (2009)

Average number of hours per year of total compulsory and non-compulsory instruction time in the curriculum for 7-8, 9-11, 12-14 and 15-year-olds

| | | Ending age of compulsory education | Age range at which over 90% of the population are enrolled | Average number of hours per year of total compulsory instruction time | | | | | Average number of hours per year of total intended instruction time | | | | |
| | | | | Ages 7-8 | Ages 9-11 | Ages 12-14 | Age 15 (typical program) | Age 15 (least demanding program) | Ages 7-8 | Ages 9-11 | Ages 12-14 | Age 15 (typical program) | Age 15 (least demanding program) |
		(1)	(2)	(3)	(4)	(5)	(6)	(7)	(8)	(9)	(10)	(11)	(12)
OECD	Australia	15	5 - 16	972	971	983	964	932	972	971	983	964	932
	Austria	15	5 - 16	690	766	913	1 005	960	735	811	958	1 050	1 005
	Belgium (Fl.)	18	3 - 17	a	a	a	a	a	831	831	955	955	448
	Belgium (Fr.)[1]	18	3 - 17	840	840	960	m	m	930	930	1 020	m	m
	Canada	16 - 18	6 - 17	m	m	m	m	m	m	m	m	m	m
	Chile	18	6 - 15	675	675	709	743	743	855	855	855	945	945
	Czech Republic[2]	15	5 - 17	624	713	871	950	683	624	713	871	950	683
	Denmark	16	3 - 16	701	803	900	930	900	701	803	900	930	900
	England	16	4 - 16	893	899	925	950	a	893	899	925	950	a
	Estonia	15	4 - 17	595	683	802	840	m	595	683	802	840	m
	Finland	16	6 - 18	608	640	777	856	a	608	683	829	913	a
	France	16	3 - 17	847	847	971	1 042	a	847	847	1 065	1 147	a
	Germany	18	4 - 17	643	794	898	912	m	643	794	898	912	m
	Greece	14 - 15	5 - 17	720	812	821	798	a	720	812	821	798	a
	Hungary	18	4 - 17	555	601	671	763	763	614	724	885	1 106	1 106
	Iceland	16	3 - 16	720	800	872	888	a	720	800	872	888	a
	Ireland	16	5 - 18	941	941	848	802	713	941	941	907	891	891
	Israel	17	4 - 16	914	991	981	964	m	914	991	981	1 101	m
	Italy	16	3 - 16	891	913	1 001	1 089	m	990	1 023	1 089	1 089	m
	Japan	15	4 - 17	709	774	868	m	a	709	774	868	m	a
	Korea	14	7 - 17	612	703	867	1 020	a	612	703	867	1 020	a
	Luxembourg	15	4 - 15	924	924	908	900	900	924	924	908	900	900
	Mexico	15	4 - 14	800	800	1 167	1 058	a	800	800	1 167	1 058	a
	Netherlands	18	4 - 17	940	940	1 000	1 000	a	940	940	1 000	1 000	a
	New Zealand	16	4 - 16	m	m	m	m	m	m	m	m	m	m
	Norway	16	3 - 17	700	756	829	859	a	700	756	829	859	a
	Poland	16	6 - 18	446	563	604	595	a	486	603	644	635	a
	Portugal	14	5 - 16	875	869	908	893	m	910	898	934	945	m
	Scotland	16	4 - 16	a	a	a	a	a	a	a	a	a	a
	Slovak Republic	16	6 - 17	687	767	813	926	926	715	785	842	926	926
	Slovenia	14	6 - 17	621	721	791	908	888	621	721	791	908	888
	Spain	16	3 - 16	875	821	1 050	1 050	1 050	875	821	1 050	1 050	1 050
	Sweden[3]	16	4 - 18	741	741	741	741	a	741	741	741	741	a
	Switzerland	15	5 - 16	m	m	m	m	m	m	m	m	m	m
	Turkey	14	7 - 13	720	720	750	810	a	864	864	846	810	a
	United States	17	6 - 16	m	m	m	m	m	m	m	m	m	m
	OECD average	16	5 - 16	749	793	873	902	860	775	821	907	941	889
	EU21 average	16	4 - 17	746	790	865	897	865	767	815	902	935	880
Other G20	Argentina[4]	17	5 - 15	m	720	744	m	m	m	m	m	m	m
	Brazil	17	7 - 15	m	m	m	m	m	m	m	m	m	m
	China	m	m	531	613	793	748	m	m	m	m	m	m
	India	m	m	m	m	m	m	m	m	m	m	m	m
	Indonesia	15	6 - 14	m	551	654	m	m	m	m	m	m	m
	Russian Federation	17	7 - 14	493	737	879	912	m	493	737	879	912	m
	Saudi Arabia	m	m	m	m	m	m	m	m	m	m	m	m
	South Africa	m	m	m	m	m	m	m	m	m	m	m	m

1. "Ages 12-14" covers ages 12-13 only.
2. Minimum number of hours per year.
3. Estimated minimum numbers of hours per year because breakdown by age not available.
4. Year of reference 2008.
Source: OECD (2011), *Education at a Glance 2011: OECD Indicators*, OECD Publishing.
Please refer to the Reader's Guide in Education at a Glance 2011 (www.oecd.org/edu/eag2011) for information concerning the symbols replacing missing data.
StatLink http://dx.doi.org/10.1787/888932465094

Figure A.8

Average class size, by type of institution and level of education (2009)

Calculations based on number of students and number of classes

		Primary education					Lower secondary education (general programs)				
			Private institutions					Private institutions			
		Public institutions	Total private institutions	Government-dependent private institutions	Independent private institutions	Total: Public and private institutions	Public institutions	Total private institutions	Government-dependent private institutions	Independent private institutions	Total: Public and private institutions
		(1)	(2)	(3)	(4)	(5)	(6)	(7)	(8)	(9)	(10)
OECD	Australia	23.2	24.8	24.8	a	**23.7**	23.0	24.7	24.7	a	**23.7**
	Austria	18.8	20.5	x(2)	x(2)	**18.9**	22.4	24.3	x(7)	x(7)	**22.6**
	Belgium	m	m	m	m	**m**	m	m	m	m	**m**
	Belgium (Fr.)	19.6	20.7	20.7	m	**20.1**	m	m	m	m	**m**
	Canada	m	m	m	m	**m**	m	m	m	m	**m**
	Chile	28.1	30.8	32.4	22.4	**29.6**	28.6	30.8	32.2	23.9	**29.7**
	Czech Republic	20.0	15.9	15.9	a	**19.9**	22.0	19.6	19.6	a	**22.0**
	Denmark	20.0	16.3	16.3	a	**19.4**	20.5	17.3	17.3	a	**19.9**
	Estonia	18.2	16.8	a	16.8	**18.1**	20.3	15.9	a	15.9	**20.1**
	Finland	19.8	18.4	18.4	a	**19.8**	20.0	21.7	21.7	a	**20.1**
	France	22.6	23.0	x(2)	x(2)	**22.7**	24.3	25.1	25.4	14.1	**24.5**
	Germany	21.7	22.0	22.0	x(3)	**21.7**	24.6	25.2	25.2	x(8)	**24.7**
	Greece	16.8	20.7	a	20.7	**17.0**	21.5	24.5	a	24.5	**21.6**
	Hungary	20.8	19.2	19.2	a	**20.7**	21.9	20.6	20.6	a	**21.7**
	Iceland	17.9	14.3	14.3	n	**17.8**	19.6	12.4	12.4	n	**19.5**
	Ireland	24.2	m	a	m	**m**	m	m	a	m	**m**
	Israel	27.4	a	a	a	**27.4**	32.2	a	a	a	**32.2**
	Italy	18.7	20.2	a	20.2	**18.8**	21.4	22.4	a	22.4	**21.5**
	Japan	28.0	32.1	a	32.1	**28.0**	32.9	35.2	a	35.2	**33.0**
	Korea	28.6	30.5	a	30.5	**28.6**	35.3	34.1	34.1	a	**35.1**
	Luxembourg	15.3	19.4	19.7	19.4	**15.6**	19.1	21.0	21.0	21.1	**19.5**
	Mexico	19.9	20.4	a	20.4	**19.9**	28.7	24.7	a	24.7	**28.3**
	Netherlands[1]	22.4	m	m	m	**m**	m	m	m	m	**m**
	New Zealand	m	m	m	m	**m**	m	m	m	m	**m**
	Norway	a	a	a	a	**a**	a	a	a	a	**a**
	Poland	19.0	11.9	11.5	12.1	**18.7**	23.5	18.0	24.4	16.2	**23.3**
	Portugal	20.2	20.8	23.2	20.0	**20.2**	22.3	24.6	23.9	25.8	**22.6**
	Slovak Republic	18.5	17.8	17.8	n	**18.4**	21.2	20.2	20.2	n	**21.1**
	Slovenia	18.5	20.2	20.2	n	**18.5**	19.8	24.0	24.0	n	**19.8**
	Spain	19.8	24.5	24.5	24.5	**21.1**	23.5	25.8	26.0	24.2	**24.3**
	Sweden	m	m	m	n	**m**	m	m	m	n	**m**
	Switzerland	19.4	m	m	m	**m**	18.7	m	m	m	**m**
	Turkey	25.8	19.2	a	19.2	**25.6**	a	a	a	a	**a**
	United Kingdom	25.7	13.0	25.7	12.9	**24.5**	21.0	15.2	19.1	10.5	**19.6**
	United States	23.8	19.3	a	19.3	**23.3**	23.2	19.1	a	19.1	**22.8**
	OECD average	21.4	20.5	20.4	20.7	**21.4**	23.5	22.8	23.0	21.3	**23.7**
	EU21 average	20.0	19.0	19.6	18.5	**19.8**	21.9	21.7	22.0	19.8	**21.9**
Other G20	Argentina[2]	25.5	26.3	29.8	24.0	**26.2**	27.8	28.1	29.7	26.9	**28.1**
	Brazil	26.5	17.7	a	17.7	**25.0**	30.2	25.0	a	25.0	**29.5**
	China	36.9	42.5	x(2)	x(2)	**37.1**	54.9	51.8	x(7)	x(7)	**54.6**
	India	m	m	m	m	**m**	m	m	m	m	**m**
	Indonesia	27.5	21.4	a	21.4	**26.4**	36.5	33.4	a	33.4	**35.3**
	Russian Federation	16.2	10.9	a	10.9	**16.2**	18.0	10.1	a	10.1	**17.9**
	Saudi Arabia	m	m	m	m	**m**	m	m	m	m	**m**
	South Africa	m	m	m	m	**m**	m	m	m	m	**m**
	G20 average	24.7	22.9	~	~	**24.5**	26.8	24.9	~	~	**26.6**

1. Year of reference 2006.
2. Year of reference 2008.
Source: OECD (2011), *Education at a Glance 2011: OECD Indicators*, OECD Publishing.
Please refer to the Reader's Guide in Education at a Glance 2011 *(www.oecd.org/edu/eag2011) for information concerning the symbols replacing missing data.*
StatLink http://dx.doi.org/10.1787/888932465170

Figure A.9 (1/2)

Teachers' salaries (2009)

Annual statutory teachers' salaries in public institutions at starting salary, after 10 and 15 years of experience and at the top of the scale, by level of education, in equivalent USD converted using PPPs

	Primary education				Lower secondary education				Upper secondary education			
	Starting salary/ minimum training	Salary after 10 years of experience/ minimum training	Salary after 15 years of experience/ minimum training	Salary at top of scale/ minimum training	Starting salary/ minimum training	Salary after 10 years of experience/ minimum training	Salary after 15 years of experience/ minimum training	Salary at top of scale/ minimum training	Starting salary/ minimum training	Salary after 10 years of experience/ minimum training	Salary after 15 years of experience/ minimum training	Salary at top of scale/ minimum training
	(1)	(2)	(3)	(4)	(5)	(6)	(7)	(8)	(9)	(10)	(11)	(12)
OECD												
Australia	34 664	48 233	48 233	48 233	34 664	48 233	48 233	48 233	34 664	48 233	48 233	48 233
Austria	30 998	36 588	41 070	61 390	32 404	39 466	44 389	63 781	32 883	35 539	45 712	67 135
Belgium (Fl.)	32 429	40 561	45 614	55 718	32 429	40 561	45 614	55 718	40 356	51 323	58 470	70 382
Belgium (Fr.)	31 545	m	44 696	54 848	31 545	m	44 696	54 848	39 415	m	57 613	69 579
Canada	m	m	m	m	m	m	m	m	m	m	m	m
Chile	15 612	19 982	22 246	29 179	15 612	19 982	22 246	29 179	16 296	20 895	23 273	30 548
Czech Republic	17 705	22 279	23 806	25 965	17 711	22 750	24 330	26 305	18 167	24 000	25 537	28 039
Denmark	46 950	52 529	54 360	54 360	46 950	52 529	54 360	54 360	47 664	62 279	62 279	62 279
England	32 189	47 047	47 047	47 047	32 189	47 047	47 047	47 047	32 189	47 047	47 047	47 047
Estonia	14 881	15 758	15 758	21 749	14 881	15 758	15 758	21 749	14 881	15 758	15 758	21 749
Finland[1]	32 692	37 632	41 415	50 461	34 707	40 550	44 294	54 181	35 743	45 444	49 237	61 089
France	24 006	31 156	33 359	49 221	27 296	33 653	35 856	51 833	27 585	33 942	36 145	52 150
Germany	46 446	m	57 005	61 787	51 080	m	62 930	68 861	55 743	m	68 619	77 628
Greece	27 951	31 858	34 209	41 265	27 951	31 858	34 209	41 265	27 951	31 858	34 209	41 265
Hungary[1]	12 045	13 838	14 902	19 952	12 045	13 838	14 902	19 952	13 572	16 211	17 894	25 783
Iceland	28 767	31 537	32 370	33 753	28 767	31 537	32 370	33 753	26 198	30 574	32 676	34 178
Ireland[1]	36 433	53 787	60 355	68 391	36 433	53 787	60 355	68 391	36 433	53 787	60 355	68 391
Israel	18 935	27 262	28 929	42 425	17 530	24 407	27 112	39 942	16 715	22 344	25 013	37 874
Italy	28 907	31 811	34 954	42 567	31 159	34 529	38 082	46 743	31 159	35 371	39 151	48 870
Japan	27 995	41 711	49 408	62 442	27 995	41 711	49 408	62 442	27 995	41 711	49 408	64 135
Korea	30 522	45 269	52 820	84 650	30 401	45 148	52 699	84 529	30 401	45 148	52 699	84 529
Luxembourg	51 799	67 340	74 402	113 017	80 053	100 068	111 839	139 152	80 053	100 068	111 839	139 152
Mexico	15 658	15 768	20 415	33 582	19 957	20 618	25 905	42 621	m	m	m	m
Netherlands	37 974	45 064	50 370	55 440	39 400	51 830	60 174	66 042	39 400	51 830	60 174	66 042
New Zealand	m	m	m	m	m	m	m	m	m	m	m	m
Norway[1]	35 593	40 392	43 614	43 861	35 593	40 392	43 614	43 861	38 950	42 258	46 247	46 495
Poland	9 186	12 809	15 568	16 221	10 340	14 520	17 732	18 479	11 676	16 585	20 290	21 149
Portugal	34 296	38 427	41 771	60 261	34 296	38 427	41 771	60 261	34 296	38 427	41 771	60 261
Scotland[1]	32 143	51 272	51 272	51 272	32 143	51 272	51 272	51 272	32 143	51 272	51 272	51 272
Slovak Republic	12 139	13 352	13 964	15 054	12 139	13 352	13 964	15 054	12 139	13 352	13 964	15 054
Slovenia	29 191	32 385	35 482	37 274	29 191	32 385	35 482	37 274	29 191	32 385	35 482	37 274
Spain	40 896	44 576	47 182	57 067	45 721	49 807	52 654	63 942	46 609	50 823	53 759	65 267
Sweden[1]	30 648	34 086	35 349	40 985	30 975	35 146	36 521	41 255	32 463	36 983	38 584	44 141
Switzerland[2]	48 853	62 903	m	76 483	55 696	71 456	m	86 418	64 450	83 828	m	98 495
Turkey	25 536	26 374	27 438	29 697	a	a	a	a	26 173	27 011	28 076	30 335
United States[1]	36 502	42 475	44 788	51 633	36 416	42 566	44 614	54 725	36 907	43 586	47 977	54 666
OECD average	29 767	36 127	38 914	48 154	31 687	38 683	41 701	51 317	33 044	40 319	43 711	53 651
EU21 average	30 150	35 912	39 735	47 883	32 306	38 721	42 967	50 772	33 553	40 204	45 442	53 956
Other G20												
Argentina	m	m	m	m	m	m	m	m	m	m	m	m
Brazil	m	m	m	m	m	m	m	m	m	m	m	m
China	m	m	m	m	m	m	m	m	m	m	m	m
India	m	m	m	m	m	m	m	m	m	m	m	m
Indonesia	1 564	m	1 979	2 255	1 667	m	2 255	2 450	1 930	m	2 497	2 721
Russian Federation	m	m	m	m	m	m	m	m	m	m	m	m
Saudi Arabia	m	m	m	m	m	m	m	m	m	m	m	m
South Africa	m	m	m	m	m	m	m	m	m	m	m	m

1. Actual salaries.
2. Salaries after 11 years of experience for Columns 2, 6 and 10.
Source: OECD (2011), *Education at a Glance 2011: OECD Indicators,* OECD Publishing.
Please refer to the Reader's Guide in Education at a Glance 2011 *(www.oecd.org/edu/eag2011) for information concerning the symbols replacing missing data.*
StatLink ᵐˢᵖ http://dx.doi.org/10.1787/888932465246

94

Figure A.9 (2/2)

Teachers' salaries (2009)

Annual statutory teachers' salaries in public institutions at starting salary, after 10 and 15 years of experience and at the top of the scale, by level of education, in equivalent USD converted using PPPs

	Ratio of salary at top of scale to starting salary			Years from starting to top salary (lower secondary education)	Salary per hour of net contact (teaching) time after 15 years of experience			Ratio of salary per teaching hour of upper secondary to primary teachers (after 15 years of experience)
	Primary education	Lower secondary education	Upper secondary education		Primary education	Lower secondary education	Upper secondary education	
	(13)	(14)	(15)	(16)	(17)	(18)	(19)	(20)
OECD								
Australia	1.39	1.39	1.39	9	55	59	61	1.10
Austria	1.98	1.97	2.04	34	53	73	78	1.47
Belgium (Fl.)	1.72	1.72	1.74	27	57	66	91	1.60
Belgium (Fr.)	1.74	1.74	1.77	27	61	67	94	1.55
Canada	m	m	m	m	m	m	m	m
Chile	1.87	1.87	1.87	30	18	18	19	1.05
Czech Republic	1.47	1.49	1.54	32	29	39	43	1.50
Denmark	1.16	1.16	1.31	8	84	84	165	1.97
England	1.46	1.46	1.46	10	74	66	66	0.89
Estonia	1.46	1.46	1.46	7	25	25	27	1.09
Finland[1]	1.54	1.56	1.71	16	61	75	90	1.46
France	2.05	1.90	1.89	34	36	56	58	1.58
Germany	1.33	1.35	1.39	28	71	83	96	1.36
Greece	1.48	1.48	1.48	33	58	80	80	1.38
Hungary[1]	1.66	1.66	1.90	40	25	25	30	1.20
Iceland	1.17	1.17	1.30	18	53	53	60	1.12
Ireland[1]	1.88	1.88	1.88	22	64	82	82	1.29
Israel	2.24	2.28	2.27	36	37	46	48	1.30
Italy	1.47	1.50	1.57	35	46	62	63	1.37
Japan	2.23	2.23	2.29	34	70	82	99	1.41
Korea	2.77	2.78	2.78	37	63	85	87	1.38
Luxembourg	2.18	1.74	1.74	30	101	177	177	1.75
Mexico	2.14	2.14	m	14	26	25	m	m
Netherlands	1.46	1.68	1.68	17	54	80	80	1.48
New Zealand	m	m	m	m	m	m	m	m
Norway[1]	1.23	1.23	1.19	16	59	67	89	1.50
Poland	1.77	1.79	1.81	10	32	37	42	1.31
Portugal	1.76	1.76	1.76	34	48	54	54	1.14
Scotland[1]	1.60	1.60	1.60	6	60	60	60	1.00
Slovak Republic	1.24	1.24	1.24	32	17	22	23	1.35
Slovenia	1.28	1.28	1.28	13	51	51	56	1.09
Spain	1.40	1.40	1.40	38	54	74	78	1.45
Sweden[1]	1.34	1.33	1.36	a	m	m	m	m
Switzerland[2]	1.57	1.55	1.53	27	m	m	m	m
Turkey	1.16	a	1.16	a	43	a	50	1.15
United States[1]	1.41	1.50	1.48	m	41	42	46	1.12
OECD average	1.64	1.64	1.64	24	51	62	71	1.34
EU21 average	1.58	1.57	1.61	24	53	65	74	1.38
Other G20								
Argentina	m	m	m	m	m	m	m	m
Brazil	m	m	m	m	m	m	m	m
China	m	m	m	m	m	m	m	m
India	m	m	m	m	m	m	m	m
Indonesia	1.44	1.47	1.41	32	2	3	3	2.16
Russian Federation	m	m	m	m	m	m	m	m
Saudi Arabia	m	m	m	m	m	m	m	m
South Africa	m	m	m	m	m	m	m	m

1. Actual salaries.
2. Salaries after 11 years of experience for Columns 2, 6 and 10.
Source: OECD (2011), *Education at a Glance 2011: OECD Indicators,* OECD Publishing.
Please refer to the Reader's Guide in Education at a Glance 2011 *(www.oecd.org/edu/eag2011) for information concerning the symbols replacing missing data.*
StatLink http://dx.doi.org/10.1787/888932465246

Figure A.10

Teachers' salaries and pre-service teacher training requirements (2009)

Annual statutory teachers' salaries at 15 years of experience and system-level information on teacher training program

		Ratio of salary after 15 years of experience (minimum training) to earnings for full-time, full-year workers with tertiary education aged 25 to 64			Duration of teacher training program in years			ISCED type of final qualification[1]			Percentage of current teacher stock with this type of qualification		
		Primary education	Lower secondary education	Upper secondary education	Primary education	Lower secondary education	Upper secondary education	Primary education	Lower secondary education	Upper secondary education	Primary education	Lower secondary education	Upper secondary education
		(1)	(2)	(3)	(4)	(5)	(6)	(7)	(8)	(9)	(10)	(11)	(12)
OECD	Australia[2]	0.85	0.85	0.85	4	4	4	5A	5A	5A	87%	91%	x(11)
	Austria	0.58	0.63	0.65	3	5.5	5.5	5A	5A	5A	94%	95%	78%
	Belgium (Fl.)	0.89	0.89	1.14	3	3	5	5B	5B	5A, 5B	98%	97%	96%
	Belgium (Fr.)	0.87	0.87	1.12	3	3	5	5B	5B	5A	100%	m	m
	Canada	m	m	m	m	m	m	m	m	m	m	m	m
	Chile	m	m	m	m	m	m	m	m	m	m	m	m
	Czech Republic	0.51	0.52	0.55	5	5	5	5A	5A	5A	87%	88%	87%
	Denmark	0.93	0.93	1.06	4	4	6	5A	5A	5A	100%	100%	100%
	England	0.81	0.81	0.81	3, 4	3, 4	3, 4	5A	5A	5A	98%	95%	95%
	Estonia	0.82	0.82	0.82	4.5	4.5	4.5	5A	5A	5A	69%	75%	81%
	Finland[2, 3]	0.85	0.91	1.01	5	5	5	5A	5A	5A	89%	89%	93%
	France[4]	0.78	0.85	0.85	5	5	5, 6	5A	5A	5A	m	m	m
	Germany	0.88	0.97	1.06	5.5	5.5, 6.5	6.5	5A	5A	5A	m	m	m
	Greece	m	m	m	4	4	4, 5	5A	5A	5A	m	96%	98%
	Hungary[3]	0.45	0.45	0.54	4	4	5	5A	5A	5A	95%	100%	100%
	Iceland[4]	0.50	0.50	0.61	3, 4	3, 4		5A	5A	5A	87%	87%	78%
	Ireland[3]	0.88	0.88	0.88	3, 5.5	4, 5	4, 5	5A, 5B	5A, 5B	5A, 5B	m	m	m
	Israel	0.75	0.70	0.64	3, 4	3, 4	3, 4	5A	5A	5A	82%	92%	86%
	Italy[5]	0.59	0.64	0.66	4	4-6	4-6	5A	5A	5A	100%	100%	100%
	Japan	m	m	m	2, 4, 6	2, 4, 6	4, 6	5A+5B, 5A, 5A	5A+5B, 5A, 5A	5A	18%, 78%, 1%	7%, 91%, 2%	72%, 28%
	Korea[5]	1.08	1.08	1.08	4	4	4	5A	5A	5A	m	m	m
	Luxembourg	0.79	1.18	1.18	3, 4	5	5	5B	5A	5A	95.6%, 4.5%	100%	100%
	Mexico	m	m	m	4	4, 6	4, 6	5A	5A, 5B	5A, 5B	96%	90%	91%
	Netherlands[5]	0.67	0.81	0.81	4	4	5, 6	5A	5A	5A	100%	100%	100%
	New Zealand	m	m	m	m	m	m	m	m	m	m	m	m
	Norway[3, 6]	0.66	0.66	0.70	4	4	4	5A	5A	5A	47%	47%	21%
	Poland[5]	0.59	0.68	0.78	3, 5	3, 5	3, 5	5A, 5B	5A	5A	99%	99%	97%
	Portugal	1.19	1.19	1.19	3, 4, 6	5, 6	5, 6	5B, 5B, 5A	5A	5A	97%	91%	93%
	Scotland[3]	0.89	0.89	0.89	4, 5	4, 5	4, 5	5A	5A	5A	m	m	m
	Slovak Republic	0.44	0.44	0.44	4, 7	5, 7	5, 7	5A	5A	5A	93%, 7%	91%, 9%	87%, 13%
	Slovenia	0.81	0.81	0.81	5	5-6	5-6	5A	5A	5A, 5B	m	m	m
	Spain[5]	1.16	1.27	1.32	3	6	6	5A	5A	5A	100%	100%	100%
	Sweden[3, 5]	0.74	0.75	0.81	3.5	4.5	4.5	5A	5A	5A	84%	84%	72%
	Switzerland[7]	m	m	m	3	5	6	5A	5A	5A	m	m	m
	Turkey	m	m	m	4-5	a	4-5	5A	a	5A	90%	a	97%
	United States[3]	0.61	0.61	0.65	4	4	4	5A	5A	5A	99%	99%	99%
	OECD average	0.77	0.81	0.85									
	EU21 average	0.78	0.83	0.88									
Other G20	Argentina	m	m	m	m	m	m	m	m	m	m	m	m
	Brazil	m	m	m	m	m	m	m	m	m	m	m	m
	China	m	m	m	m	m	m	m	m	m	m	m	m
	India	m	m	m	m	m	m	m	m	m	m	m	m
	Indonesia	m	m	m	m	m	m	m	m	m	m	m	m
	Russian Federation	m	m	m	m	m	m	m	m	m	m	m	m
	Saudi Arabia	m	m	m	m	m	m	m	m	m	m	m	m
	South Africa	m	m	m	m	m	m	m	m	m	m	m	m

1. Tertiary-type A programs are largely theory-based and are designed to provide qualifications for entry into advanced research programs and professions with high knowledge and skill requirements. Tertiary-type B programs are classified at the same level of competence as tertiary-type A programs but are more occupationally oriented and usually lead directly to the labor market.
2. Year of reference 2010 for Columns 10 to 12.
3. Actual salaries for Columns 1, 2 and 3.
4. Year of reference 2006 for Columns 1, 2 and 3.
5. Year of reference 2008 for Columns 1, 2 and 3.
6. Year of reference 2007 for Columns 1, 2 and 3.
7. Salaries after 11 years of experience for Columns 1, 2 and 3.
Source: OECD (2011), *Education at a Glance 2011: OECD Indicators,* OECD Publishing.
Please refer to the Reader's Guide in Education at a Glance 2011 *(www.oecd.org/edu/eag2011) for information concerning the symbols replacing missing data.*
StatLink ᵐˢᵖ http://dx.doi.org/10.1787/888932465265

Figure A.11

Organization of teachers' working time (2009)

Number of teaching weeks, teaching days, net teaching hours, and teachers' working time over the school year, in public institutions

	Number of weeks of instruction			Number of days of instruction			Net teaching time in hours			Working time required at school in hours			Total statutory working time in hours		
	Primary education	Lower secondary education	Upper secondary education, general programs	Primary education	Lower secondary education	Upper secondary education, general programs	Primary education	Lower secondary education	Upper secondary education, general programs	Primary education	Lower secondary education	Upper secondary education, general programs	Primary education	Lower secondary education	Upper secondary education, general programs
	(1)	(2)	(3)	(4)	(5)	(6)	(7)	(8)	(9)	(10)	(11)	(12)	(13)	(14)	(15)
OECD															
Australia	40	40	40	197	197	193	874	812	797	1 201	1 204	1 186	a	a	a
Austria	38	38	38	180	180	180	779	607	589	a	a	a	1 776	1 776	a
Belgium (Fl.)	37	37	37	178	179	179	801	687	642	926	a	a	a	a	a
Belgium (Fr.)	38	38	38	183	183	183	732	671	610	a	a	a	a	a	a
Canada	m	m	m	m	m	m	m	m	m	m	m	m	m	m	m
Chile	40	40	40	191	191	191	1 232	1 232	1 232	1 760	1 760	1 760	1 760	1 760	1 760
Czech Republic	40	40	40	189	189	189	832	624	595	a	a	a	1 664	1 664	1 664
Denmark[1]	42	42	42	200	200	200	648	648	377	648	648	377	1 680	1 680	1 680
England[1]	38	38	38	190	190	190	635	714	714	1 265	1 265	1 265	1 265	1 265	1 265
Estonia	39	39	39	175	175	175	630	630	578	1 540	1 540	1 540	a	a	a
Finland	38	38	38	188	188	188	677	592	550	a	a	a	a	a	a
France[1]	35	35	35	m	m	m	918	642	628	a	a	a	a	a	a
Germany	40	40	40	193	193	193	805	756	713	a	a	a	1 775	1 775	1 775
Greece	36	32	32	177	157	157	589	426	426	1 140	1 170	1 170	a	a	a
Hungary	37	37	37	181	181	181	597	597	597	a	a	a	1 864	1 864	1 864
Iceland[1]	36	36	35	176	176	171	609	609	547	1 650	1 650	1 720	1 800	1 800	1 800
Ireland	37	33	33	183	167	167	915	735	735	1 036	735	735	a	a	a
Israel	43	42	42	183	176	176	788	589	524	1 069	802	704	a	a	a
Italy	39	39	39	172	172	172	757	619	619	a	a	a	a	a	a
Japan[1]	40	40	40	201	201	198	707	602	500	a	a	a	1 899	1 899	1 899
Korea	40	40	40	220	220	220	836	618	605	a	a	a	1 680	1 680	1 680
Luxembourg	36	36	36	176	176	176	739	634	634	900	828	828	a	a	a
Mexico	42	42	36	200	200	172	800	1 047	843	800	1 167	971	a	a	a
Netherlands	40	m	m	195	m	m	930	750	750	a	a	a	1 659	1 659	1 659
New Zealand	m	m	m	m	m	m	m	m	m	m	m	m	m	m	m
Norway	38	38	38	190	190	190	741	654	523	1 300	1 225	1 150	1 688	1 688	1 688
Poland	37	37	37	181	179	180	489	483	486	a	a	a	1 480	1 464	1 472
Portugal	37	37	37	175	175	175	875	770	770	1 289	1 289	1 289	1 464	1 464	1 464
Scotland	38	38	38	190	190	190	855	855	855	a	a	a	1 365	1 365	1 365
Slovak Republic	38	38	38	187	187	187	832	645	617	m	m	m	1 560	1 560	1 560
Slovenia	40	40	40	190	190	190	690	690	633	a	a	a	a	a	a
Spain	37	37	36	176	176	171	880	713	693	1 140	1 140	1 140	1 425	1 425	1 425
Sweden	a	a	a	a	a	a	a	a	a	1 360	1 360	1 360	1 767	1 767	1 767
Switzerland	m	m	m	m	m	m	m	m	m	m	m	m	m	m	m
Turkey	38	a	38	180	a	180	639	a	567	870	a	756	1 808	a	1 808
United States[1]	36	36	36	180	180	180	1 097	1 068	1 051	1 381	1 381	1 378	1 913	1 977	1 998
OECD average	38	38	38	186	185	183	779	701	656	1 182	1 198	1 137	1 665	1 660	1 663
EU21 average	38	38	37	184	181	181	755	659	628	1 124	1 108	1 078	1 596	1 594	1 580
Other G20															
Argentina[2]	36	36	36	170	171	171	680	1 368	1 368	m	m	m	m	m	m
Brazil	40	40	40	200	200	200	800	800	800	800	800	800	800	800	800
China	35	35	35	175	175	175	m	m	m	m	m	m	m	m	m
India	m	m	m	m	m	m	m	m	m	m	m	m	m	m	m
Indonesia	44	44	44	251	163	163	1 255	734	734	m	m	m	m	m	m
Russian Federation[1]	34	35	35	164	169	169	615	507	507	a	a	a	a	a	a
Saudi Arabia	m	m	m	m	m	m	m	m	m	m	m	m	m	m	m
South Africa	m	m	m	m	m	m	m	m	m	m	m	m	m	m	m

1. Actual teaching and working time.
2. Year of reference 2008.
Source: OECD (2011), *Education at a Glance 2011: OECD Indicators*, OECD Publishing.
Please refer to the Reader's Guide in Education at a Glance 2011 *(www.oecd.org/edu/eag2011) for information concerning the symbols replacing missing data.*
StatLink http://dx.doi.org/10.1787/888932465398

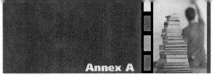

Figure A.12

Number of teaching hours per year (2000, 2005-09)

Net statutory contact time in hours per year in public institutions by level of education from 2000, 2005 to 2009

		Primary level						Lower secondary level						Upper secondary level					
		2000	2005	2006	2007	2008	2009	2000	2005	2006	2007	2008	2009	2000	2005	2006	2007	2008	2009
		(1)	(2)	(3)	(4)	(5)	(6)	(7)	(8)	(9)	(10)	(11)	(12)	(13)	(14)	(15)	(16)	(17)	(18)
OECD	Australia	882	888	884	877	873	874	811	810	818	815	812	812	803	810	817	813	810	797
	Austria	m	774	774	774	779	779	m	607	607	607	607	607	m	589	589	589	589	589
	Belgium (Fl.)	826	806	797	806	810	801	712	720	684	691	695	687	668	675	638	645	649	642
	Belgium (Fr.)	804	722	724	724	724	732	728	724	662	662	662	671	668	664	603	603	603	610
	Canada	m	m	m	m	m	m	m	m	m	m	m	m	m	m	m	m	m	m
	Chile	m	m	864	860	m	1 232	m	m	864	860	m	1 232	m	m	864	860	m	1 232
	Czech Republic	650	813	854	849	849	832	650	647	640	637	637	624	621	617	611	608	608	595
	Denmark[1]	640	640	648	648	648	648	640	640	648	648	648	648	560	560	364	364	364	377
	England[1]	m	m	m	631	654	635	m	m	m	714	722	714	m	m	m	714	722	714
	Estonia	630	630	630	630	630	630	630	630	630	630	630	630	578	578	578	578	578	578
	Finland	656	677	677	677	677	677	570	592	592	592	592	592	527	550	550	550	550	550
	France[1]	907	918	910	914	926	918	639	639	634	632	644	642	611	625	616	618	630	628
	Germany	783	808	810	806	805	805	732	758	758	758	756	756	690	714	714	714	715	713
	Greece	609	604	604	590	593	589	426	434	429	426	429	426	429	430	421	423	429	426
	Hungary	583	583	583	583	597	597	555	555	555	555	597	597	555	555	555	555	597	597
	Iceland[1]	629	671	671	671	671	609	629	671	671	671	671	609	464	560	560	560	560	547
	Ireland	915	915	915	915	915	915	735	735	735	735	735	735	735	735	735	735	735	735
	Israel	731	731	731	731	731	788	579	579	579	579	579	589	524	524	524	524	524	524
	Italy	744	739	735	735	735	757	608	605	601	601	601	619	608	605	601	601	601	619
	Japan[1]	635	578	m	705	709	707	557	505	m	600	603	602	478	429	m	498	500	500
	Korea	865	883	864	848	840	836	570	621	588	612	616	618	530	605	596	599	604	605
	Luxembourg	m	774	774	774	739	739	m	642	642	642	634	634	m	642	642	642	634	634
	Mexico	800	800	800	800	800	800	1 182	1 047	1 047	1 047	1 047	1 047	m	848	843	843	848	843
	Netherlands	930	930	930	930	930	930	867	750	750	750	750	750	867	750	750	750	750	750
	New Zealand	985	985	985	985	985	m	968	968	968	968	968	m	950	950	950	950	950	m
	Norway	713	741	741	741	741	741	633	656	654	654	654	654	505	524	523	523	523	523
	Poland	m	m	m	m	513	489	m	m	m	m	513	483	m	m	m	m	513	486
	Portugal	815	855	860	855	855	875	595	564	757	752	752	770	515	513	688	684	752	770
	Scotland	950	893	893	855	855	855	893	893	893	855	855	855	893	893	893	855	855	855
	Slovak Republic	m	m	m	m	m	832	m	m	m	m	m	645	m	m	m	m	m	617
	Slovenia	m	697	697	682	682	690	m	697	697	682	682	690	m	639	639	626	626	633
	Spain	880	880	880	880	880	880	564	713	713	713	713	713	548	693	693	693	693	693
	Sweden	a	a	a	a	a	a	a	a	a	a	a	a	a	a	a	a	a	a
	Switzerland	884	m	m	m	m	m	859	m	m	m	m	m	674	m	m	m	m	m
	Turkey	639	639	639	639	639	639	a	a	a	a	a	a	504	567	567	567	567	567
	United States[1]	m	1 080	1 080	1 080	1 097	1 097	m	1 080	1 080	1 080	1 068	1 068	m	1 080	1 080	1 080	1 051	1 051
	OECD average	773	781	792	780	770	779	693	696	711	706	696	701	620	653	662	657	649	656
	OECD average for countries with data available for all reference years	764	772	773	770	771	771	679	681	684	683	685	684	609	625	618	616	622	623
	EU21 average for countries with data available for all reference years	770	776	778	775	777	778	659	662	668	665	669	670	629	635	626	623	632	634
Other G20	Argentina	m	m	m	m	680	m	m	m	m	m	1 368	m	m	m	m	m	1 368	m
	Brazil	800	800	800	800	800	800	800	800	800	800	800	800	800	800	800	800	800	800
	China	m	m	m	m	m	m	m	m	m	m	m	m	m	m	m	m	m	m
	India	m	m	m	m	m	m	m	m	m	m	m	m	m	m	m	m	m	m
	Indonesia	m	m	m	m	1 260	1 255	m	m	m	m	738	734	m	m	m	m	738	734
	Russian Federation[1]	m	615	615	615	615	615	m	507	507	507	507	507	m	507	507	507	507	507
	Saudi Arabia	m	m	m	m	m	m	m	m	m	m	m	m	m	m	m	m	m	m
	South Africa	m	m	m	m	m	m	m	m	m	m	m	m	m	m	m	m	m	m

1. Actual teaching and working time.

Source: OECD (2011), *Education at a Glance 2011: OECD Indicators*, OECD Publishing.

Please refer to the Reader's Guide in Education at a Glance 2011 *(www.oecd.org/edu/eag2011) for information concerning the symbols replacing missing data.*

StatLink http://dx.doi.org/10.1787/888932465417

Figure A.13

Participation of teachers in professional development in the previous 18 months (2007-08)

Participation rates, average number of days and average of compulsory days of professional development undertaken by teachers of lower secondary education in the 18 months prior to the survey

	Percentage of teachers who undertook some professional development in the previous 18 months		Average days of professional development across all teachers		Average days of professional development among those who participated		Average percentage of professional development days taken that were compulsory	
	%	(S.E.)	Mean	(S.E.)	Mean	(S.E.)	%	(S.E.)
Australia	96.7	(0.43)	8.7	(0.19)	9.0	(0.20)	47.3	(1.17)
Austria	96.6	(0.37)	10.5	(0.17)	10.9	(0.16)	31.4	(0.66)
Belgium (Fl.)	90.3	(0.73)	8.0	(0.38)	8.8	(0.42)	33.6	(0.95)
Brazil	83.0	(1.21)	17.3	(0.70)	20.8	(0.79)	40.2	(1.17)
Bulgaria	88.3	(1.17)	27.2	(1.65)	30.8	(2.04)	46.9	(2.11)
Denmark	75.6	(1.26)	9.8	(0.34)	12.9	(0.40)	34.6	(1.43)
Estonia	92.7	(0.50)	13.1	(0.29)	14.2	(0.31)	49.2	(1.20)
Hungary	86.9	(1.77)	14.5	(0.50)	16.7	(0.41)	46.1	(1.58)
Iceland	77.1	(1.10)	10.7	(0.44)	13.9	(0.56)	49.9	(1.30)
Ireland	89.7	(0.78)	5.6	(0.21)	6.2	(0.21)	41.4	(0.99)
Italy	84.6	(0.76)	26.6	(0.98)	31.4	(1.17)	40.0	(1.08)
Korea	91.9	(0.59)	30.0	(0.57)	32.7	(0.55)	46.9	(0.85)
Lithuania	95.5	(0.40)	11.2	(0.21)	11.8	(0.21)	56.6	(0.98)
Malaysia	91.7	(0.67)	11.0	(0.32)	11.9	(0.33)	88.1	(0.64)
Malta	94.1	(0.75)	7.3	(0.25)	7.8	(0.26)	78.4	(1.07)
Mexico	91.5	(0.60)	34.0	(1.60)	37.1	(1.78)	66.4	(1.22)
Norway	86.7	(0.87)	9.2	(0.30)	10.6	(0.34)	55.5	(1.25)
Poland	90.4	(0.67)	26.1	(1.10)	28.9	(1.20)	41.0	(1.14)
Portugal	85.8	(0.87)	18.5	(0.89)	21.6	(1.01)	35.1	(0.99)
Slovak Republic	75.0	(1.13)	7.2	(0.30)	9.6	(0.38)	44.1	(1.19)
Slovenia	96.9	(0.35)	8.3	(0.20)	8.6	(0.20)	60.5	(0.93)
Spain	100.0	(0.03)	25.6	(0.51)	25.6	(0.51)	66.8	(0.99)
Turkey	74.8	(2.09)	11.2	(0.52)	14.9	(0.65)	72.8	(1.65)
TALIS average	88.5	(0.20)	15.3	(0.14)	17.3	(0.16)	51.0	(0.25)

Source: OECD (2009), *Creating Effective Teaching and Learning Environments: First Results from TALIS,* OECD Publishing.

StatLink http://dx.doi.org/10.1787/607807256201

Figure A.14

Amount of professional development undertaken by teachers in the previous 18 months (2007-08) – teacher characteristics

Average number of days of professional development undertaken by teachers of different characteristics [among those teachers of lower secondary education who took some professional development]

	Female teachers		Male teachers		Teachers aged under 30 years		Teachers aged 30-39 years		Teachers aged 40-49 years		Teachers aged 50+ years	
	Mean	(S.E.)	Mean	(S.E.)	Mean	(S.E.)	Mean	(S.E.)	Mean	(S.E.)	Mean	(S.E.)
Australia	9.0	(0.24)	9.0	(0.28)	9.0	(0.52)	8.9	(0.41)	9.1	(0.34)	9.1	(0.31)
Austria	11.2	(0.20)	10.3	(0.23)	12.4	(0.72)	10.5	(0.47)	11.3	(0.25)	10.5	(0.25)
Belgium (Fl.)	8.5	(0.55)	9.5	(0.48)	8.7	(0.62)	8.8	(0.79)	8.6	(0.61)	9.2	(0.88)
Brazil	20.7	(0.88)	21.2	(1.02)	22.2	(1.51)	22.3	(1.15)	19.7	(0.85)	17.0	(1.40)
Bulgaria	30.7	(2.00)	31.5	(3.79)	27.3	(5.36)	34.2	(4.29)	33.6	(4.21)	26.8	(1.67)
Denmark	13.4	(0.53)	12.3	(0.68)	17.3	(3.02)	13.4	(0.70)	15.8	(1.07)	10.3	(0.50)
Estonia	14.6	(0.36)	11.6	(0.51)	15.3	(1.19)	16.8	(0.80)	15.2	(0.55)	11.8	(0.36)
Hungary	16.6	(0.52)	16.9	(1.28)	15.4	(1.05)	16.3	(0.95)	18.3	(0.80)	15.4	(1.29)
Iceland	14.4	(0.68)	12.7	(0.83)	11.5	(1.41)	12.9	(0.84)	15.2	(0.96)	14.2	(0.99)
Ireland	6.0	(0.23)	6.7	(0.45)	5.8	(0.49)	6.6	(0.49)	6.8	(0.45)	5.7	(0.30)
Italy	30.5	(1.12)	34.8	(2.52)	64.1	(12.08)	50.1	(3.36)	30.4	(1.54)	24.1	(1.04)
Korea	34.2	(0.69)	30.0	(0.91)	43.3	(1.61)	36.7	(1.01)	30.3	(0.82)	24.3	(1.51)
Lithuania	12.1	(0.24)	10.1	(0.46)	11.2	(0.75)	11.5	(0.41)	12.5	(0.34)	11.4	(0.31)
Malaysia	11.8	(0.39)	12.3	(0.44)	12.0	(0.56)	11.7	(0.43)	12.2	(0.37)	11.9	(0.65)
Malta	7.9	(0.39)	7.6	(0.32)	7.7	(0.51)	7.5	(0.42)	8.6	(0.86)	7.9	(0.50)
Mexico	39.9	(2.17)	33.9	(2.72)	48.5	(5.64)	41.8	(3.88)	34.5	(2.27)	28.1	(2.26)
Norway	10.9	(0.49)	10.1	(0.47)	10.2	(0.95)	10.4	(0.58)	12.6	(0.86)	9.7	(0.55)
Poland	29.9	(1.40)	25.6	(1.60)	35.2	(3.22)	33.2	(2.08)	25.5	(1.45)	17.9	(1.64)
Portugal	20.3	(1.06)	24.8	(1.95)	38.5	(5.51)	21.3	(1.29)	20.2	(1.12)	17.7	(2.21)
Slovak Republic	9.9	(0.43)	8.3	(0.61)	9.8	(1.05)	9.7	(0.52)	10.9	(0.53)	8.5	(0.45)
Slovenia	8.7	(0.23)	8.3	(0.34)	9.4	(0.54)	9.7	(0.49)	8.4	(0.25)	7.2	(0.26)
Spain	26.7	(0.64)	24.2	(0.60)	29.4	(1.51)	25.7	(0.91)	26.8	(0.73)	23.0	(0.69)
Turkey	13.6	(0.82)	16.2	(1.29)	16.9	(1.13)	13.6	(0.74)	14.4	(1.91)	10.6	(1.18)
TALIS average	**17.5**	**(0.18)**	**16.9**	**(0.29)**	**20.9**	**(0.72)**	**18.9**	**(0.34)**	**17.4**	**(0.28)**	**14.4**	**(0.23)**

	Teachers with qualification at ISCED level 5B or below		Teachers with an ISCED level 5A Bachelor degree		Teachers with an ISCED level 5A Master degree or a higher level of qualification	
	Mean	(S.E.)	Mean	(S.E.)	Mean	(S.E.)
Australia	9.8	(1.24)	8.7	(0.20)	10.6	(0.51)
Austria	11.3	(0.22)	14.1	(2.72)	10.2	(0.25)
Belgium (Fl.)	8.6	(0.44)	15.5	(4.03)	8.0	(0.72)
Brazil	18.9	(2.00)	20.8	(0.87)	24.8	(2.87)
Bulgaria	28.0	(4.37)	28.4	(3.40)	32.3	(2.93)
Denmark	12.8	(4.47)	12.4	(0.39)	18.7	(1.83)
Estonia	14.7	(1.02)	13.3	(0.43)	14.9	(0.43)
Hungary	23.2	(6.28)	17.1	(0.53)	15.7	(0.59)
Iceland	10.4	(0.79)	15.1	(0.74)	17.8	(2.41)
Ireland	5.9	(0.66)	5.9	(0.25)	7.9	(0.65)
Italy	28.4	(1.53)	26.3	(3.81)	32.0	(1.25)
Korea	55.5	(11.32)	31.5	(0.65)	34.4	(0.82)
Lithuania	11.1	(0.54)	11.5	(0.32)	12.5	(0.34)
Malaysia	10.5	(0.65)	12.0	(0.34)	13.6	(0.76)
Malta	7.6	(0.57)	7.8	(0.30)	8.0	(0.67)
Mexico	27.4	(2.62)	36.4	(2.26)	53.1	(5.31)
Norway	16.0	(3.02)	9.9	(0.39)	12.7	(0.81)
Poland	28.7	(8.87)	27.5	(4.46)	29.0	(1.21)
Portugal	21.1	(3.54)	19.8	(1.07)	35.3	(3.34)
Slovak Republic	12.4	(2.90)	9.9	(2.81)	9.6	(0.37)
Slovenia	7.7	(0.22)	9.3	(0.31)	14.0	(2.98)
Spain	23.8	(2.20)	22.1	(1.22)	26.2	(0.49)
Turkey	10.6	(1.07)	15.0	(0.76)	19.3	(2.95)
TALIS average	**17.6**	**(0.80)**	**17.0**	**(0.41)**	**20.0**	**(0.41)**

Denotes categories that include less than 5% of teachers.

Source: OECD (2009), *Creating Effective Teaching and Learning Environments: First Results from TALIS,* OECD Publishing.

StatLink ⟨⟩ http://dx.doi.org/10.1787/607807256201

Figure A.15

Amount of professional development undertaken by teachers in the previous 18 months (2007-08) – school characteristics

Average number of days of professional development undertaken by teachers in schools of different characteristics [among those teachers of lower secondary education who took some professional development]

	Teachers in public schools		Teachers in private schools		Teachers in schools in a village		Teachers in schools in a small town		Teachers in schools in a town		Teachers in schools in a city		Teachers in schools in a large city	
	Mean	(S.E.)	Mean	(S.E.)	Mean	(S.E.)	Mean	(S.E.)	Mean	(S.E.)	Mean	(S.E.)	Mean	(S.E.)
Australia	8.9	(0.24)	9.2	(0.32)	10.1	(0.57)	9.4	(0.74)	9.0	(0.35)	8.8	(0.40)	9.0	(0.32)
Austria	11.0	(0.19)	10.2	(0.55)	11.3	(0.44)	10.2	(0.24)	12.1	(0.58)	11.2	(0.45)	11.3	(0.40)
Belgium (Fl.)	12.2	(1.31)	7.6	(0.34)	15.6	(4.07)	7.7	(0.46)	9.1	(0.86)	10.3	(0.88)	a	a
Brazil	21.1	(0.91)	19.0	(1.36)	22.8	(3.01)	19.5	(1.18)	20.2	(1.42)	21.3	(1.23)	20.2	(1.19)
Bulgaria	30.9	(2.08)	20.5	(9.36)	27.5	(3.54)	32.9	(6.88)	32.1	(2.56)	30.6	(3.18)	30.2	(2.55)
Denmark	13.4	(0.49)	12.4	(0.99)	11.7	(0.98)	14.0	(1.45)	12.1	(0.77)	15.0	(1.37)	15.4	(1.74)
Estonia	14.2	(0.31)	14.9	(3.11)	13.9	(0.45)	14.1	(0.76)	14.8	(0.85)	14.3	(0.64)	a	a
Hungary	16.6	(0.50)	17.0	(0.81)	16.7	(1.17)	17.6	(1.06)	16.2	(1.04)	17.0	(0.91)	16.0	(0.81)
Iceland	14.3	(0.65)	6.9	(2.27)	13.3	(0.71)	14.9	(1.21)	15.4	(1.37)	13.3	(1.09)	a	a
Ireland	6.4	(0.33)	5.7	(0.35)	5.9	(0.45)	5.9	(0.40)	6.2	(0.57)	6.7	(0.97)	5.9	(0.51)
Italy	30.8	(1.20)	44.5	(7.40)	30.4	(2.91)	33.0	(2.38)	29.5	(1.48)	29.2	(2.43)	35.3	(3.84)
Korea	34.3	(0.76)	25.1	(1.29)	32.9	(2.74)	33.0	(2.12)	32.2	(1.58)	32.2	(1.43)	33.1	(0.94)
Lithuania	11.8	(0.22)	11.4	(1.58)	10.9	(0.32)	11.7	(0.54)	12.3	(0.53)	12.2	(0.38)	a	a
Malaysia	12.0	(0.33)	10.0	(1.45)	12.1	(0.60)	11.6	(0.47)	12.3	(0.96)	11.9	(1.04)	13.4	(0.41)
Malta	7.5	(0.34)	8.2	(0.36)	8.6	(0.78)	7.9	(0.33)	7.6	(0.54)	a	a	a	a
Mexico	35.3	(1.57)	44.0	(6.21)	30.6	(7.64)	38.6	(4.31)	35.6	(3.13)	32.2	(2.47)	38.4	(2.43)
Norway	10.7	(0.36)	7.1	(1.14)	11.8	(0.78)	10.4	(0.64)	10.6	(0.59)	8.7	(0.57)	a	a
Poland	29.0	(1.26)	27.9	(3.86)	26.5	(1.32)	31.7	(3.33)	28.1	(1.92)	29.7	(3.70)	45.1	(7.16)
Portugal	21.9	(1.22)	17.9	(1.49)	23.8	(2.18)	20.2	(2.00)	22.9	(1.74)	19.9	(3.23)	18.0	(3.57)
Slovak Republic	9.7	(0.39)	10.0	(1.19)	10.6	(1.07)	9.4	(0.66)	8.9	(0.46)	10.3	(1.19)	a	a
Slovenia	8.6	(0.21)	a	a	8.9	(0.42)	8.4	(0.29)	9.0	(0.63)	8.6	(0.73)	a	a
Spain	27.1	(0.62)	21.1	(0.79)	25.4	(1.50)	27.0	(0.88)	25.3	(0.86)	25.5	(1.28)	24.6	(1.18)
Turkey	15.0	(0.72)	14.9	(1.13)	15.1	(2.42)	17.4	(3.05)	14.9	(1.48)	14.4	(0.83)	15.8	(1.32)
TALIS average	**17.5**	**(0.18)**	**16.6**	**(0.66)**	**17.2**	**(0.50)**	**17.7**	**(0.46)**	**17.2**	**(0.28)**	**17.4**	**(0.34)**	**22.1**	**(0.44)**

Denotes categories that include less than 5% of teachers.
Source: OECD (2009), *Creating Effective Teaching and Learning Environments: First Results from TALIS,* OECD Publishing.
StatLink http://dx.doi.org/10.1787/607807256201

Figure A.16

Types of professional development undertaken by teachers (2007-08)

Percentage of teachers of lower secondary education undertaking specified professional development activities in the previous 18 months

	Courses and workshops		Education conferences and seminars		Qualification programs		Observation visits to other schools		Professional development network		Individual and collaborative research		Mentoring and peer observation		Reading professional literature		Informal dialogue to improve teaching	
	%	(S.E.)	%	(S.E.)	%	(S.E.)	%	(S.E.)	%	(S.E.)	%	(S.E.)	%	(S.E.)	%	(S.E.)	%	(S.E.)
Australia	90.6	(0.81)	64.0	(1.34)	11.7	(0.80)	22.2	(1.42)	60.1	(1.38)	36.6	(1.21)	48.6	(1.30)	82.4	(1.09)	93.7	(0.70)
Austria	91.9	(0.56)	49.2	(0.97)	19.9	(0.68)	10.3	(0.55)	37.6	(0.98)	25.9	(0.82)	18.4	(0.84)	89.4	(0.57)	91.9	(0.60)
Belgium (Fl.)	85.2	(0.89)	32.6	(1.33)	17.8	(0.83)	15.1	(1.06)	25.7	(1.05)	31.8	(0.87)	22.1	(0.92)	79.6	(0.98)	91.3	(0.71)
Brazil	80.3	(1.31)	61.0	(1.52)	40.8	(1.27)	32.5	(1.03)	21.9	(0.95)	54.7	(1.17)	47.5	(1.37)	82.5	(0.78)	94.2	(0.58)
Bulgaria	73.7	(2.07)	42.2	(3.44)	50.2	(2.56)	22.5	(2.03)	19.8	(2.22)	24.5	(1.73)	35.4	(3.01)	93.5	(0.96)	94.7	(0.70)
Denmark	81.2	(1.33)	41.6	(1.56)	15.4	(1.47)	10.4	(0.92)	43.5	(1.65)	52.3	(1.51)	17.5	(1.66)	77.3	(1.50)	90.4	(0.89)
Estonia	92.5	(0.66)	50.6	(1.29)	27.7	(0.96)	62.8	(1.37)	42.8	(1.16)	26.6	(1.00)	31.5	(1.35)	87.7	(0.85)	93.8	(0.58)
Hungary	68.7	(1.66)	39.9	(1.64)	26.1	(1.13)	34.6	(2.15)	43.7	(1.83)	17.0	(0.84)	46.7	(1.93)	88.4	(1.11)	79.1	(1.39)
Iceland	72.1	(1.30)	52.1	(1.25)	18.8	(1.02)	60.0	(1.27)	82.6	(1.11)	18.2	(1.08)	33.4	(1.16)	82.8	(1.05)	94.9	(0.65)
Ireland	85.7	(0.88)	42.0	(1.41)	11.4	(0.67)	7.6	(0.75)	51.1	(1.20)	26.3	(1.17)	18.2	(1.12)	60.3	(0.96)	87.4	(0.81)
Italy	66.3	(1.10)	43.5	(1.03)	10.8	(0.50)	16.0	(0.89)	20.0	(0.75)	56.5	(0.92)	27.4	(0.93)	66.2	(0.81)	93.1	(0.46)
Korea	85.0	(0.86)	46.9	(1.24)	27.5	(0.88)	66.8	(1.26)	39.6	(1.00)	50.1	(1.03)	69.4	(1.15)	52.5	(1.06)	90.0	(0.63)
Lithuania	95.7	(0.43)	67.6	(1.10)	43.9	(1.16)	57.1	(1.21)	37.6	(1.05)	48.1	(1.00)	39.7	(1.16)	93.5	(0.50)	96.7	(0.38)
Malaysia	88.6	(0.71)	32.4	(0.93)	22.0	(1.01)	30.0	(1.40)	47.8	(1.25)	21.7	(1.08)	41.8	(1.26)	61.5	(1.63)	95.7	(0.36)
Malta	90.2	(0.96)	51.8	(1.88)	18.1	(1.36)	14.8	(1.23)	39.0	(1.70)	37.4	(1.85)	16.5	(1.19)	61.1	(1.90)	92.3	(1.05)
Mexico	94.3	(0.57)	33.1	(1.23)	33.5	(1.21)	30.5	(1.30)	27.5	(1.13)	62.9	(1.05)	38.1	(1.37)	67.4	(1.05)	88.9	(0.86)
Norway	72.5	(1.40)	40.4	(1.61)	17.6	(0.71)	19.1	(1.49)	35.3	(1.55)	12.3	(0.72)	22.0	(1.50)	64.1	(1.12)	94.0	(0.57)
Poland	90.8	(0.77)	64.3	(1.18)	35.0	(0.95)	19.7	(0.84)	60.7	(1.43)	40.0	(1.08)	66.7	(1.40)	95.2	(0.46)	95.8	(0.36)
Portugal	77.0	(0.91)	51.6	(1.31)	29.5	(0.87)	26.4	(1.03)	15.0	(0.82)	47.1	(1.15)	14.6	(0.84)	73.3	(0.97)	94.2	(0.49)
Slovak Republic	50.1	(1.45)	38.2	(1.38)	38.1	(1.28)	33.1	(1.41)	34.6	(1.46)	11.8	(0.83)	64.8	(1.27)	93.2	(0.64)	95.9	(0.48)
Slovenia	88.1	(0.70)	74.7	(1.05)	10.2	(0.65)	7.7	(0.58)	71.9	(1.38)	22.5	(0.97)	29.1	(0.87)	86.4	(0.73)	97.0	(0.35)
Spain	83.9	(0.86)	36.2	(1.10)	17.2	(0.62)	14.7	(0.75)	22.6	(0.84)	49.2	(0.96)	21.4	(1.00)	68.1	(0.93)	92.6	(0.49)
Turkey	62.3	(1.51)	67.8	(1.99)	19.2	(1.09)	21.1	(1.66)	39.4	(1.67)	40.1	(1.35)	32.2	(2.15)	80.6	(2.14)	92.8	(0.82)
TALIS average	**81.2**	**(0.23)**	**48.9**	**(0.32)**	**24.5**	**(0.23)**	**27.6**	**(0.26)**	**40.0**	**(0.28)**	**35.4**	**(0.24)**	**34.9**	**(0.30)**	**77.7**	**(0.23)**	**92.6**	**(0.14)**

Source: OECD (2009), *Creating Effective Teaching and Learning Environments: First Results from TALIS,* OECD Publishing.
StatLink http://dx.doi.org/10.1787/607807256201

Figure A.17

Teachers who wanted to participate in more development than they did in the previous 18 months (2007-08)

Percentage of teachers of lower secondary education who wanted to take more professional development than they did in the previous 18 months, by certain teacher and school characteristics

	All teachers		Female teachers		Male teachers		Teachers aged under 40 years		Teachers aged 40+ years		Teachers with qualification below ISCED level 5A		Teachers with qualification at ISCED level 5A Bachelor degree		Teachers with qualification at ISCED level 5A Masters degree or higher		Teachers in public schools		Teachers in private schools	
	%	(S.E.)	%	(S.E.)	%	(S.E.)	%	(S.E.)	%	(S.E.)	%	(S.E.)	%	(S.E.)	%	(S.E.)	%	(S.E.)	%	(S.E.)
Australia	55.2	(1.37)	57.9	(1.67)	51.3	(1.89)	59.0	(1.70)	52.5	(1.70)	24.6	(11.05)	55.0	(1.37)	58.9	(2.83)	55.5	(1.49)	54.8	(2.49)
Austria	44.7	(0.93)	46.0	(1.17)	41.9	(1.36)	48.8	(1.83)	43.5	(1.00)	40.3	(1.18)	41.8	(8.01)	51.9	(1.43)	43.9	(1.01)	53.4	(2.05)
Belgium (Fl.)	30.5	(0.98)	32.3	(1.40)	26.5	(2.50)	34.9	(1.22)	25.6	(1.34)	30.4	(1.02)	23.0	(3.04)	36.0	(3.42)	32.7	(1.17)	29.7	(1.36)
Brazil	84.4	(0.77)	85.9	(0.88)	80.5	(1.30)	85.8	(1.05)	82.6	(1.21)	86.4	(2.41)	83.9	(0.85)	83.3	(3.56)	84.8	(0.89)	83.6	(1.52)
Bulgaria	68.9	(1.77)	69.5	(1.62)	65.8	(4.77)	70.9	(2.83)	68.0	(1.87)	67.6	(4.25)	71.6	(3.98)	68.5	(2.33)	68.9	(1.78)	64.5	(12.29)
Denmark	47.6	(1.39)	49.6	(1.93)	44.8	(2.50)	47.3	(2.41)	47.8	(1.90)	18.0	(6.30)	47.8	(1.37)	52.9	(5.58)	48.0	(1.80)	45.8	(3.01)
Estonia	48.7	(1.07)	48.6	(1.16)	49.2	(2.38)	48.3	(1.90)	48.8	(1.26)	48.7	(2.89)	49.8	(1.74)	47.8	(1.49)	48.6	(1.10)	50.4	(9.40)
Hungary	40.2	(2.00)	39.9	(2.45)	41.0	(2.10)	41.1	(3.19)	39.6	(1.81)	39.3	(18.39)	38.6	(2.07)	44.6	(2.22)	40.1	(1.63)	40.3	(5.22)
Iceland	37.9	(1.47)	40.6	(1.93)	32.0	(2.36)	36.3	(2.23)	39.0	(1.84)	36.5	(2.33)	39.4	(1.80)	32.9	(5.74)	37.5	(1.61)	35.0	(12.03)
Ireland	54.1	(1.37)	55.7	(1.54)	50.7	(2.56)	54.8	(1.87)	53.5	(1.61)	46.5	(5.83)	54.6	(1.45)	53.6	(2.85)	53.6	(2.28)	53.8	(1.81)
Italy	56.4	(0.98)	58.4	(1.08)	49.2	(1.78)	57.0	(1.85)	56.2	(1.07)	54.0	(2.38)	62.9	(3.09)	56.1	(1.07)	56.5	(1.03)	48.5	(5.20)
Korea	58.2	(1.16)	60.5	(1.28)	54.1	(1.92)	67.6	(1.57)	52.5	(1.53)	68.1	(13.27)	58.5	(1.42)	57.6	(1.72)	59.6	(1.41)	50.8	(3.98)
Lithuania	44.7	(1.10)	45.4	(1.12)	40.9	(2.80)	47.9	(1.79)	43.3	(1.28)	44.0	(2.18)	45.2	(1.40)	44.2	(1.84)	45.0	(1.10)	31.6	(6.43)
Malaysia	82.9	(0.95)	83.8	(1.10)	81.1	(1.30)	86.5	(1.12)	77.3	(1.28)	75.0	(2.21)	83.9	(1.05)	85.8	(2.12)	83.0	(0.97)	66.9	(11.42)
Malta	43.3	(1.79)	44.4	(2.33)	41.4	(3.10)	42.5	(2.22)	44.6	(3.04)	40.5	(4.26)	43.3	(1.99)	48.0	(5.52)	41.1	(2.44)	47.7	(2.04)
Mexico	85.3	(0.85)	86.3	(1.04)	84.1	(1.15)	88.0	(1.04)	83.3	(1.15)	80.8	(3.10)	86.1	(0.88)	86.6	(2.15)	85.7	(0.80)	84.8	(3.28)
Norway	70.3	(1.13)	72.5	(1.43)	67.1	(1.76)	70.3	(1.72)	70.4	(1.45)	52.6	(12.23)	71.1	(1.36)	68.6	(2.11)	70.6	(1.16)	72.9	(8.17)
Poland	43.6	(1.04)	45.1	(1.28)	38.9	(2.07)	49.5	(1.54)	37.3	(1.26)	40.7	(8.80)	47.5	(4.38)	43.3	(1.07)	43.5	(1.01)	45.2	(7.26)
Portugal	76.2	(0.91)	77.5	(1.04)	73.1	(1.56)	77.3	(1.22)	75.1	(1.43)	70.7	(4.35)	76.0	(0.99)	79.8	(2.52)	77.0	(0.98)	66.0	(3.51)
Slovak Republic	43.2	(1.34)	44.3	(1.37)	38.6	(2.98)	48.4	(1.90)	39.6	(1.78)	38.4	(7.68)	47.3	(15.00)	43.6	(1.40)	42.6	(1.35)	46.3	(3.89)
Slovenia	35.1	(1.18)	34.9	(1.23)	36.0	(2.38)	39.5	(1.82)	32.2	(1.36)	28.8	(1.48)	40.7	(1.50)	36.0	(7.85)	34.9	(1.14)	a	a
Spain	60.6	(1.02)	63.8	(1.28)	56.4	(1.43)	68.6	(1.59)	56.0	(1.29)	47.6	(3.83)	56.5	(2.53)	62.0	(1.16)	60.6	(1.23)	59.5	(2.31)
Turkey	48.2	(2.21)	51.3	(2.13)	44.8	(3.22)	51.2	(2.40)	37.2	(3.56)	26.2	(5.62)	48.8	(2.23)	58.8	(6.69)	48.4	(2.51)	41.6	(3.71)
TALIS average	**54.8**	**(0.27)**	**56.3**	**(0.32)**	**51.7**	**(0.49)**	**57.5**	**(0.40)**	**52.4**	**(0.36)**	**48.1**	**(1.47)**	**55.4**	**(0.85)**	**56.6**	**(0.74)**	**54.9**	**(0.31)**	**53.3**	**(1.26)**

Denotes categories that include less than 5% of teachers.

Source: OECD (2009), *Creating Effective Teaching and Learning Environments: First Results from TALIS,* OECD Publishing.

StatLink ⟨⟩ http://dx.doi.org/10.1787/607807256201

Figure A.18

Teachers' high professional development needs (2007-08)

*Percentage of teachers of lower secondary education indicating they have a "High level of need"
for professional development in the following areas and overall index of need*

	Overall index of development need (Maximum=100)[1]		Content and performance standards		Student assessment practices		Classroom management		Subject field		Instructional practices	
	Index	(S.E.)	%	(S.E.)	%	(S.E.)	%	(S.E.)	%	(S.E.)	%	(S.E.)
Australia	44	(0.35)	8.3	(0.64)	7.5	(0.60)	5.2	(0.52)	5.0	(0.53)	3.6	(0.40)
Austria	51	(0.31)	13.9	(0.69)	12.2	(0.53)	13.6	(0.64)	14.8	(0.59)	18.6	(0.75)
Belgium (Fl.)	47	(0.39)	12.0	(0.65)	15.6	(0.74)	12.1	(0.59)	17.5	(0.74)	14.1	(0.77)
Brazil	58	(0.55)	23.1	(1.31)	21.1	(1.15)	13.7	(0.98)	14.9	(1.06)	14.8	(1.06)
Bulgaria	50	(0.59)	25.7	(2.33)	16.1	(1.45)	12.7	(1.46)	21.2	(1.53)	18.3	(1.67)
Denmark	44	(0.59)	17.1	(1.25)	13.6	(0.97)	2.3	(0.55)	4.6	(0.54)	4.7	(0.57)
Estonia	55	(0.49)	17.7	(0.95)	10.4	(0.65)	13.4	(0.76)	22.6	(1.01)	18.2	(0.78)
Hungary	45	(0.51)	9.2	(0.55)	5.9	(0.51)	3.3	(0.36)	7.4	(0.64)	14.7	(0.81)
Iceland	52	(0.48)	7.3	(0.74)	14.3	(1.00)	11.6	(0.90)	10.3	(0.91)	8.2	(0.76)
Ireland	49	(0.48)	6.7	(0.52)	8.2	(0.77)	6.4	(0.59)	4.1	(0.49)	5.4	(0.60)
Italy	63	(0.30)	17.6	(0.69)	24.0	(0.83)	18.9	(0.84)	34.0	(0.75)	34.9	(0.89)
Korea	70	(0.30)	26.8	(0.92)	21.5	(0.79)	30.3	(0.91)	38.3	(0.96)	39.9	(0.91)
Lithuania	62	(0.41)	39.2	(1.01)	37.3	(1.03)	27.9	(0.96)	43.4	(0.89)	44.5	(0.90)
Malaysia	72	(0.64)	49.8	(1.59)	43.8	(1.43)	41.6	(1.41)	56.8	(1.53)	55.2	(1.47)
Malta	48	(0.57)	8.1	(1.00)	7.2	(0.82)	5.3	(0.78)	6.7	(0.86)	3.9	(0.60)
Mexico	50	(0.59)	13.7	(0.77)	15.0	(0.83)	8.8	(0.66)	11.0	(0.88)	12.3	(0.92)
Norway	55	(0.51)	12.9	(0.85)	21.9	(1.29)	7.7	(0.66)	8.6	(0.70)	8.2	(0.61)
Poland	49	(0.50)	11.9	(0.74)	12.8	(0.77)	17.6	(0.95)	17.0	(0.87)	17.5	(0.75)
Portugal	56	(0.31)	9.8	(0.62)	6.9	(0.51)	5.8	(0.47)	4.8	(0.43)	7.7	(0.54)
Slovak Republic	48	(0.56)	8.2	(0.66)	9.0	(0.57)	9.8	(0.81)	17.2	(0.96)	13.4	(0.89)
Slovenia	57	(0.35)	13.4	(0.67)	22.3	(0.89)	24.0	(0.79)	15.9	(0.78)	19.9	(0.80)
Spain	49	(0.44)	6.0	(0.38)	5.8	(0.42)	8.1	(0.57)	5.0	(0.47)	5.5	(0.39)
Turkey	43	(0.72)	9.8	(0.81)	9.2	(0.90)	6.7	(1.29)	8.9	(0.93)	9.0	(0.92)
TALIS average	**53**	**(0.10)**	**16.0**	**(0.20)**	**15.7**	**(0.19)**	**13.3**	**(0.18)**	**17.0**	**(0.18)**	**17.1**	**(0.18)**

	ICT teaching skills		Teaching special learning needs students		Student discipline and behavior problems		School management and administration		Teaching in a multicultural setting		Student counseling	
	%	(S.E.)	%	(S.E.)	%	(S.E.)	%	(S.E.)	%	(S.E.)	%	(S.E.)
Australia	17.8	(0.94)	15.1	(0.98)	6.6	(0.71)	5.9	(0.53)	4.0	(0.43)	7.3	(0.61)
Austria	23.8	(0.64)	30.3	(0.94)	32.6	(1.03)	3.9	(0.37)	10.0	(0.68)	13.1	(0.65)
Belgium (Fl.)	14.8	(0.72)	12.8	(0.76)	11.8	(0.71)	2.4	(0.31)	3.7	(0.46)	11.0	(0.68)
Brazil	35.6	(1.33)	63.2	(1.21)	26.5	(1.12)	20.0	(0.78)	33.2	(1.22)	20.7	(1.14)
Bulgaria	26.9	(1.58)	24.4	(1.47)	14.9	(1.82)	8.5	(0.95)	15.5	(2.35)	10.4	(1.30)
Denmark	20.1	(1.67)	24.6	(1.44)	9.8	(1.21)	3.9	(0.49)	7.1	(0.98)	5.5	(0.66)
Estonia	27.9	(0.91)	28.1	(0.95)	23.6	(1.02)	4.6	(0.37)	9.7	(0.77)	21.5	(0.95)
Hungary	23.0	(1.15)	42.0	(1.57)	31.2	(1.50)	3.4	(0.96)	10.7	(0.68)	8.4	(0.83)
Iceland	17.3	(1.08)	23.2	(1.16)	20.0	(0.97)	7.9	(0.84)	14.0	(0.92)	12.9	(0.86)
Ireland	34.2	(1.30)	38.3	(1.32)	13.9	(0.98)	11.8	(0.94)	24.3	(1.31)	24.9	(1.33)
Italy	25.8	(0.81)	35.3	(1.05)	28.3	(1.04)	8.6	(0.49)	25.3	(0.85)	19.7	(0.87)
Korea	17.7	(0.67)	25.6	(0.88)	34.6	(0.92)	10.8	(0.62)	10.4	(0.61)	41.5	(1.04)
Lithuania	36.1	(0.93)	25.4	(0.95)	24.3	(0.89)	9.8	(0.68)	9.8	(0.79)	18.6	(1.09)
Malaysia	43.8	(1.18)	25.9	(1.08)	41.6	(1.41)	29.9	(1.14)	30.3	(1.35)	35.1	(1.21)
Malta	22.8	(1.51)	34.4	(1.56)	10.5	(1.18)	12.9	(1.31)	14.0	(1.36)	15.8	(1.29)
Mexico	24.9	(1.09)	38.8	(1.27)	21.4	(1.04)	11.9	(0.71)	18.2	(0.93)	25.9	(1.12)
Norway	28.1	(1.19)	29.2	(1.04)	16.5	(0.93)	5.8	(0.57)	8.3	(0.75)	7.8	(0.63)
Poland	22.2	(0.90)	29.4	(1.28)	23.5	(0.94)	7.8	(0.57)	6.6	(0.58)	25.4	(1.01)
Portugal	24.2	(0.89)	50.0	(1.06)	17.4	(0.88)	18.2	(0.90)	17.0	(0.73)	8.5	(0.61)
Slovak Republic	14.8	(0.97)	20.1	(0.97)	19.2	(1.26)	4.8	(0.46)	4.6	(0.52)	7.9	(0.58)
Slovenia	25.1	(0.81)	40.4	(1.09)	32.0	(1.04)	7.0	(0.59)	9.9	(0.68)	21.1	(0.83)
Spain	26.2	(1.08)	35.8	(1.04)	18.3	(0.76)	14.2	(0.64)	17.5	(0.73)	12.0	(0.62)
Turkey	14.2	(0.85)	27.8	(1.70)	13.4	(1.44)	9.3	(0.78)	14.5	(1.10)	9.5	(1.16)
TALIS average	**24.7**	**(0.23)**	**31.3**	**(0.25)**	**21.4**	**(0.23)**	**9.7**	**(0.15)**	**13.9**	**(0.21)**	**16.7**	**(0.20)**

1. Index derived from aggregating the development need for each teacher over all of the aspects of their work: 3 points for a high level of need; 2 points for a moderate level of need, 1 point for a low level of need and no points for cases where teachers noted no development need at all. These were then aggregated and divided by the maximum possible score of 33 and multiplied by 100.
Source: OECD (2009), *Creating Effective Teaching and Learning Environments: First Results from TALIS,* OECD Publishing.
StatLink http://dx.doi.org/10.1787/607807256201

Figure A.19

Support for professional development undertaken by teachers (2007-08)

Percentage of those teachers of lower secondary education who undertook professional development and received the following types of support

	Teacher contribution to the cost of professional development undertaken						Teacher received scheduled time		Teacher received salary supplement	
	Paid none of the costs		Paid some of the costs		Paid all of the costs					
	%	(S.E.)	%	(S.E.)	%	(S.E.)	%	(S.E.)	%	(S.E.)
Australia	74.5	(1.24)	24.3	(1.24)	1.2	(0.26)	85.5	(0.86)	5.5	(0.57)
Austria	43.7	(1.00)	49.7	(1.01)	6.6	(0.45)	89.0	(0.72)	11.7	(0.68)
Belgium (Fl.)	81.4	(1.32)	15.3	(1.10)	3.2	(0.46)	78.1	(1.63)	2.2	(0.49)
Brazil	54.8	(1.59)	26.9	(1.36)	18.3	(1.22)	56.2	(1.67)	10.9	(0.88)
Bulgaria	73.4	(2.06)	20.5	(2.16)	6.1	(0.68)	40.4	(1.88)	8.1	(0.91)
Denmark	77.3	(1.45)	16.3	(1.13)	6.4	(0.93)	71.8	(2.34)	9.2	(1.64)
Estonia	72.5	(0.98)	25.6	(0.93)	2.0	(0.28)	64.2	(1.37)	12.0	(0.88)
Hungary	71.5	(1.99)	20.5	(1.76)	8.0	(0.76)	44.4	(2.95)	5.9	(0.85)
Iceland	67.8	(1.34)	27.8	(1.42)	4.5	(0.61)	70.3	(1.39)	17.9	(1.24)
Ireland	79.3	(1.03)	17.5	(0.99)	3.2	(0.46)	94.7	(0.53)	5.8	(0.67)
Italy	68.7	(1.04)	13.7	(0.65)	17.6	(0.78)	30.9	(1.38)	9.6	(0.74)
Korea	27.1	(1.07)	58.5	(1.06)	14.4	(0.79)	24.3	(0.94)	19.8	(1.02)
Lithuania	65.2	(1.75)	30.0	(1.48)	4.8	(0.57)	69.1	(1.26)	6.5	(0.58)
Malaysia	43.5	(1.52)	52.7	(1.54)	3.9	(0.38)	88.6	(0.80)	2.5	(0.31)
Malta	87.1	(1.29)	10.6	(1.18)	2.2	(0.51)	78.2	(1.62)	48.7	(1.94)
Mexico	43.2	(1.31)	38.0	(1.12)	18.8	(1.14)	71.1	(1.52)	2.9	(0.45)
Norway	79.8	(1.14)	17.0	(1.05)	3.3	(0.44)	66.3	(1.56)	7.2	(0.74)
Poland	44.2	(1.30)	45.1	(1.12)	10.7	(0.85)	57.0	(1.68)	5.4	(0.61)
Portugal	50.3	(1.43)	25.2	(1.14)	24.5	(1.24)	25.1	(1.68)	2.0	(0.33)
Slovak Republic	70.4	(1.37)	24.1	(1.21)	5.5	(0.57)	69.2	(1.47)	28.3	(1.72)
Slovenia	85.3	(0.91)	13.7	(0.87)	1.0	(0.22)	79.3	(1.28)	29.7	(1.18)
Spain	54.8	(1.33)	29.6	(1.00)	15.6	(0.87)	29.5	(1.48)	3.3	(0.41)
Turkey	82.9	(1.87)	12.1	(1.90)	5.0	(0.95)	61.2	(2.96)	6.9	(1.19)
TALIS average	**65.2**	**(0.29)**	**26.7**	**(0.27)**	**8.1**	**(0.15)**	**62.8**	**(0.34)**	**11.4**	**(0.20)**

Source: OECD (2009), *Creating Effective Teaching and Learning Environments: First Results from TALIS*, OECD Publishing.
StatLink ▬▬ http://dx.doi.org/10.1787/607807256201

Figure A.20

Frequency of mentoring and induction programs (2007-08)

Percentage of teachers of lower secondary education whose school principal reported the existence of induction processes and mentoring programs for teachers new to the school

	Existence of formal induction process in school						Existence of a mentoring program or policy in school					
	Yes, for all teachers new to the school		Yes but only for those in their first teaching job		No formal induction process		Yes, for all teachers new to the school		Yes but only for those in their first teaching job		No formal mentoring process	
	%	(S.E.)	%	(S.E.)	%	(S.E.)	%	(S.E.)	%	(S.E.)	%	(S.E.)
Australia	93.1	(2.41)	5.6	(2.21)	1.3	(0.96)	70.4	(4.59)	23.8	(4.27)	5.8	(1.84)
Austria	32.1	(3.15)	23.6	(2.61)	44.3	(2.99)	23.0	(2.73)	23.0	(2.64)	54.1	(3.24)
Belgium (Fl.)	94.4	(1.69)	3.9	(1.21)	1.7	(1.08)	90.5	(2.08)	8.8	(2.02)	0.7	(0.49)
Brazil	19.8	(2.38)	6.5	(1.42)	73.7	(2.46)	17.7	(2.11)	11.7	(2.03)	70.7	(2.91)
Bulgaria	53.2	(4.94)	30.7	(6.13)	16.2	(3.85)	29.6	(3.95)	53.5	(4.87)	16.9	(3.51)
Denmark	47.7	(5.22)	23.5	(4.51)	28.8	(3.81)	62.6	(4.52)	27.0	(3.77)	10.4	(2.65)
Estonia	23.1	(3.68)	59.1	(4.19)	17.8	(3.14)	25.8	(3.49)	64.9	(3.81)	9.2	(1.98)
Hungary	34.8	(5.06)	46.4	(5.26)	18.8	(3.46)	44.8	(4.50)	44.2	(4.68)	11.0	(2.40)
Iceland	72.8	(0.17)	15.7	(0.13)	11.5	(0.12)	44.7	(0.17)	48.4	(0.16)	6.9	(0.04)
Ireland	83.7	(3.67)	7.2	(2.68)	9.0	(2.64)	63.8	(4.21)	10.7	(2.44)	25.5	(4.10)
Italy	36.6	(2.87)	34.4	(2.91)	29.0	(2.81)	26.3	(2.70)	61.3	(2.99)	12.4	(2.16)
Korea	33.6	(3.33)	49.8	(3.75)	16.6	(3.03)	26.8	(3.76)	44.3	(4.37)	29.0	(4.18)
Lithuania	17.1	(2.61)	14.0	(2.49)	68.9	(3.26)	29.0	(3.59)	50.6	(4.08)	20.4	(3.13)
Malaysia	43.0	(3.62)	40.9	(4.00)	16.2	(2.87)	45.0	(3.71)	38.1	(3.82)	16.9	(2.61)
Malta	25.3	(0.17)	11.8	(0.11)	62.9	(0.18)	22.4	(0.18)	12.3	(0.12)	65.3	(0.20)
Mexico	22.7	(3.35)	14.7	(2.91)	62.6	(3.94)	19.2	(3.47)	20.4	(3.52)	60.5	(4.14)
Norway	29.9	(3.83)	18.3	(3.25)	51.8	(4.27)	43.3	(3.85)	25.4	(3.67)	31.3	(3.67)
Poland	14.3	(3.13)	79.4	(3.63)	6.3	(2.15)	23.5	(3.97)	71.9	(4.32)	4.6	(1.87)
Portugal	73.1	(3.52)	4.2	(1.69)	22.7	(3.20)	41.3	(4.48)	20.4	(3.53)	38.3	(4.32)
Slovak Republic	62.1	(3.85)	35.5	(3.67)	2.4	(1.53)	26.4	(4.06)	71.3	(4.22)	2.4	(1.32)
Slovenia	41.1	(3.83)	51.5	(4.06)	7.4	(2.01)	23.5	(3.55)	64.6	(4.02)	11.9	(2.65)
Spain	20.9	(3.22)	15.7	(2.71)	63.4	(3.70)	17.6	(2.77)	18.1	(2.74)	64.3	(3.60)
Turkey	50.2	(5.27)	16.2	(4.04)	33.6	(5.10)	22.3	(4.85)	69.6	(5.51)	8.1	(3.22)
TALIS average	**44.5**	**(0.73)**	**26.5**	**(0.70)**	**29.0**	**(0.62)**	**36.5**	**(0.75)**	**38.4**	**(0.76)**	**25.1**	**(0.60)**

Source: OECD (2009), *Creating Effective Teaching and Learning Environments: First Results from TALIS*, OECD Publishing.
StatLink ▬▬ http://dx.doi.org/10.1787/607807256201

Figure A.21 (1/2)

Recruitment of principals, 2006-07, public schools

	Level of decision making		Criteria		Procedure
	Level of decision making on hiring the principal	How autonomously is the decision taken?	Eligibility criteria	Selection criteria	Recruitment procedure
Australia	State government	In full autonomy	Teaching qualification Teaching experience Experience in school-wide leadership and management responsibilities	m	m
Austria	State government or provincial government (depending on type of school)	Within a framework set by the central government	Teaching qualification Teaching experience	Seniority as a teacher. Management/leadership experience Quality of work proposal for the school Vision/values for school leadership Additional qualifications	Interview Presentation of work proposal Assessment center Potential analysis
Belgium (Fl.)	School boards	m	Teaching qualification	At the discretion of school boards	At the discretion of school boards
Belgium (Fr.)	Provincial / regional authorities	In full autonomy	Teaching qualification Teaching experience	m	Interview "Brevet de chef d'établissement"
Chile	Local authorities	Within a framework set by the central government	Teaching qualification Teaching experience (5 years)	Quality of work proposal for the school	Public contest Presentation of work proposal
Denmark	Local authorities	In full autonomy	Pedagogical qualification Teaching experience	Management/leadership experience Interpersonal skills assessed in interview Vision/values for school leadership	Interview
England	School, school board or committee	After consultation with local authorities	Candidate must hold or be working towards NPQH	At the discretion of school governing bodies	At the discretion of school governing bodies
Finland	Local authority	In full autonomy	Teaching qualification Teaching experience Knowledge of educational administration assessed in exam Other formal qualifications	At the discretion of local authorities	At the discretion of local authorities
France (secondary schools)	Central government	After consultation with provincial/regional authorities	Teaching qualification Teaching experience (5 years)	Knowledge and skills assessed in exam and interview	National exam ("concours") Interview
Hungary	Local authorities	After consultation with school	Teaching qualification Teaching experience (5 years) (As of 2015: successful completion of school leadership training)	Quality of work proposal for the school (application document)	Application document with work proposal for the school
Ireland	School, school board or committee	With involvement/ approval of Trustees or Patron	Teaching qualification Teaching experience (5 years)	Management/leadership experience Interpersonal and other skills assessed in interview Vision/values for school leadership Additional academic qualifications	Public competition Interview

...
105

Figure A.21 (2/2)
Recruitment of principals, 2006-07, public schools

	Level of decision making		Criteria		Procedure
	Level of decision making on hiring the principal	**How autonomously is the decision taken?**	**Eligibility criteria**	**Selection criteria**	**Recruitment procedure**
Israel	m	m	Teaching qualification, (Master's degree for high school leadership positions) Teaching experience Successful completion of a two-year leadership preparation program	Management/leadership experience Vision/values for school leadership	Questionnaire Personal evaluation Interview
Korea	Provincial/regional authorities	Within a framework set by the central government	m	m	Promotion or Invitation
Netherlands	School, school board or committee	In full autonomy	None	m	m
New Zealand	School, school board or committee	In full autonomy	Current registration as a teacher	At the discretion of the Board of Trustees	At the discretion of the Board of Trustees
Northern Ireland	School, school board or committee	m	Teaching qualification	Management/leadership experience Vision/values for the school Personal skills and professional knowledge assessed in interview Additional qualification (may include PQH(NI))	Interview (often including presentation of a pre-selected topic)
Norway	Local authorities	Within a framework set by the central government	At the discretion of local authorities	At the discretion of local authorities	Interview
Portugal	School, school board or committee	In full autonomy	Management experience or training on school management	Candidates without experience in school management need to have an academic qualification in school management (250 hours)	Election (as of 2008, the school board will designate principals)
Scotland	Local authorities	m	m	m	m
Slovenia	School, school board	In full autonomy	Teaching qualification. Teaching experience (5 years) Acquired second promotion title of first promotion (5 years) Headship licence (can be acquired up to one year after starting the post	Opinions of teaching staff, local community, parents and Minister must be sought by the school governing body before selection	Presentation of work proposals for the school
Spain	School, school board or committee	Within a framework set by state governments	Teaching qualification Teaching experience as a civil servant teacher (5 years) Current employment as a state school teacher Successful completion of school leadership training or at least 2 years leadership experience	Date of application Seniority as a teacher Management/leadership experience Quality of work proposal for the school Preference is given to candidates from the school Additional academic qualifications	Presentation of work proposal for the school Assessment of academic and professional merits
Sweden	Local authorities	In full autonomy	Educational experience ("pedagogical insight")	At the discretion of local authorities	Interview

106

Figure A.22

Reasons for not participating in more professional development (2007-08)

Percentage of teachers of lower secondary education who wanted more professional development and gave the following reasons for not undertaking more

	Reason for not undertaking more professional development											
	Did not have the pre-requisites		Too expensive		Lack of employer support		Conflict with work schedule		Family responsibilities		No suitable professional development	
	%	(S.E.)	%	(S.E.)	%	(S.E.)	%	(S.E.)	%	(S.E.)	%	(S.E.)
Australia	3.2	(0.59)	32.6	(1.61)	26.5	(1.52)	61.7	(1.93)	27.6	(1.73)	40.5	(1.80)
Austria	2.6	(0.46)	18.0	(0.93)	9.3	(0.79)	41.5	(1.34)	29.0	(1.21)	64.2	(1.15)
Belgium (Fl.)	3.6	(0.86)	11.8	(1.33)	10.9	(1.40)	43.2	(1.69)	40.6	(1.70)	38.8	(1.73)
Brazil	5.1	(0.46)	51.0	(1.46)	24.6	(1.35)	57.8	(1.46)	18.4	(0.92)	27.0	(1.22)
Bulgaria	7.0	(1.61)	34.6	(2.41)	2.9	(0.47)	24.4	(1.46)	16.6	(1.22)	48.3	(2.35)
Denmark	1.8	(0.44)	29.6	(1.94)	38.3	(1.76)	23.7	(1.90)	15.4	(1.21)	42.1	(1.99)
Estonia	4.2	(0.62)	35.1	(1.59)	15.3	(1.30)	60.5	(1.65)	25.2	(1.35)	52.3	(1.61)
Hungary	5.6	(0.85)	46.9	(2.40)	23.0	(1.90)	40.3	(1.88)	24.5	(1.77)	25.9	(1.89)
Iceland	1.8	(0.70)	18.6	(1.61)	6.7	(1.18)	43.0	(2.41)	35.4	(1.99)	47.0	(2.36)
Ireland	5.5	(0.75)	12.2	(0.96)	13.9	(1.47)	42.6	(1.53)	29.4	(1.57)	45.2	(1.83)
Italy	5.1	(0.44)	23.5	(1.23)	5.8	(0.50)	43.1	(1.47)	40.8	(1.38)	47.2	(1.37)
Korea	11.9	(0.95)	19.9	(0.98)	8.7	(0.93)	73.3	(1.26)	32.7	(1.30)	42.2	(1.28)
Lithuania	7.7	(0.90)	25.7	(1.45)	15.9	(1.19)	46.7	(1.63)	26.4	(1.20)	53.2	(1.60)
Malaysia	28.4	(1.38)	22.2	(1.41)	13.7	(1.14)	58.9	(1.30)	31.3	(1.32)	45.9	(1.25)
Malta	4.7	(1.06)	18.4	(2.06)	10.2	(1.73)	38.8	(2.37)	45.4	(2.85)	40.5	(2.84)
Mexico	17.2	(1.07)	49.0	(1.44)	21.1	(1.01)	48.7	(1.31)	37.4	(1.29)	20.3	(0.97)
Norway	2.5	(0.38)	31.6	(1.36)	26.4	(1.79)	50.4	(1.44)	26.5	(1.37)	30.0	(1.36)
Poland	3.4	(0.51)	51.2	(1.72)	12.3	(1.20)	40.7	(1.90)	32.6	(1.63)	38.7	(1.84)
Portugal	6.5	(0.63)	36.3	(1.14)	10.4	(0.66)	65.5	(1.26)	35.6	(1.28)	48.2	(1.23)
Slovak Republic	9.5	(0.96)	18.8	(1.48)	12.8	(1.32)	38.2	(1.95)	20.6	(1.35)	58.0	(1.81)
Slovenia	3.7	(0.74)	35.9	(1.57)	18.2	(1.48)	47.8	(1.75)	22.3	(1.25)	32.6	(1.52)
Spain	6.7	(0.67)	19.2	(0.99)	6.3	(0.66)	50.3	(1.23)	48.4	(1.43)	38.4	(1.25)
Turkey	16.9	(2.03)	12.4	(1.48)	11.9	(1.51)	34.7	(3.47)	31.2	(2.68)	46.6	(2.22)
TALIS average	**7.2**	**(0.19)**	**28.5**	**(0.32)**	**15.0**	**(0.27)**	**46.8**	**(0.37)**	**30.1**	**(0.33)**	**42.3**	**(0.36)**

Source: OECD (2009), *Creating Effective Teaching and Learning Environments: First Results from TALIS,* OECD Publishing.
StatLink ⌐╜ http://dx.doi.org/10.1787/607807256201

ORGANISATION FOR ECONOMIC CO-OPERATION AND DEVELOPMENT

The OECD is a unique forum where governments work together to address the economic, social and environmental challenges of globalisation. The OECD is also at the forefront of efforts to understand and to help governments respond to new developments and concerns, such as corporate governance, the information economy and the challenges of an ageing population. The Organisation provides a setting where governments can compare policy experiences, seek answers to common problems, identify good practice and work to co-ordinate domestic and international policies.

The OECD member countries are: Australia, Austria, Belgium, Canada, Chile, the Czech Republic, Denmark, Estonia, Finland, France, Germany, Greece, Hungary, Iceland, Ireland, Israel, Italy, Japan, Korea, Luxembourg, Mexico, the Netherlands, New Zealand, Norway, Poland, Portugal, the Slovak Republic, Slovenia, Spain, Sweden, Switzerland, Turkey, the United Kingdom and the United States. The European Commission takes part in the work of the OECD.

OECD Publishing disseminates widely the results of the Organisation's statistics gathering and research on economic, social and environmental issues, as well as the conventions, guidelines and standards agreed by its members.

OECD PUBLISHING, 2, rue André-Pascal, 75775 PARIS CEDEX 16
(98 2012 02 1P) ISBN 978-92-64-17421-4 – No. 59973 2012

CPSIA information can be obtained at www.ICGtesting.com
Printed in the USA
BVOW020934150812

297945BV00003B/2/P